"Robert Pagliarini does an excellent job integrating the financial as well and the psychological impact of sudden wealth with the added benefit of clear, tactical, and common sense strategies. If you want to protect your good fortune, this is a must read!"

> – **JOAN DIFURIA**, co-founder of the Money, Meaning, & Choices Institute, who coined the term "Sudden Wealth Syndrome"

"Robert Pagliarini's insights can help you achieve a better relationship with your money and build a team that can help you manage it the smart way. I've already given this book to one friend and plan to give it to many others."

> – **LIZ WESTON**, Nationally-syndicated personal finance columnist and author

"Worried and nervous about how to handle a windfall? *The Sudden Wealth Solution* is the definitive financial and psychological guide that shows you how to take control and use sudden wealth to create a happier and fuller life."

> – **ELIZABETH LOMBARDO**, Ph.D., best-selling author of *Better than Perfect: 7 Strategies to Crush Your Inner Critic and Create a Life You Love*

"In *The Sudden Wealth Solution*, Pagliarini offers an invaluable resource for coping with and keeping a financial windfall. I highly recommend this book."

> – **BRAD KLONTZ**, Psy.D., CFP ®, financial psychologist, and co-author of *Mind Over Money: Overcoming the Money Disorders that Threaten Our Financial Health*

"As a communication specialist, I am very sensitive to tone. What I found most delightful about *The Sudden Wealth Solution* by Robert Pagliarini is that he doesn't talk *over* or *at* you or for much of the book, even *to* you. Instead he talks *"with"* you about finance and money, which makes it so much less daunting and so much more pleasurable to learn all that he has to teach you."

> – **MARK GOULSTON**, author of *Just Listen: Discover the Secret to Getting Through to Absolutely Anyone*

"As the CEO of a trust company, I can tell you from working with clients there are significant financial, tax, legal, and psychological challenges of new wealth. Robert has taken his years of experience as a sudden wealth advisor and condensed it into a comprehensive system that turns sudden wealth into lasting wealth. *The Sudden Wealth Solution* is an absolute must read if you are coming into money."

– **THERESA FETTE**, CEO of Provident Trust Group

"*The Sudden Wealth Solution* is a must read for a myriad of folks from lottery winners to professional athletes, to those involved in academia to lawyers and judges, as well as to large settlement recipients. The necessity to save, create and maintain a sustainable lifestyle is of critical importance to one's financial and mental health. Compulsive spending of sudden wealth often leads to unfortunate and unintended results. This book is a roadmap to success. Congratulations Robert Pagliarini for your efforts and your contribution to society as a whole."

– **KAREN MEYERS**, MBA/JD, CSSC, MEd, CLU, FLMI, CPCU, Co-Founder of The Certified Structured Settlement Consultant Program & Assistant Visiting Professor, Miami University

THE
SUDDEN
WEALTH
SOLUTION

ALSO BY ROBERT PAGLIARINI

THE SIX-DAY FINANCIAL MAKEOVER (St. Martin's Press)

THE OTHER 8 HOURS (St. Martin's Press)

THE
SUDDEN
WEALTH
SOLUTION

12 PRINCIPLES
TO TRANSFORM
SUDDEN WEALTH
INTO
LASTING WEALTH

ROBERT PAGLIARINI

HARBINGER PRESS

Harbinger Press

ISBN: 978-0-9905715-6-8

Library of Congress Control Number: has been applied for

This book is printed on acid-free paper.

Printed in the United States of America

Note To The Reader

This book is intended to provide general guidelines that are for informational purposes only and is sold with the understanding that the publisher and author are not engaged in rendering professional services or in providing specific investment advice. The application of general guidelines involving regulatory, accounting, and legal practices, which may differ from locality to locality and which are constantly changing, is highly dependent on an evaluation of individual facts and specific circumstances. With regard to any decisions that can potentially have significant financial, legal, tax, or other consequences, no book can take the place of individualized professional advice. Readers should not regard this book as a substitute for consulting with a competent lawyer, accountant, or other financial professional, as appropriate to the nature of their particular situation. Different types of investments involve varying degrees of risk and there can be no assurance that the future performance of any specific investment, investment strategy, or product discussed in this book will be profitable or suitable for any one reader's portfolio. If readers have any questions regarding the applicability of any investment strategy or product discussed in this book to their particular financial situation, they should consult with a professional advisor.

CONTENTS

SECTION I
THE 12 PRINCIPLES OF SUDDEN WEALTH

SECTION II
THE SUDDEN WEALTH EVENTS

FOREWORD

We all wish to find the pot of gold at the end of every rainbow. For some, finding the pot of gold is one thing, but keeping it is another matter.

Before I started writing my books or began to give seminars on value investing, or even long before I learned how to understand the market from The Best – Warren Buffett, I was in the music business.

I saw firsthand what happens when instant success arrives to those who could write a song and carry a tune. I wish I could share what it's like when a hook of a song blossoms into a monster hit.

In an instant, life changes. Battered old cars and cramped one-bedroom apartments are exchanged for stretch limousines, private jets, and L.A. mansions. Just as quickly, the cost of this new lifestyle skyrockets and this overnight success underlines how hard they have worked for their place in the sun. Hanger-ons and groupies feed their egos. Along the way, they collect expensive hobbies but soon, the shadows of their own personal demons grow in size and depth.

The music industry is a brutal place. What worked last year might fail this year. I've seen more than my share of musicians whose second album tanked when it arrived on the shelves. In quick succession, concert dates are canceled, calls to the record label are never returned, and the money dries up. Expensive toys are repossessed, fair weather friends disappear, and mansions are foreclosed. Sadly, life becomes another battered old car and another cramped one-bedroom apartment. Survivors play the "would-a, could-a, should-a game" for the rest of their lives.

What takes place in entertainment takes place everywhere else. Approximately 80% of those who play professional sports will go broke within five years of retirement. For every ingénue that appears on screen as this year's "It Girl," there's a whole busload of pretty young things who arrive daily, primed to take her place. The number of former child actors who fall down a black hole of misfortune is so pervasive that it becomes cliché. Lottery winners whose payouts have evaporated after a series of bad choices are heartbreaking. Closer to home, a long layoff can turn a comfortable existence into something scary.

But it does not have to be this way. Windfalls should be life-changing for all of the good reasons. With the right tools, we can turn even a modest inheritance into something substantial that will carry us through our lives. Robert's book helps us to get out of our own way; he helps us think through the right choices so that new windfalls, large and small, don't end up in our rear view mirror as distant memories.

Not everyone wins the lottery or has a wealthy uncle who drops dead. However, from time to time, windfalls do show up at our front door . . . but the first thing we should unpack is ourselves. How we handle these moments will say a great deal about our emotional intelligence when it comes to financial matters. Robert's book gives us the skills to ensure that our good fortune stays with us for life.

The next generation will bring the largest transfer of wealth in our nation's history. Baby Boomers, who themselves are getting closer to retirement, will inherit $12 trillion from their depression-era parents. As Baby Boomers come to their end, they will leave an additional $30 trillion in inheritance to Millennials.

Robert's book is the bible of sudden wealth. So read it now!

Mary Buffett
May 2014

READ THIS FIRST

Do you want access to exclusive content, videos, worksheets, tax, legal & financial tips, and breaking news?

VISIT SUDDENWEALTHSOLUTION.COM FOR THE LATEST INFORMATION

ARE YOU AN ADVISOR?

We want you! We are looking for financial advisors, attorneys, CPAs, therapists and other service professionals who are currently serving or want to serve sudden wealth recipients to join our growing nationwide community of experts dedicated to working with sudden wealth recipients.

▶ Receive referrals to sudden wealth recipients in your area looking for advice

▶ Network with other professionals

▶ Learn the latest tax, legal, and financial strategies

▶ Get access to exclusive content

▶ Watch educational videos and listen to podcasts

▶ Download forms and worksheets to help you work with clients

INTRODUCTION
THE SUDDEN WEALTH PRINCIPLES

Everything changes. Those are the words I've heard time and time again over the past two decades from my clients who became sudden wealth recipients. Sudden wealth is a roller coaster ride of emotions – from the highest highs to the lowest lows. Sudden wealth is often portrayed as creating dire consequences for its recipients, but it can be an amazing opportunity that improves your life and those around you. I've worked with enough sudden wealth clients over the years to see patterns – what works and what doesn't. With proper guidance, and a willingness to stick to the 12 Principles outlined in this book, you can avoid the common pitfalls that so often destroy money, and instead transform your sudden wealth into lasting wealth to create a better life for yourself and others.

Sudden wealth can come from luck, such as from a lottery win, or from years of effort, such as from a business sale. It can come from a loss, such as an inheritance, divorce, or lawsuit settlement, or it can from a gain, such as from stock options or sports/entertainment contracts. Although the sources of sudden wealth are unique, they all share something in common. Many people who become responsible for a great deal of money overnight feel overwhelmed by the financial, legal, and tax decisions they face, confused as to what they should do, and a deep weight because of their new responsibility. They feel unprepared for the job and are unsure of who to trust.

While everyone focuses on the "wealth" in sudden wealth, it's often not about the money. The issues surrounding sudden wealth can be highly emotional and charged. The reason so many people lose their sudden wealth so quickly is not because they make bad financial decisions, it's because they make emotional decisions that, more often than not, are bad financial decisions. Why?

Sudden Wealth Curse?

If you just lost a loved one and are expecting an inheritance or lawsuit settlement, the sudden wealth may seem more like a curse than an opportunity. With time and proper guidance, your sudden wealth can truly be an opportunity – regardless of how you received it.

There are a lot of things in life that you can prepare for, but getting more money than you've ever dreamed of overnight can turn even the most stable and grounded person's life upside down, because it's impossible to prepare for. You can imagine what the Grand Canyon will look like, but it's entirely different when the view takes your breath away as you are sitting on the edge looking down at it in real life.

Most of us experience gradual wealth – the accumulation of money over months, years, and even decades. If we've planned well, we have a portfolio we're responsible for overseeing and managing. This "nest egg" represents years of effort, sacrifice, and decisions. It has become our child. We nurture it. We do our best raising it. We may lose sleep worrying about it. As we watch it grow, we are also developing new skills and maturity to become a better parent. We also become more sophisticated in the other areas of our finances.

Early on, we may have been able to file our taxes with a simple 1040-EZ form, but then we graduate to TurboTax, and then to having an accountant prepare our taxes. We'll upgrade our insurance coverage over the years and hire an attorney to write our will and other estate documents. In short, we grow with our money. It's a gradual process that spans decades. We make more, we learn more. It's a gradual ride up.

Fish Out Of Water

What do Eddie Murphy in *Beverly Hills Cop*, Tom Hanks in *Big*, Paul Hogan in *Crocodile Dundee*, and Daryl Hannah in *Splash* all have in common? They all, with the latter quite literally, are fish out of water. The "fish out of water" storyline is a popular one in books and movies, where the character is thrust into a new and unfamiliar environment. It's popular because it provides comedy and drama. We like to see the crazy situations that develop when a poor backwoods family is transplanted to Beverly Hills after striking oil on their land, or when basketball bad boy Dennis Rodman is sent to the boardroom to discuss business with Donald Trump. It's fun to watch, but not so fun to experience.

If gradual wealth is a smooth escalator ride that can take decades to reach the top, sudden wealth is a rocket trip straight to the top in seconds. Your circumstances have changed overnight, and you've had no chance to adapt or to grow. To make matters more difficult, you're often forced to make immediate financial, legal, and tax decisions that can have permanent and dramatic consequences. Emotions run high and stress can get the best of you. And if that were not enough, we may feel pressure from those closest to us—our family and friends. They may offer support and encouragement or even offer advice, but they're often no better prepared for the situation than you are. Their support, if it is unwanted, can strain relationships, causing even more anxiety and stress on an already highly charged situation.

With the onslaught of responsibility, anxiety, decisions, and strained relationships, we can make poor decisions, lash out at those we love, or freeze with uncertainty and paralysis. Although some people handle this rapid shift better than others, to many, the dream of a windfall can feel more like a nightmare.

But sudden wealth shouldn't be doom and gloom. Although it's often portrayed as creating dire consequences for its recipients, money can also provide freedom.

THE POWER OF MONEY

A few years ago, I saw a TV show called *Lockup*. It's a documentary style program that films the stories and lives of inmates in the country's most infamous and dangerous prisons. The behind-the-scenes look in these prisons fascinated me, but having watched a dozen or more episodes, the prisons and the stories bled together . . . except for one. It is not the story of an inmate, but a prison guard. A year before the cameras arrived, this guard – a woman – was brutally attacked by an inmate. She was badly beaten. She was punched in her face and kicked over and over again. She suffered countless broken bones, a broken jaw, and nearly died. She spent several months in a hospital bed struggling to stay alive. Tubes were required to do all of the things you and I do without thinking. Miraculously, over months and through painful rehabilitation, she regained her strength. As the tubes were removed and the scars healed, the trauma still lived on inside her head through nightmares, flashbacks, and panic attacks. Even in the safety of her hospital bed, she could not shake the fear.

Money Doesn't Solve All Problems, It Upgrades Them

Commuting three hours a day when you have a debilitating and painful disease to a job where your boss constantly yells at you is a problem. Having your sister pressure you to pay for your nephew's braces is also a problem, albeit an upgraded problem. Don't box yourself into the corner thinking you need to choose between money and happiness. You can have both. They are not mutually exclusive. It's not money or meaning, it's money and meaning.

But here she was — back from the dead — with tears streaming down her face and wearing her guard uniform, walking back through the prison gates to the place that almost took her life. Trembling, she tells the camera that she has no choice. She ran out of money and couldn't find a job doing anything else. She did it so she could pay her rent and buy groceries. She did it so she could survive. She did it for the money.

She is not alone. There are billions of people on this planet who are suffering in a job because they have no other option. Survival is a beautiful thing, but what is required to survive is often soul-crushing. Women and children suffer sexual, emotional, and physical abuse to earn just enough to survive. I've counseled women who were in abusive relationships, but felt they couldn't leave because they had no money.

Sudden wealth isn't going to solve all of your problems. The truth is, everyone has problems, issues, and irritations. It doesn't matter who you are or how much money you have. The wealthiest are not immune to life's challenges and setbacks. Sudden wealth

> *Sudden wealth can be the catalyst that helps you create a better life.*

will create problems you never even knew you could have, but it can also give you a voice. Money provides options and freedom. Money can give you the power to shape your life on your terms. It can purchase food, stability, security, shelter, education, and medicine.

We are experts at living life by default. Our lifestyle is dictated by our finances. Our bank accounts set the bar for what we can do. But what happens when we receive sudden wealth and there is no longer a bar? When we can do whatever we want? This is why sudden wealth can feel so liberating but also so foreign. When you can do anything, what will you choose?

Sudden wealth can be an amazing opportunity that can give you the ability to pay off lingering debt, save for retirement, or even re-create the life of your dreams. For many, it's a once in a lifetime opportunity to start over – to erase some of the mistakes of their financial past and get back on track. This is the promise of *The Sudden Wealth Solution* – to help you transform sudden wealth into lasting wealth and to create a better life.

THE 12 PRINCIPLES
OF SUDDEN WEALTH

Sudden wealth can turn your life upside down. Clients have described it as being stripped of everything that they are used to and comfortable with, and then being dropped into a strange environment. Imagine traveling to a foreign land where you don't know the language, rules, laws, or customs. Furthermore, imagine you don't know anyone and you have trouble communicating with your friends and family back home. Exciting? Maybe. Unnerving? Absolutely.

I like to travel to exotic places around the world. These trips are a short vacation from my normal responsibilities. Each trip is an exciting adventure and there are very few things I look forward to more in my life. But when the wheels hit the ground back in the U.S., I immediately feel a sense of relief. The thrill I experienced from the unfamiliar is now replaced by the comfort of familiarity. I can relax. A 737 and about 15 hours makes it possible for me to return home, but for sudden wealth recipients, it can take months or even years for them to feel comfortable with their new position and responsibilities.

Some sudden wealth recipients manage their stress and uncertainty well, while others struggle – some never fully adapting to their sudden wealth and the changes it entails. One of the key differences between those who manage this process effectively and those who do not is how they view their role in the process.

Sudden wealth recipients who take a passive role tend to struggle. They view themselves not as a participant in the process, but as an observer. They sit back and let the situation control them. They wait to be told what to do. They accept the suggestions and advice of others because they are not comfortable asking questions or making decisions for themselves. Sudden wealth recipients who take control and own the situation fare much better than the ones who sit back and hope others will take care of it for them.

WHAT SURVIVORS DO DIFFERENTLY

What does a plane crash and sudden wealth have in common? In the first few days of a windfall, sudden wealth recipients can experience shock and disassociation. Both are highly charged events that spike our adrenaline and cortisol levels and initiate a flight, freeze, or fight response. Contrary to Hollywood movies, research shows that we don't panic, but instead freeze and respond to the crisis with paralysis. Author and researcher of *The Unthinkable: Who Survives When Disaster Strikes and Why*, Amanda Ripley, writes in *Time Magazine*, "Panic is rare. The bigger problem is that people do too little, too slowly. They sometimes shut down completely, falling into a stupor."[1]

The solution, say the experts, is to keep emotions under control, but maybe even more importantly, to live in the moment and to react based on what is actually happening. Instead of asking, "Why me?" survivors focus on the facts and ask better questions, such as, "What is happening right now and what can I do about it?"

The sudden wealth recipients who respond best to their windfall are those who control their emotions, accurately assess the situation, and take responsibility for doing what is required. Fortunately, you don't have to have all of the answers. It's completely normal and understandable that as a result of your sudden wealth, you will be in new situations and not know what to do.

> *Taking control doesn't mean you have to have all of the answers or that you need to make decisions. Taking control means you are not going to passively sit back and let the events unfold before your eyes.*

Former Navy SEAL, Cade Courtley, who trains people in how to survive disasters, says, "Don't wait for someone to come and rescue you. As an officer in the military, I was always told . . . you can't sort of wait for somebody to help you out. You can't expect somebody will be there to assist[2]."

For almost everyone, sudden wealth is a novel and awkward experience. Most people just do not have the experience or knowledge to deal with the situation they find themselves in. It's okay to feel like a foreigner in a strange land, but you cannot be passive. At best, passivity leads to indecisiveness, and at worst, to being taken advantage of. If you don't assume control, others will. If you're lucky, they will have your best interests at heart, but they may not.

Instead of letting sudden wealth happen to you, stand up, take charge, and own it. Whether you have just learned you will be coming into sudden wealth or if you did years ago, it's never too late to take control. Here's how you can get into the driver's seat…

BUILD YOUR CONFIDENCE

To minimize the "freeze" response, or inclination to defer responsibility to others, you need to have the belief that you can handle whatever comes at you. Psychologists call this self-efficacy – this is the strength of your belief in yourself, whether that be your ability to handle a task, reach a goal, or succeed in a certain situation. Even if you have limited financial, tax, or legal experience, your positive belief that you will rise to the occasion and manage the situation will promote a more successful outcome. Here are a few ideas on how to build your confidence…

SMALL SUCCESSES

One of the best ways to build your confidence is to get a few small successes under your belt. Reading this book is an achievement and should be celebrated. Researching and contacting a few attorneys is a success. Telling a family member "Not now" when they ask for a loan is an achievement. Signing up for a personal finance workshop is a small success. Attending a Debtors Anonymous meeting to learn how to control your spending is a success. Focus on small steps you can take – with one building on the other.

FIND A ROLE MODEL

The research shows that those with a mentor can achieve greater financial success[3]. As a sudden wealth recipient, if you can find a good role model you may be able to successfully navigate through the financial maze a little easier. Have your attorney or financial advisor share stories of their clients who have taken control and used their sudden wealth to create a better life. These vicarious experiences can boost your own self-confidence.

REVIEW PAST SUCCESSES

Chances are, you've never experienced sudden wealth before, but you probably have countless experiences where you mastered a difficult task or achieved a challenging goal. Re-experience as many of these successes as possible, as each one will further validate your ability to succeed in new or demanding situations, even if you started with fear and hesitation.

ASK OTHERS

Have a best friend or close family member give you a pep talk. Ask them to give you specific examples of past successes and why they think you can step up to the task of managing your windfall.

VISUALIZATION

Mental practice has been shown to have a positive and significant effect on performance[4]. Visualize taking control of your situation and making your life a success. Even this structured daydreaming can have a positive impact on your confidence.

KNOWLEDGE IS POWER

Have you ever choked or been unable to breath? Imagine being in a small tent on the side of one of the world's tallest mountains in the middle of Africa and not being able to breathe. Medical help is days away. It's just you and the mountain. Can you imagine the panic? What do you do?

This happened to me. I was two days into a seven day climb on Mt. Kilimanjaro in Africa, and I stopped breathing in the middle of the night. But I didn't panic. Instead, I smiled. Why? I knew what to expect. Before the trip, and almost accidentally, I discovered a high-altitude phenomenon known as periodic breathing, where your body stops breathing intermittently throughout the night as it adjusts to the lower oxygen content. I smiled on the mountain in the middle of the night because I knew what to expect. What could have been a terrifying event – thinking I was going to die or that something was terribly wrong with me – turned into an appreciation for knowledge. Fear is often the result of uncertainty, simply not knowing what is happening or what will happen next.

Sudden wealth is no different. Much of the anxiety sudden wealth recipients feel is not knowing what comes next. You are better able to deal with your wealth if you understand what stage you are at as you can anticipate what comes next. This allows you to feel more comfortable with your situation, which will help you make more rational and less emotional decisions. I've found that when clients understand the stages, they can better appreciate where they are and can feel more confident about knowing that whatever they are experiencing is normal.

Pro Tip

I learned in the SEALs the importance of mastering four skills that build an unbeatable mind and emotional resiliency. These skills will work equally well if you find yourself newly wealthy and are dealing with the shock, sharks, and dizzying array of opportunities to sift through.

1. Set SMART-FITS goals. You must have a plan, and your plan must have goals that fit you and are SMART. So take time to sit quietly and get very clear about what your goals are for your wealth. Put the potential goals through a filter of questions that answer: Does the goal FIT you in terms of your personality and skills? Is the goal IMPORTANT enough that you will want to focus your valuable time and energy on it? Is the TIMING right for this goal? Too soon or too late and you will fail. Finally, is the goal SIMPLE to understand and execute? Select only those goals that meet these standards, then state them in a Specific, Measurable, Achievable, Realistic, and Time-bound (SMART) manner for optimal success.

2. Use visualization. You can win in your mind before starting to work on your goals. Develop intricate and emotion-filled mental imagery of your desired character as a newly wealthy person (i.e., healthy, happy, powerful, balanced, in-control, inspired, and charitable) and also the end-state of the specific goals you select.

3. Be positive and optimistic! Negativity destroys performance and attracts negative people and events into your life. SEALs are eternally optimistic and positive that they will achieve mission success, and so should you be. Learn to control your mind and to feed the courage dog with positive self-talk.

4. Learn to breathe better. Seriously, deep diaphragmatic breathing will negate stress in your life and turn you into the calm, cool character you need to be when dealing with your new found wealth. Inhale to a count of 4, hold your breath for a count of 4, exhale for a count of 4, and hold the exhale for a count of 4. Do this when you wake up in the morning for 10 minutes and whenever you feel stressed during the day.

~ Mark Divine, former Navy SEAL and author of *The Way of the Seal*

WHAT SUDDEN WEALTH STAGE ARE YOU IN?

STAGE 1: PRE-MONEY

Stage 1 is when you know you will be receiving sudden wealth but you don't have it yet. For example:

Inheritance. Your aunt recently passed away and left you a large inheritance, but you don't have the money yet.

Divorce. You are going through a divorce and you know you will be responsible for your share of the assets, but the divorce hasn't been finalized.

Lawsuit. You and your attorneys are negotiating a settlement but no documents have been signed.

Stock options. You've been granted a significant amount of stock options and the company you work for has gone public, but you have to wait six months before you can exercise the options and sell the stock.

Lottery. You have the winning ticket, but you haven't yet claimed the jackpot.

KEY CHARACTERISTICS

Stage 1 can last a few days in the case of a lottery win, a few months in the case of an inheritance, business sale, or stock options, or years in the case of a lawsuit or divorce. Stage 1 is all about the anticipation of sudden wealth. You almost have it. You can see and almost touch it, but it's just beyond your reach. This stage is characterized by a whirlwind of emotions. Clients are usually excited about the possibilities. They think about all the things they want to do and people they want to help. They'll usually start mentally spending the money – thinking about the new car they want to buy, the home improvement project they can now afford, and the family reunion trip to Hawaii they want to plan. And sometimes, they may even start actually spending the money they don't yet have.

Stage 1 can be an exciting time for clients, and relations with family and friends is usually quite positive. But for some clients in this stage, the excitement of the situation and the seemingly endless possibilities becomes too much. Instead of embracing the opportunity, they become overwhelmed by it. It is not uncommon for sudden wealth recipients in this stage to have difficulty sleeping, to have erratic swings in emotions, and ironically, to feel an overwhelming sense of doom. And for the sudden wealth recipient who experiences these things, it only makes matters worse. They are getting a large sum of money that can change their lives and everyone around them is elated. Intellectually, they know they should be happy as well, but because they are feeling more apprehension than excitement, they often think there is something wrong with them or are undeserving of the money. You may hear them cry out, "What is wrong with me?" or "Why am I like this?" at the contradiction of knowing they should be happy but feel nothing but worry and gloom. Their feeling that there is something wrong with them can produce a painful cycle that drives the sudden wealth recipient deeper and deeper into despair.

Post Sudden Wealth Stress Syndrome?

Some Stage I sudden wealth recipients experience post-traumatic stress symptoms such as re-experiencing the event (e.g., checking the winning lottery numbers over and over), hyperarousal (e.g., poor concentration or irritability), emotional numbing (e.g., lack of interest), or a sense of helplessness. In these situations, you should seek professional help from a licensed therapist.

If they become overwhelmed by their new situation and their feelings, they may try to hide their feelings or even hide themselves from others because they don't want to look crazy. They may retreat by turning off their phone and not leaving the house or by turning to drugs or alcohol. But, of course, this doesn't have to be their fate. Simply knowing that sudden wealth recipients who are in Stage 1 experience a wide range of emotions and thoughts that are completely normal often goes a long way in helping them realize that whatever they are feeling is completely normal, and that they are not flawed.

TAKE CONTROL TIPS

Create a wishlist. Chances are you are already thinking about what you want to do with the money you will be receiving. Keep it up! Dream and brainstorm as much as you can about what you'd like to do. In the next chapter, you'll learn more about creating a wishlist, but for now, simply get a pad and write down your ideas as they come to you.

Write down questions for advisors. Stage 1 can be frustrating because you will have more questions than answers. That's okay. Jot down all of your questions as they come to you. When you meet with your advisors, you can have all of your questions answered.

Research advisors. Sudden wealth can be complicated and full of tax, legal, and financial issues. You will need experts to help you navigate these issues. "Sudden Wealth Principle 3: Get Help" is dedicated to helping you find the very best advisors for your situation.

Find a confidant. I strongly recommend that you keep your sudden wealth as private as possible, but you should have at least one confidant – either a family member or close friend – that you can talk to about what you're experiencing and feeling. You don't need to share the economics of your sudden wealth, but you need to be able to talk about your fears with someone who knows and understands you.

Get a therapist. If you find that you are becoming overwhelmed with the situation or don't want to talk to a friend or family member, consider talking to a therapist. These sessions are confidential, and you can get a professional to help you work through some of the issues that may not be appropriate to discuss with family or friends.

Manage your stress. Stage 1 can be exciting, but it is still highly stressful. Consider taking daily walks, meditating, or doing other things that will help reduce your stress.

THINGS TO AVOID

Making unnecessary decisions. Depending on the type of sudden wealth event, there may only be a handful of decisions you need to make during Stage 1. In the next chapter, "Sudden Wealth Principle 2: Slow Down," you will learn which decisions you should make and which you should avoid. Bottom line, unless it is necessary, hold off on making a decision.

Spending money. There will be plenty of time to figure out what you want to do with your money, but Stage 1 is not that time. You still need to know how much you will get after taxes and how much you can comfortably spend. If you are tempted, write it on your wishlist.

Promising anything or making commitments. Stage 1 is too early to make any financial or non-financial commitments. Don't make promises to friends and family. Again, it is too early to know what you have and what you can spend.

Sharing news with others. Keep your sudden wealth situation private. The fewer people who know, the better. You'll receive less unsolicited advice and you won't feel the pressure from others.

Retreating. Although you don't want to broadcast to the world your situation, you should avoid hiding. Stay social and engage in the activities you always have. This will help you stay structured, and the social connection will help draw you out from within yourself.

Self-medicating with alcohol/drugs. It's understandable that you want to take the edge off a situation that, by all accounts, can be one of the most stressful experiences anyone will face. Even though drinking or drugs will certainly do the trick, it's not sustainable and will only make your situation worse. There are many more healthful alternatives, such as exercise, talking to friends, or therapy, that are more effective and will set you up better for the later sudden wealth stages.

The Ultimate Control

The problem with many sudden wealth recipients is they lack appropriate money confidence. The quickest and easist way to get control and to gain confidence is to participate in our online wealth prep course. Through videos, drawings, and real world examples, you'll gain the money confidence and skills you need to make the right financial decisions so that your sudden wealth becomes lasting wealth. Go to suddenwealthsolution.com to get wealth ready!

STAGE 2: POST-MONEY

Stage 1 ends and Stage 2 begins when you receive the money. It is no longer about anticipating the money or wondering how much money you will receive. The money is in the account. You can see it and touch it. This is an important distinction from Stage 1, where clients will often feel that something will happen and they won't get the money. In Stage 2, all of those fears are removed. In most cases, Stage 2 typically lasts one to six months.

KEY CHARACTERISTICS

If Stage 1 is all about thinking and preparing, Stage 2 is all about planning and doing. It is during this stage that clients usually hire advisors (although there can be compelling reasons to engage these advisors before the money arrives to take advantage of tax, legal, and financial issues that may not be available once you receive the money).

Stage 2 is when you and your advisors establish goals and objectives, open accounts, make investments, determine your spending plan, protect the assets, complete your estate plan, consider charitable planning, and develop a tax strategy for the new money and ongoing taxes. Stage 2 is where you put the plan that you and your advisors have created into action. There are often many meetings, phone calls, and emails as your advisors and you work through the details of the sudden wealth. Paperwork is plentiful in this stage — agreements with your advisors, investment and bank account applications, insurance documents, trusts, business entities, and a myriad of other forms are often required. This planning and implementation can be time consuming. It is easy for your life to be hijacked by meetings and decisions – all of which are deemed urgent and important.

Stage 2 is still often exciting for the client, if not a bit overwhelming. It is during Stage 2 where you can accurately determine how much money you really have after paying taxes and fees. The reality of your opportunity sets in once you start working with your advisors and planning your future. But the excitement can quickly fade if you feel too overwhelmed by the activity and decisions. And frankly, most lawyers, accountants, and financial advisors don't slow down long enough to clearly explain what they are doing. This can leave the client feeling that they are not even a participant in the process, that things are happening beyond their control on issues they don't understand. If this occurs, many clients freeze. They stop returning emails and start missing meetings. In an effort to regain some sense of control, they check out. This places the whole planning process on hold and can cause irreparable tax, legal, and financial problems. To avoid this, it's important to work with good advisors and to slow things down.

TAKE CONTROL TIPS

Go slowly. It's paramount to your immediate sanity as well as your long-term success to not go too fast or do things until you are comfortable with them. The sudden wealth process is not new to your advisors (or at least it shouldn't be!). They work with people just like you for 50 hours a week for decades, so they may go faster than you want. Go slowly. On most issues, there is no rush.

You are normal. Whatever you are feeling is probably perfectly normal. Like in Stage 1, talk to a friend or family member, or if you prefer, find a licensed therapist if you are having difficulty adapting to the demands of the situation.

Keep your routine. Stage 2 can be unnerving. It can turn someone's life upside down for a period with all of the planning and implementation. It's important to continue doing the things that ground you and make you feel good. For example, if you normally exercise each morning, don't schedule calls or meetings with your advisors during this time. Stick to your normal daily structure as much as possible.

THINGS TO AVOID

Spending blind. Don't make the mistake of spending more money than you can afford. How much you can afford to spend will depend on many factors and may take some time to determine. While you and your advisors are determining your taxes and how much you will have, avoid making any financial decisions.

Shutting down. Again, the demands of Stage 2 can be stressful. Sudden wealth often throws clients into unfamiliar situations in which they never expected to be involved. Although sudden wealth is viewed as an opportunity, Stage 2 can be overwhelming. Avoid retreating by taking things slowly. Read and re-read Sudden Wealth Principle 2. Share it with your advisors. This is your money and your life. Even though it may not always feel like it, you are in control. Don't let overly eager advisors go too quickly.

Locking up your money. If you are working with good advisors, this won't happen. Avoid investing in things that unnecessarily lock up your assets. Avoid "red" investments discussed in "Sudden Wealth Principle 11: Grow Wealth."

STAGE 3: MAINTENANCE

Stage 3 is the continuous process of monitoring the plan you've set in place, investing your assets, and tracking your progress against measurable criteria. The plan you created in Stage 2 provides the foundation. Stage 3 is making sure the goals and objectives you set are still relevant, you are hitting the targets, you are minimizing your ongoing taxes, and that your portfolio is allocated correctly and your investments are appropriate, depending on the existing and projected financial and economic forecast.

KEY CHARACTERISTICS

Stage 3 is when things slow down. Accounts are open and investments made. You can now settle into the life you designed in Stage 2. You know how much you can spend and the limitations of what you can do financially. The meetings and phone calls with your advisors have slowed. What once seemed like it would never end, has. You are now able to concentrate more on work or activities you previously did. However, if you no longer need to work, you may have more time and resources than you've ever had in your life before. This is a critical point for many sudden wealth recipients.

For those who can quit their jobs, many are able to create new meaning and purpose and are able to thrive in their new life. They may find activities and projects that fill their days and their souls. For others with plenty of money and time but no direction, this transition is not as smooth. Some experience a sense of emptiness or void because even though they have few responsibilities and can do whatever they want, they don't find purposeful activities to fill their time. This is addressed in much greater detail in "Sudden Wealth Principle 8: Create a Better Life," but for now, understand that whatever you are feeling is normal and that there are tools and strategies to help you create a life full of meaning and satisfaction.

TAKE CONTROL TIPS

Be willing to make changes. Stage 3 is a continuous process of evaluating and tweaking. The "plan" that encompassed so much of your time in Stage 2 is not meant to be static. All financial plans need to be dynamic and change based on the changing circumstances of your life as well as what's happening in the economy and with your investments. Don't become passive or get hung-up on keeping things the same. A good plan is a moving target that requires small and sometimes big changes.

THINGS TO AVOID

Being reactive or passive. Change is the only constant. It is easy to become spooked by the markets and the media and want to make radical changes to your plan and investments, but these emotional reactions are usually detrimental to your longer-term plan. Adapt and shift the plan, but make sure you do it for the right reasons.

TAKE THE LEAD

Knowledge about sudden wealth can give you a boost of confidence, but it's just as important to take action when appropriate. There are several things you can do to become more active throughout the sudden wealth process, regardless of what stage you are in.

Use a Q list. Sudden wealth creates more questions than answers, and if you're not careful, it is easy to become confused and feel out of the loop with the decisions and plans your advisors are recommending. One of the best things you can do to feel more in control is to keep a list of questions for your advisors. I suggest to clients that they use the same notepad they use for their wishlist. The same rules apply – capture any question you have, whether you think it is big, small, smart, or dumb, and do it immediately. Be sure to keep all of your questions in one place.

Stick to a Schedule. Don't let sudden wealth control you. As mentioned earlier, as best as you can, stick to the same schedule you had pre-money. You may have more meetings with advisors and phone calls, but try to wake up at the same time and do as many of the same things you did before you received the money.

Schedule weekly calls with advisors. Anxiety is usually the result of worrying about the unknown. Too much anxiety is detrimental to our health and our ability to think rationally and make sound decisions. The elixir to anxiety is knowledge, of knowing what's going on and what to expect. This is why scheduling weekly calls with your advisors is so important. During these mandatory calls, you can check in with them on what is happening and get answers to your list of question. If you have the right advisors, they will encourage these calls and will be happy to explain everything that is going on and answer your questions. If not, don't ever forget that your advisors work for you. You pay them to provide you a service. If they are not willing or want to rush these calls, consider finding an advisor who better understands the psychology of sudden wealth.

Sleep on it. There are few, if any, tax, legal, or financial decisions you don't have time to sleep on. Ask your advisors if you can make your decision in the morning. Make a point of waiting a night before making any decisions. When in doubt, ask your advisors if you can take a day to think about it.

The goal of "Sudden Wealth Principle 1: Take Control" is to not become caught up in the moment and to let the situation and your emotions get the best of you. It's about helping you take a step back from the emotional chaos of the situation and to replace what can be the deluge of decisions and details with something more manageable. Stress is not our friend when we need to make logical, rational decisions. By taking control, you can engage more of your analytical brain while minimizing your primitive fight or flight response.

DRIVER VERSUS PASSENGER

Sudden wealth can create an interesting power dynamic. On one hand, it's your money and your life, your advisors work for you, you are in charge and you call the shots; you are the driver. On the other hand, most sudden wealth recipients aren't comfortable enough with the tax code, laws, or financial strategies to make smart decisions. You must rely on your team to guide you; you are the passenger.

The driver vs. passenger is a critical distinction. Some sudden wealth recipients go too far one way or the other. For example, they may throw their hands up in the air and relinquish all control to their team because they feel confused and overwhelmed. Or on the flipside, they become involved in every detail and make it difficult for the experts to do their jobs. Both scenarios are disastrous. The key is to identify the areas where you will be the driver and the other areas where you will be the passenger. Here's what I've found to work best.

Be the driver when it comes to defining your goals, objectives, and vision. Sometimes, well-meaning attorneys, CPAs, and financial planners will place a higher emphasis on form over function. They may devise sophisticated strategies that are financially correct, but in doing so, compromise your overall vision and desire for simplicity. They may dazzle you with big words and highly technical details, but make sure you are vocal about what you want.

It also makes sense to be the driver when it comes to setting expectations for your team. It is worth repeating: Your advisors work for you. It doesn't matter how little education or experience you have or how many letters they have after their name, you pay them to perform a service. As a result, you should set expectations, such as how often to meet, how they should best communicate with you, and how well they should explain things.

Be the driver as it relates to asking questions and ensuring you understand what is happening. Every question you have is valid and deserves an explanation. Most people only experience one sudden wealth event in their lives, but their advisors may handle hundreds or even thousands. What is "obvious" or "common sense" to them, may not be to you. Don't be shy about asking a lot of questions or having your advisors explain things until you understand them.

You shouldn't attempt to be the driver in every situation, however. There is a reason you are hiring the best attorneys, CPA, and financial advisor you can find. They have decades (or should!) of knowledge and experience. You're paying them, so let them do their jobs. This means giving them the freedom to explore different strategies, to have conference calls with the other members of your team, and to keep an open-mind to their ideas and advice.

I've found that the best client relationships are the ones where the client paints the big picture of what they want and hope to achieve and then lets the advisors craft the strategy about how to make that happen. Focus on the destination while you let your team figure out how to best get you there.

PROACTIVELY CONTACT FRIENDS/FAMILY

For highly publicized sudden wealth events, such as a lottery, sports/entertainment contract, stock options, or some lawsuits, your friends and family may be all over you with advice and questions. To avoid much of this and to establish control, I've found a successful solution that is both direct and caring. Send this email/letter to your friends and family:

"Thank you for reaching out to me. As you can imagine, life has been very crazy for me lately. I'm sorry that I haven't been able to get back to you, but I want you to know I appreciate our relationship. I'm working with my advisory team. Once I'm able to come up for air, I will give you an update. At this point, I don't need any advice or suggestions, but if this changes, I will let you know. Again, thank you for your understanding while I sort everything out. I look forward to being able to catch up with you soon."

GET HELP

If I've learned anything over the past nearly two decades working with sudden wealth recipients, it is that you can't do it alone. If I won the lottery tomorrow, I guarantee I'd get help. It makes no sense trying to do it all yourself – there are just too many tax, legal, and financial issues. Regardless of what sudden wealth stage you are in, but especially if you are in 'Stage 1: Pre-Money', get advisors on your team as soon as possible. Why? You could save yourself millions of dollars. For example, if you are expecting $5 million from a lawsuit judgment, you may actually receive more money if you settle the case for $3 million. How is that possible? Punitive damages are taxed differently than compensatory damages. It pays to have a good tax lawyer on your team as early as possible. Read "Sudden Wealth Principle 3: Get Help" to find the right team for you.

Don't confuse taking control with taking action or making decisions. We are terrible at making decisions under stress, and if there is anything sudden wealth provides in spades, it is stress. Sometimes, control is making the decision to not make any decisions and to slow down, which leads us to Sudden Wealth Principle 2 . . .

Know which decisions you need to make and which you can delay.

Sudden wealth has been described as a frenzy of emotions, decisions, and requests. Clients have expressed that they feel like a "fish out of water," where everything is foreign to them. It's been described as going to bed and waking up in an unfamiliar land where no one speaks their language, yet it's vital to be able to communicate. One client said it's similar to the feeling you have when you are dreaming and can't move – a feeling of agitation and uneasiness, of knowing you should be doing something but not knowing how.

Sudden wealth recipients experience a wide range of emotions – from joy to guilt and euphoria to panic – sometimes on the same day. These wild swings are not conducive to creating a state where you can make the best decisions, and further, these emotional swings are just not fun to experience. The better you are at being able to stay relaxed and focused on what matters most in your life, the better you will feel. But don't count on your friends or family to help you gain perspective or slow things down. They're often caught up in the same heightened emotional state as you! They are vicariously experiencing the same highs and lows as you, and in some cases, they may have their own agenda for your sudden wealth.

If your advisors aren't familiar with the psychological effects of sudden wealth, they may be of little help. Most just don't understand the need to slow down. Bottom line, it's up to you to slow everything down to a pace at which you are comfortable.

This Sudden Wealth Principle provides a bridge and the structure between the early stages when everything feels chaotic and it's hard to concentrate and make a decision to the point where you feel more comfortable and in control. Think of the recommendations in this chapter as tools for a healthy and smooth transition into sudden wealth and coping strategies for the demands it places on you. One client referred to this process as getting his "sea legs."

Fortunately, humans are perfectly adapted to handle a wide range of experiences and environments, but sudden wealth can stretch our abilities, sometimes past the breaking point, because we cannot prepare for it. The sudden wealth event can come out of nowhere, and we are thrust into unfamiliar territory where we are required to make instant life-changing decisions. We just weren't designed for this. Worse still, the high anxiety of the situation actually makes it harder for us to adapt and make these decisions.

We like to think we are rational creatures who look at all the facts, make analytical comparisons, and arrive at sensible decisions, but that's just not how we are wired. We are highly emotional beings, and it turns out, highly irrational – especially when under stress.

Sudden wealth forces us into an unfamiliar situation, piles on stress, and does all of this overnight. If we don't take a step back and slow things down, we can make all kinds of bad decisions. When emotions take over, logic and thoughtful consideration go out the window. And even though we can't change our wiring overnight, by understanding our limitations and learning strategies to slow the process, we can minimize mistakes and bad decisions.

SUDDEN WEALTH STRESS AND MAKING DECISIONS

Quick, how do you say "thank you" in Spanish? Even if you don't speak Spanish, almost everyone knows it's *gracias*. What if I told you I studied Spanish for six months but couldn't answer that question? Here's what happened. I listened to audio programs, practiced with flashcards, and read intently every day, but I didn't have anyone to practice with. After several months, I had my chance. I went to a Mexican restaurant, eager to practice my new language skills. I began with "Habla Espanol?" but then things went downhill. I became self-conscious and immediately felt my mouth go dry and my heart beating rapidly in my chest. Words escaped me. I couldn't even order a glass of water or say thank you in Spanish. It was a meltdown. But why would a seemingly innocuous situation like ordering food in a restaurant cause so much stress and prevent me from remembering simple phrases?

Would you trust a lizard to help you decide whether it makes sense to take your $48 million lottery win as a lump-sum or an annuity?

Or how about deciding whether to quit your job and buy a lake front house or to keep working and buy an ocean view house? Obviously, we'd never consult a lizard for these important decisions . . . or, would we? Neuroscientists and behavioral economists may disagree with you.

According to researchers, our brain is actually comprised of three areas, or what they call the triune brain, meaning three brains. The first and most primitive of these areas is called the reptilian brain. Our reptilian brain, also called our lizard brain by many, controls our breathing, heartbeat, and other critical functions. Our lizard brain does one thing very well . . . it keeps us alive! It's not the part of the brain charged with thoughtful planning and analysis. No, its job is making quick decisions that ensure our survival. On the Savannah, our lizard brain is the most important thing we have to prevent us from being lunch. In today's less life-or-death world, the lizard brain is still important, but it has a hard time distinguishing between the stress of being chased by a lion and the stress of sudden wealth.

Have you ever been in a dangerous situation or a car accident? Do you become nervous before you give a speech? You can thank the second area of our brain, called the limbic brain, or the monkey brain, for this. Why monkey? Think of the limbic brain as being most responsible for thoughts and emotions. The limbic brain controls the release of hormones such as adrenaline and is critical to emotional memories, which is why the highly emotional events from your past stand out and you forget the hum drum experiences.

The third area of the brain is the neocortex, which is the analytical part of your brain that controls planning, organizing, and looking objectively and logically at a situation. If the monkey brain can be identified as a five year old throwing a tantrum, then certainly the neocortex is best represented by the coolness and composure of Star Trek's Dr. Spock.

Have you ever been in an argument with someone where you remained calm and tried to use logic to explain your point, but the other person was loud and worked up? How did your logic work for you? I'm sure that with your analysis of the facts in a rational manner, the other person quickly calmed down and was able to understand your perspective. Not exactly? And now you can begin to see the limits of our rational brain. It works great when all three brains get along but in highly stressful situations, when our hormones and emotions are high, it becomes overpowered by the less logical parts of our brain.

So what does all of this have to do with sudden wealth? More than you think. The sudden wealth experience – especially in Stage 1 and

Stage 2 — is highly charged and highly emotional. Even though we are in no physical danger, our hormones start pumping and our lizard and monkey brains take over, just like in a heated argument. It's the same response you might feel if you are pulled over by the police. It happens automatically and instantly, but unlike a speeding ticket, where the rush subsides after a few minutes, your logical and rational brains can be hijacked for weeks or months during a sudden wealth event. The quality of our life is based on the decisions we make. If we are making decisions based on prehistoric (i.e., lizard) and emotional (i.e., monkey) thinking, we can undermine our finances and relationships.

What's the solution? Some advisors suggest eliminating any decisions during the first six months of receiving sudden wealth. Although this is a noble goal, it is not practical. Making no decisions can be just as destructive as making too many decisions and can cost you millions of dollars in extra taxes and legal and financial problems. It shouldn't be about making decisions or not making decisions. It's about making the right decisions and delaying the others. You don't want to feel paralyzed from making decisions, so it's important to distinguish the decisions you can and should make versus the decisions you shouldn't make immediately after experiencing a sudden wealth event.

Use the guide below to determine the types of decisions you can make and the ones you should avoid:

GREEN DECISIONS

These are safe decisions that you (and your lizard/monkey brain!) should be okay making:

1. Researching and hiring advisors (e.g., attorney, CPA, financial advisor)

2. Researching and implementing tax minimization strategies

3. Working with a therapist

4. Creating a wishlist

5. Opening bank/investment accounts

6. Doing some basic estate planning

7. Upgrading your property and casualty insurance policies

8. Buying personal umbrella liability insurance

9. Continuing to pay your bills as normal

YELLOW DECISIONS

You have to be careful with these decisions. Work with your advisors and get their feedback before making these decisions:

1. If you should take some time off from work
2. Talking to the media
3. Moving in with your partner
4. Investing in CDs, short-term bonds, and other liquid and conservative investments
5. Talking to friends and family about your sudden wealth
6. Travelling
7. Taking the lump sum or annuity in a lottery win
8. Taking an ex-spouse to court for child custody or financial support issues
9. Asset protection strategies that do not involve giving up control over your assets
10. Moving to a different state
11. Signing any forms or documents
12. Paying off any tax liens
13. Pre-paying any bills

RED DECISIONS

Generally speaking, these decisions should be avoided for several months and only after you and your advisors have gone through your entire plan:

1. Whether you can quit your job
2. Buying a new car
3. Contributing to a child's college savings account
4. If you should move
5. If you should give money to charity
6. If and how much you can give to friends and family
7. How your money should be invested
8. Getting married or divorced

9. Promising/committing to help friends and family pay for things (e.g., college, car, new business)

10. Buying life insurance or annuities

11. Irrevocable gifting or transferring of assets to minimize taxes or for asset protection

12. Transferring any money or assets to someone else (including your children)

13. Committing to an employment agreement

14. Paying off any liabilities (including credit cards and loans from family/friends)

As a rule of thumb, if the decision is not a tax or legal issue related to your sudden wealth, it's best if you can wait. This will give you time to sink in to the new situation and to get your bearings while the stress of the sudden wealth fades, allowing your rational brain to take over.

Emotions And Spending

Do you like to shop when you feel stressed? You're not alone. Research suggests that emotions play an important role in self-control and impulsive purchasing. A study in the *Journal of Consumer Reports* concludes, "Coping with stress may also involve making difficult choices under uncertain conditions. All these will deplete the self's resources and leave the self more vulnerable to impulsive behavior, including impulsive purchases" (Baumeister, 2002[5]). But it's not just stress that can lead to impulsive buying, excitement can as well. In a 2008 report in the *Seoul Journal of Business*, the research suggested that, "Arousal, which is the degree to which one feels stimulated, excited and frenzied, is most strongly related to impulsive buying" (Yi[6]). Be careful.

HOW YOU CAN TAKE CONTROL

Here's how you can take control and slow the rush of decisions and emotions to a more manageable pace . . .

USE A WISHLIST

This was discussed in the last chapter, but it is one of the most important things you can do to slow things down. Instead of making emotional "must buy now" decisions with your lizard/monkey brain, the wishlist slows things down. It buys you time so you can think with a clearer head, while still validating your desires and ideas. For the wishlist to be successful, write down anything that comes to you that you want to do with the new money. This includes what you want to buy (e.g., new house, car, boat), what you want to experience (e.g., go back to school, travel), what you want to do for others (e.g., gift money, donate to charity, start a foundation), and thoughts on how you envision your new life. Don't second guess yourself. If you think it, write it. There is no need to prioritize or categorize these yet. Just get them out of your head and on paper (or computer) for now.

Make sure that no matter where you are, you are able to capture your ideas. It's important to have one central place for all of your ideas. I send clients a Moleskine notepad, where they can write all of their ideas. If you have a long commute, consider buying a small digital recorder for the car. Some clients prefer an electronic tool for capturing their ideas. Smartphones are great for this. Evernote (www.evernote.com) is a wonderful app I've used for years. Also, you can easily record audio notes in the car with most new phones. The three important rules for a wishlist are (1) write everything down no matter how small, big, or ridiculous you think it is, (2) as soon as the idea pops in your head, capture it – don't wait – and (3) keep all of your ideas in one place, either on a notepad or electronically.

PHONE A FRIEND

Better yet, get together with friends. Continue to socialize. Lean on them for support and encouragement. These interactions are good for the soul and can keep things in perspective. If we become too stressed or myopic in our own lives, we may lack the desire to socialize, but this is when we need the connection the most.

EXERCISE

Research shows that daily exercise can be as effective in treating depression and anxiety as prescription medication. It's a natural mood booster and relaxant. Incorporate some form of daily exercise into your schedule. It can be as simple as a morning walk or an after dinner bike ride. Exercise is one of the easiest ways to slow down and to keep our lizard/monkey brains at bay.

STRESS REDUCTION STRATEGIES

To slow the barrage of requests and decisions and to clear your head, try yoga, meditation, praying, or just conscious deep breathing.

Many sudden wealth recipients have found solace engaging in these calming activities.

KEEP WHAT WORKS

"Everything changes" is how one unhappy sudden wealth recipient described her experience. A sudden wealth event can get us thinking about all of the things we want to buy and do with our new lives, but everything doesn't have to change. In fact, not everything should change. Money is a tool that can better your life, but the key word is "better." Sudden wealth recipients who are most unhappy are the ones who radically changed their lives after getting the money. They threw out what wasn't working with what was. They'll reminisce about the "good old days" when their lives were less complicated. But the money alone didn't change their lives, they did. You'll learn how to create your best life in "Sudden Wealth Principle 8: Create a Better Life," but for now, and before things change, take an inventory of what you like about your pre-money life.

What gave you happiness and a sense of accomplishment? When do you feel the most connected to your purpose? What activities, big or small, do you enjoy? What rituals do you appreciate? Who is important to you? Don't just casually consider your answers, document them. Be very clear on what you want to keep and incorporate into your "new" life. Headline your notepad "What I want to keep the same" and get to work. Talk to family members and friends and ask them what they don't want to change. This process will not only ensure you create the best life you can, but it also forces you to appreciate what you have, which can provide the pause you need when emotions run high and things become too hectic.

SEEK A HIGHER AUTHORITY

If you are religious, talk to your spiritual leader. Share your concerns and your excitement. He or she may offer encouragement and help ground you to your beliefs and a higher purpose.

SEEK LIKE-MINDED SUPPORT

Sudden wealth can be isolating. It can be a lonely experience if you think it is all up to you and that no one understands what you are going through. Do exactly what you are doing right now – getting support from someone who understands your situation and what you are going through – through books or through "support" groups. Join one of the groups we hold with clients and non-clients; you can talk to others who have experienced sudden wealth and can hear their story and what worked for them.

Get more sudden wealth tips and encouragement on the go. Listen to Sudden Wealth Radio, the first and only broadcast to discuss the tax, legal, financial, and psychological issues of sudden wealth. Get more information at www.suddenwealthsolution.com.

GET PROFESSIONAL HELP

The best few hundred dollars a month you can spend is on a licensed therapist – at least for the first few months while you are adjusting to your sudden wealth. Even if you have an understanding family and great friends, sometimes it is nice to be able to talk to someone who doesn't come with any baggage or agenda and is in no way connected to the financial decisions you are going to make. Objectivity and a fresh perspective can be just what you need to reduce stress and to slow things down.

VOLUNTEER

Do you really want to gain perspective and get grounded? Volunteer for a few hours a week. Your life may feel turned upside down, but spend a couple of hours in a children's shelter or soup kitchen and you'll appreciate the quality of your problems. Volunteering won't improve your situation, but it will improve your perspective – something we can easily lose when we get into the weeds of all of the tax, legal, and financial details.

FIND YOUR PEAK

When do you perform at your best? Circadian rhythms are natural daily cycles we experience. Research shows we are better equipped at handling certain tasks at different times during the day. For example, most of us experience a cognitive and energy decline between the hours of 2pm and 5pm. This is the familiar afternoon slump where productivity and concentration drops. Managing the tax, legal, and financial issues of sudden wealth can be challenging enough, so why make it harder for yourself by scheduling meetings and calls when you are cognitively least equipped? If you have the flexibility in your day, schedule advisor calls and meetings during peak cognitive functioning, which, for most people, is in the morning – between 7am and 11am.

TAKE CARE OF YOURSELF

The sudden wealth experience is similar in a lot of ways to competitive sports. To perform your best, you need to be in peak condition. No, this doesn't mean you need to train for a marathon, but it does mean you should take care of yourself. Again, this process can be challenging, so you might as well give yourself all the advantages you can to not only survive the process, but to also enjoy it. Eat a healthy diet, avoid over-drinking, and try to get at least eight hours of sleep a night. The better you feel, the better your decisions.

Take A Trip

If you have a highly publicized sudden wealth event such as a lottery win or lawsuit, it may be best to take a trip to avoid the media frenzy. The trip should not be a vacation but a retreat, where you spend a couple of days with your family and team of advisors plotting your future. It is remarkable how much can be accomplished in these day or multi-day retreats. In one memorable retreat I spearheaded, the winner of a large lawsuit brought his family and extended family – there were no less than 25 of us in a family room. When we started the retreat, the anxiety and uncertainty were high, but by the end, in addition to gaining a few pounds from all of the home-cooked dishes they prepared, we had a plan and everyone felt secure and comfortable. Although I don't recommend eating as much as I did, I strongly encourage you to set aside a day or two with your advisors to make preparations for your sudden wealth.

KEEP IT PRIVATE

It is in your best interest not to divulge too much information to too many people. Sounds obvious, but you'd be surprised how often sudden wealth recipients can't contain their excitement and will share everything with family and friends. This is a mistake, especially early on. The sudden wealth is too new, and you are still trying to figure things out. You don't need other people's unsolicited recommendations or even their enthusiasm. This will just cloud your judgment and make the job of slowing things down even more difficult. At most, choose one or two people, who you know well and who you trust, if you need to share your news. And even then, there's no need to get into the details of your situation or how much money you will be receiving. Lean on them for emotional support, not tax, legal, or financial advice.

Although it's important to slow down and to adjust to your new reality, you may be faced with several tax, legal, and financial decisions that require your immediate attention. It's time to get some help . . .

GET HELP

As a sudden wealth recipient, you are likely to be barraged by tax, legal, and financial issues. The only method to successfully navigate your way through the complexity is to have a team of experts who are the best at what they do. I've specialized in financial planning and investment management for sudden wealth recipients for almost two decades, but if I won the lottery tomorrow, you can bet one of the first things I'd do is build my advisory team. There is too much at stake not to have the best minds and latest strategies available to you.

So often, when I start working with a sudden wealth client months or years after they received their money, I cringe at the tax, legal, or financial strategies they could have employed if only they had better advice. If you win the daily scratcher for $1,000 or if you receive a $5,000 insurance settlement, there are limited options for which you can take advantage. But if your sudden wealth is significant, there is a whole world of options and strategies that can potentially save you not just a little, but a lot of money. How much? I once watched a client write a $15 million check to the IRS for federal income tax. Sounds like a disaster, but if she hadn't hired a team of experts, that check would have been closer to $25 million. By working with the right specialists, she was able to save close to $10 million of state and federal income tax. If her team had been made of a typical CPA, a general business attorney, and normal financial planner, she would have left millions of dollars on the table. That $10 million of "found" money over her lifetime could be worth over $100 million if invested. As they say, "A billion here, a billion there, and pretty soon, you're talking about real money."

The goal for this chapter is for you to become familiar with who should be on your team, what roles they each play, what their qualifications should be, and the most challenging of all, how to find them.

WHO SHOULD BE ON YOUR TEAM?

Each sudden wealth type has its own unique characteristics and tax, legal, and financial challenges, which are highlighted in Section II of this book. Therefore, not all sudden wealth events require the same type of experts. At a minimum, you should expect to have at least the following three advisors: attorney, CPA, and a financial planner. These three advisors represent the foundation – what I call *the advisor triad*. Think of them as three legs of a stool. You need all three to form a stable base where you can be secure in knowing the tax, legal, and financial issues are being addressed.

ATTORNEY

A good attorney (no pun intended) is worth his weight in gold. The problem is knowing what type of attorney you need. There are thousands of specialties within the legal profession – from criminal to copyright to bankruptcy to divorce to real estate and everything in between. Think of law as being similar to the medical field where "doctor" is a generic term used for anyone who has gone to medical school. You wouldn't go to a dermatologist for an appendectomy and you wouldn't want to hire a business attorney for tax matters.

The following are the types of attorneys you may need:

TAX ATTORNEY

Depending on the type of sudden wealth you receive, you may need the specialized knowledge of a tax attorney on your team. For large sums coming from lawsuit judgment/settlement, business sale, stock options, sports/entertainment contract, and to a lesser extent, the lottery, a tax attorney will be invaluable.

The tax attorney will play a highly specialized role. She will ensure you are taking advantage of all the tax minimization strategies possible. Even if you have a CPA on your team, which you should and which we'll discuss below, you will still need a tax attorney. Why? A CPA has a broad knowledge of taxes whereas the tax attorney understands the tax laws and may be highly specialized in just one area of tax law. For example, if you are expecting a large lawsuit settlement, there are tax attorneys who focus exclusively on the tax issues of damages. If you are expecting hundreds of thousands or millions of dollars, you will need a tax attorney to cut your tax bill as low as legally possible.

The tax attorney is a hired gun who works with you for a limited amount of time, usually a few weeks to a few months, in an effort to minimize the amount of tax you pay the year you receive the sudden wealth. It pays to bring the tax attorney in as early as possible, ideally even before you receive the money, because they can advise you on how to structure the business sale, judgment, etc., in the best tax manner possible. After you pay taxes that first year, their job is usually done and the CPA calculates your taxes thereafter.

ESTATE ATTORNEY

Estate attorneys, also called trust and estate attorneys, specialize in minimizing estate/gift taxes and drafting documents that address the distribution of your assets before and after death. Stage 2 is usually a good time to bring in the estate attorney. Unlike the tax attorney, whom you will probably never need to speak to after their initial work, you will have the need to continue your relationship with your estate attorney.

ASSET PROTECTION ATTORNEY

Money is a magnet for lawsuits. The more money you have, the greater the chance someone (and their attorney) will see you as a target. There are legal ways to shield your assets and to protect yourself against lawsuits, and this is where the knowledge of an asset protection attorney is needed. Some asset protection attorneys focus on this area exclusively, but you'll often see estate attorneys provide asset protection to clients. If you find the right estate attorney, they can do both effectively. If your estate attorney is less qualified in asset protection, this is an area where it can make sense to hire a specialist.

GENERAL BUSINESS ATTORNEY

A general business attorney may have their hands in different areas of law, but they can be a valuable member of your team, if only to help you find more specialized attorneys. The problem I see clients run into is when they hire a general business attorney to do everything – reduce taxes, draft trusts, set up LLCs, etc. I've had clients come to me after they had the same attorney not only help them with divorce but also draft their estate plan and create a buy-sell agreement for their company. It doesn't matter how smart or seemingly qualified an attorney appears, one person cannot effectively practice three areas of law. Avoid this by hiring a specialist.

There are a few things you should consider when hiring an attorney. The first was already discussed. Make sure you hire a specialist in the area(s) you need rather than a one-size-fits-all legal generalist. Specialists will cost more, and you may have to hire more than one, but they should pay for themselves many times over.

Second, does it make more sense to hire an attorney from a big firm or a small firm? I think the same rule applies to music. You don't download songs because Universal Music Group is the record label, you download the artist you like. Law firms are a collection of attorneys. Don't hire the firm, hire the attorney. Some of the very best attorneys in the country have firms with fewer than 10 employees.

Cost is another issue to consider. Many sudden wealth recipients are aghast at the retainers and fees their advisory team charges – it is not at all uncommon for the first year's advisory fees to exceed the annual income of the client before their sudden wealth. There are two ways to pay less in fees. You can hire an advisory team that is subpar or you can choose to go it alone and come up with your own tax, legal, and financial strategies. Obviously, these are both terrible options. This doesn't mean that you should pay more than what is fair, and it doesn't mean that just because someone charges more that they are better. We'll discuss this further later in this chapter, but for now, start to become comfortable with the idea that you may be paying a considerable amount of money to your attorneys and other advisors.

Lastly, each state regulates the attorneys who are licensed to practice law in their state. An attorney only licensed in California cannot provide legal advice if you live in Missouri, so it's important that your attorney is licensed to practice law in your state.

CPA

A CPA, or Certified Public Accountant, is a broad designation provided to someone who has passed a comprehensive exam administered by the National Association of State Boards of Accountancy and who meets additional state education and experience requirements. A CPA, like an attorney, is regulated by the state, so it's important that you work with a CPA who is qualified in the state in which you live.

CPAs perform a vast range of services – from auditing to forensic accounting to corporate finance. The CPA you hire should be focused on tax, specifically tax minimization and preparation. The CPA is not a hired gun you bring in for a limited time to help address a specific issue. Your CPA will be a long-term and critical member of your advisory team. You'll work with them throughout the year to minimize state and federal income taxes and they'll help you calculate your estimated taxes and prepare your tax returns.

The year you receive the sudden wealth and the year following typically require more sophisticated tax planning. It is during this time you may have not only a CPA but a tax attorney on your team. Your income tax and tax planning/preparation bills will undoubtedly be higher during these years. After this period, things usually become a lot simpler. The amount of tax and tax advisory fees you pay often drops substantially.

CPAs can be sole practitioners, work for one of the "big four" accounting firms, or fall somewhere in between. CPAs will also typically specialize in personal returns (tax matters for individuals) or business returns (tax matters for companies). If you have or plan on operating a business, a firm larger than one person may have more depth of services and research to support your needs.

FINANCIAL ADVISOR

The third leg of the stool, and completing the advisory triad, is the financial advisor. A good financial advisor will work with you even before you receive the money. They will be a critical resource to help prepare you for the money and help you create a comprehensive financial plan. A financial advisor well-versed in the tax and legal aspects of sudden wealth can be an important part of your team – working with and suggesting tax minimization, asset protection, and other advanced strategies with the other members of your team. And, of course, once you have received the money, your financial advisor will manage your assets and provide ongoing reporting, monitoring, and adjustments to your plan and investments.

The complaint of many sudden wealth clients is that they are paying all of these experts but that no one knows what the others are doing – the CPA doesn't know what the estate attorney is doing and is not aware of what the insurance guy is recommending. This can lead to inefficiency, extra fees for you, sub-optimal planning, and gaping holes in your estate, asset protection, and financial plan.

I've learned that to create a comprehensive financial plan, someone has to step up and manage it, but what usually happens is the attorneys and CPA have their heads in the details and the client has to manage everyone and everything. Not only should the client not have to take on this job, especially with what they are paying their advisors, but they also are often not qualified to know who to bring in or even what questions to ask.

A good financial advisor should not only play a critical role in the early stages of sudden wealth, but I've found that they are best equipped to be the person managing the other advisors, coordinating and overseeing the plan, and the person you call first when there is a question. When the financial advisor fills this role, they are called the "financial quarterback" because they see all of the moving parts of the client's tax, legal, and financial life. They are the ones who can identify when to bring in other experts and make sure all of your financial bases are covered.

But why is the financial advisor best equipped for this role? Many aren't, and that is why it's important to work with a comprehensive financial planner, someone who can provide expertise in the areas of insurance, cash-flow management, retirement planning, taxes, estate planning, asset protection, and investments. Sounds like a tall order, and it is. Most financial advisors are simply not qualified (regardless of what their websites, TV ads, or brochures claim), but you'll learn how to separate the pros from the amateurs.

8 RULES TO EVALUATE A FINANCIAL ADVISOR

There are many types of financial advisors. Or is it financial planner? Certified Financial Planner™? Investment Advisor? Wealth manager? And this is where things can become confusing. The financial industry has a whole lot of people calling themselves different things and purporting to provide a wide range of services. Unlike an attorney or CPA, who have state bodies regulating their profession, anyone can call themselves a financial advisor, financial planner, or any number of other titles. "Buyer beware" couldn't be more apt, but by the end of this section, you'll have a much better understanding of the financial industry and the type of financial advisor you should hire to be part of your team.

Criteria 1 – Hire a Fiduciary

Here's how to eliminate 90% of potential financial advisors. There are two broad categories of advisors – fiduciaries and non-fiduciaries. Simply put, fiduciaries are legally obligated to put their clients' interests first, whereas non-fiduciaries can offer advice that is not in your interest as long as it is "suitable" to you. Clearly, it behooves you to work with an advisor who will always put your interests first – ahead of their own interests and of the firm they work for. Surprisingly (or maybe not so surprisingly), almost all of the big brokerage firms you see advertising on TV are not fiduciaries. They can put their (financial) interests ahead of the client, and this is perfectly acceptable, as long as they meet the minimum requirement of it being suitable to you. Don't settle for suitable. Hire a fiduciary.

Criteria 2 – Hire a Certified Financial Planner™ Practitioner

The Certified Financial Planner™ (CFP®) designation is earned by passing a comprehensive exam, completing a series of courses, agreeing to a code of ethics, and having three years' worth of professional experience in financial planning. The CFP® mark is arguably the most recognized comprehensive financial planning designation available. Are there other designations? Yes, literally hundreds. Some are good and some bordering on the inane (e.g., Life Underwriter Training Council Fellow, Chartered Mutual Fund Counselor, etc.). A CFP® shows that the advisor has at least a basic level of comprehensive planning – an understanding of tax, estate planning, investments, insurance, college and retirement planning, and cash-flow management. Are there bad financial advisors with the CFP®? Yes. Are there good financial advisors without the CFP®? Yes. But as a rule of thumb, I highly recommend the advisor you work with have the CFP®.

Criteria 3 – Look for Advanced Education/Training

The CFP® represents the minimal amount of training from which to begin your advisor search. It's like thinking you're qualified to race in the Indy 500 because you have a driver's license. It's a good starting point but with your financial life on the line, don't settle for the minimum. Look for your advisor to have advanced designations or degrees including a JD (law degree), CPA/EA (tax), CFA/CIMA (portfolio design and investment analysis), master's degree in tax, financial planning, economics, or finance, an MBA with an emphasis in finance/investments, or the PFS/CPWA (financial planning). Additionally, because sudden wealth is a highly specialized field, look for those financial advisors who have experience in, and focus their practice on, serving sudden wealth recipients.

Criteria 4 – Stick to the 10,000 Hour Rule

Psychologist Anders Ericsson has studied what makes great performers such great performers. His conclusion? Practice. Lots of practice, actually. The 10,000 hours of practice rule has emerged as a rule-of-thumb for how much practice is required to develop an expertise in a field of study. It often requires at least 10 years in one's profession to begin to have mastery. Again, this is a generality, but if I'm hiring a doctor or any specialist, I will only hire someone with at least ten years of experience, and when you are hiring a financial advisor, attorney, or CPA, I strongly recommend you do the same.

Criteria 5 – Avoid Commission-Only Advisors

There are many different ways in which to pay for financial advice. You can pay by the hour, based on a percentage of assets the advisor manages for you (referred to as "AUM" or assets under management), a flat monthly retainer, commissions, or any combination of the above. Commission-only advisors – nowadays usually stockbrokers and insurance salespeople – should be avoided. Their entire financial livelihood is based on selling you something. You want your advisory team to be objective and to be your partner, not your adversary. Stick with a fee-based advisor who charges an AUM fee and may receive incidental commissions on insurance products or a fee-only advisor who receives no commissions. For years, I expounded on the merits of the fee-only model, but after years of referring insurance business to less competent advisors who earned the commission, I now see the benefit of a single advisor handling all aspects of the financial planning process.

Criteria 6 – Check for a Clean Record

Do a background check on your advisor to ensure there are no regulatory or legal infractions against him. Use the following websites to check on the status of their license and regulatory history:

FINRA: suddenwealthsolution.com/check-your-advisor

SEC: suddenwealthsolution.com/check-your-advisor

CFP® Board: suddenwealthsolution.com/check-your-advisor

Don't Blindly Trust; Verify Instead

Do not rely on the bio your advisor provides you or that is on his website. If he claims to be a CFP® practitioner, verify it. If he claims he went to Yale, verify it. It takes just a moment, but it can save you dearly. Retired NFL star Ricky Williams learned this the hard way. He is suing his financial advisor for absconding with $6 million from his account and lying about being an attorney and a graduate of Harvard Business School. Don't blindly trust; verify instead.

Criteria 7 – Check Their Form ADV

Every Registered Investment Advisory firm must complete a document that discloses details about the firm, their clients, their experience, and other valuable information. This is a treasure trove of information as you evaluate advisors. Things to look for are an experienced team (at least 10 years of experience), good education and credentials, a focus on high net-worth individuals and sudden wealth recipients, no negative legal issues, and a large pool of investor assets they manage – at least $500 million to $1 billion as a starting point. You can request a copy of the firm's Form ADV from the company itself or by going to suddenwealthsolution/check-your-advisor.

Criteria 8 – Ask the Right Questions by Using AdvisorFit

After watching one too many episodes of the TV show *American Greed*, where unsuspecting people got bilked out of their life savings by unscrupulous advisors, I knew I had to do something to protect people from those who prey on the less financially sophisticated. This was the birth of AdvisorFit (www.advisorfit.com), a free online question and analysis tool for screening potential financial advisors. AdvisorFit helps clients ask the right questions, and just as importantly, understand the answers they receive from perspective advisors.

Help Evaluating Your Advisors

Evaluate potential financial advisors by asking them the right questions. Use AdvisorFit (www.advisorfit.com) to leave no question un-asked. Here are a few sample questions AdvisorFit uses:

- How did you respond to the 2008-2009 recession and financial crisis and what would you have done differently?

- Do you or a related party have ownership or financial interest in the entity that houses my account?

- What are the sources of your compensation?

Here's how it works. Once you find an advisor you are interested in screening, go to the AdvisorFit website and enter their email address. The advisor will receive a detailed questionnaire, and once they complete it, you will receive their answers and an analysis of their answers that may help you better understand their approach and whether they are a good fit for your needs. It doesn't guarantee you'll find the best advisor, but it goes a long way by asking the tough questions.

OTHER ADVISORS YOU MAY WANT ON YOUR TEAM

The financial triad represents your core team, but there may be others you may want to consider, including the following:

Bookkeeper. A bookkeeper can help keep you financially organized. They can pay your bills, balance your accounts, and work with your CPA to make tax preparation easier.

Business manager. Business managers often serve Hollywood celebrities and athletes. They pay their client's bills, file tax returns, and can even perform concierge services such as handling vacation plans, disputing credit card charges, and managing home projects.

Insurance advisors. After a sudden wealth event, you will need additional insurance. At the minimum, you will want excess personal liability insurance (i.e., umbrella liability policy), but if you purchase a larger house, buy a new car, or want to have a policy to pay estate taxes, you will need insurance. There are two types of insurance advisors – agents and brokers. An agent works for one insurance company and can only sell you their brand of insurance. A broker, on the other hand, can shop your policy among the top 20 or more insurance companies. Therefore, I recommend you use an insurance broker. Also, you can further divide insurance advisors between property/casualty and personal. Property/casualty advisors provide advice on policies such as home-owner's, auto, umbrella, boat, renters, business liability, etc. whereas personal insurance advisors focus on health, life, and disability. If your insurance broker claims to be an expert in both, be cautious. Although it's all insurance, the two areas are highly specialized. Insurance is not an area to be lax. I recommend seeking insurance advisors who specialize.

HOW BEST TO WORK WITH YOUR ADVISORS

The best ingredients do not necessarily make the best meal. You can have the best advisors in the world in their respected fields, but if they don't have a clear leader, communicate effectively, agree on an overall strategy, or generally play well together, it will be a mess. A mess can undermine the viability of the client's financial plan and cre-ate unnecessary stress for the client at a time when their advisors should be working to make the client's life easier and stress-free. Ulti-mately, when the advisory team doesn't operate smoothly, it hurts the client. This is why it is so important to have someone managing the process and leading the team – holding the members accountable, dri-ving the plan forward, integrating the tax, legal, and financial issues, and ensuring constant communication among the advisors and to the client.

Sometimes the leader is the client, but often it is the financial advisor. Regardless of who assumes this role, there are several strategies to make the team work better and for the client to feel like an integral part of the process.

CHOOSE THE LEADER

As early as possible, make the decision about who will be the leader responsible for overseeing the plan and for managing the advi-sory team. If that person is you, great. Let your team know you are tak-ing on this role. If it's not you, identify the person on your team responsible for this – the attorney, CPA, or financial advisor. Don't assume someone will step up on their own to assume control and lead. It is your responsibility to identify this person and to have a conversa-tion with them and the team.

DRIVER VERSUS PASSENGER

As was discussed in chapter one, know when to be the driver and when to be the passenger. Be the driver on the overall goals and objectives – the "what" – but be the passenger on the specifics of your plan – the "how." Lean on your advisors for their experience and knowledge of the tax code, laws, and strategies while you shape the direction of the plan.

SET COMMUNICATIONS EXPECTATIONS

As good as we advisors are at what we do, our ability to read the minds of others is lacking. If you have a preference in how your advisor communicates with you (e.g., phone call, email, text, etc.) and how often, let them know. What are the best hours to contact you? At work or after hours? How early can they call in the morning? Some clients like the details and want to do a great deal of communication, whereas others want less. For example, if you want a weekly phone call and an email summary each time your advisors work on your case, set this expectation with your advisors. A competent sudden wealth advisor will ask you, but if yours doesn't, it's up to you to let them know. In the past, I've made the mistake of assuming what clients want, but not now. I explicitly ask their preferred form of communication and how often they want updates.

DETERMINE AND DISCUSS YOUR COMMUNICATION STYLE

Imagine that you are a quiet person who likes to analyze the details and take your time to make a decision, but your attorney is loud, excitable, and gives you a brief summary and then pushes you to make a quick decision. Or maybe you are a big picture person who quickly makes decisions but are working with a highly detailed and methodical advisor who feels the need to explain not just their recommendation but also how they came to that conclusion. In either case, it won't take long for you to feel disconnected, and maybe even frustrated and angry. You certainly won't feel listened to or respected. Your advisor may be one of the best in the country, but if they don't better match their communication style with yours, it not only won't be an enjoyable experience, but you also may not listen to or implement the advice they provide. It's difficult to separate the advice from the advisor.

The most common breakdown in the advisor relationship is the result of unmatched communication styles, when the advisor thinks, communicates, and makes decisions in a certain way that doesn't match the advisor's style. When you find a good match, you will feel the difference. It's like matching the radio tuner to the exact station – the communication will come through loud and clear. If you don't have a good match, all you'll hear is static.

The experts in your advisor triad are going to work with you for years. You'll share things with them that no one else may know. You want to build a relationship, and the best way to do that is if they understand how best you communicate and make decisions. The responsibility is on your advisors to match your style, not for you to match your advisors'. To better help them understand how you tick, complete the Communication Preferences form (suddenwealthsolution.com) and share it with them.

Keeping Your Advisor From "Going Rogue"

I received a call from a woman who apologized for calling because she wasn't sure why she called or what she needed. She said she had been working with an investment advisor at a large bank for several years. She said her performance had been great but that she didn't understand her statements or even what she was investing in. She told me she was 68 years old and that the only assets she had was her house and her investments with this advisor. She made a point to tell me she was more concerned about losing money than making money and that her advisor told her she had a "conservative allocation." I told her to send me her statements so I could have a look at how she was invested. Within 20 seconds of reviewing her statements, I knew she had a problem. Her large portfolio was invested 98.8% in stocks, and of those stocks, the majority were in high-tech investments and many in Chinese Internet companies. The strange thing was that the advisor hadn't always been so aggressive with her portfolio.

After reviewing older statements, it was clear that the advisor became more and more aggressive the longer he worked with her. What started out as an appropriate allocation turned into a high-flying, risk-it-all, allocation. Because the advisor had a discretionary account — a common type of investment account where an advisor can buy and sell at will — he was able to shift not only the investments but also the allocation from sane to insane. The advisor went rogue with her portfolio. But why? Why did the advisor take so much risk?

Sometimes, it is to make up for earlier losses or bad investments — the familiar Las Vegas strategy of doubling down to try to make back losses. But that's not always the reason. Sometimes advisors become too confident in their abilities and think they cannot lose. Simply, they forget their client's goals and objectives and instead focus on their own goals and objectives. Fortunately, she took immediate action and didn't get hurt, but when an advisor goes rogue, it can wipe out a portfolio overnight.

To prevent your advisor from going rogue, pay close attention to the trades she makes in your account, the statements you receive, the risk you are taking, and the overall allocation of your total portfolio. If you don't have the time or expertise to do this yourself, consider using a service that will do this for you. Go to wealthdefend.com to learn about *WealthDefend* — a completely independent service that doesn't replace your advisors but instead provides ongoing monitoring of your performance, risk, and asset allocation to make sure you are not falling behind, paying too much in fees, or that your investment advisor doesn't go rogue with your hard-earned money.

PET PEEVES

Are there certain things your advisors do that annoy you? Maybe you're a stick-to-the-facts kind of person and you become annoyed when they talk about their weekend plans with your charge-by-the-minute attorney. Or maybe you have a tight calendar but your financial advisor always seems to call three or four minutes late. These seemingly little things aren't little at all. They are a big deal, and if they continue unaddressed, they can undermine a good relationship. Complete the Pet Peeve form (suddenwealthsolution.com) and share it with your team.

Don't worry about being "difficult." At the end of the day, you're helping your advisors communicate and work with you in the most ideal and unobstructed way possible so you can make good decisions. This is what you need and what your advisors want.

WEEKLY CALLS

As a reminder, schedule weekly calls with your advisors as you get closer to receiving the money and even more frequently after you receive the money. This weekly call, sometimes just 10 or 15 minutes, is where you can ask the questions from your written log and get updates from your advisors. These calls can help you feel connected to the important issues and your team.

Connect With Others

We have a small but growing list of professional advisors in the areas of tax, law, investments, financial planning, and coaching/counseling, who have specific expertise in navigating the issues of sudden wealth. We'd be happy to put you in touch with the right people. Contact us at suddenwealthsolution.com

HOW TO FIND GOOD ADVISORS

There are approximately 1.2 million attorneys, 700,000 CPAs, and several hundred thousand financial advisors in the United States. How can you find the best three for your needs? As you can imagine, this isn't always easy! Here are a few guidelines you can consider as you start your search.

DON'T LOOK HERE FOR AN ADVISOR

"Best Advisors" lists. There are countless lists of so-called best financial advisors or attorneys in the country, but most are meaningless. The criteria can be skewed to favor some advisors over others, and in some cases, an advisor with little experience can qualify for a list if they pay a hefty application fee.

Television. Don't hire an attorney, CPA, or financial advisor just because they are on TV. Good advisors do make it on TV, but not all advisors who are on TV are good. I've done my share of TV shows, so I know first-hand how it works. For some shows, the vetting process is detailed – they really only want the best of the best. On other shows, they just want a warm body. If you get an advisor from TV, you may be getting a good advisor or maybe just a good marketer. If you see someone on TV, who you think may be a good fit for your needs, do your research and follow the guidelines in this chapter to make sure he's qualified to provide advice, not just look good on TV.

Local bank. Sudden wealth requires sophistication and highly specialized knowledge. No matter how friendly the branch manager at your local bank is, she/he probably doesn't have the experience or technical ability to best advise you. The best advisor for your needs may be in the local branch of your bank but chances are, they aren't. Do you think the country's wealthiest individuals work with the teller or branch manager of their local bank? Neither should you. Willy Sutton robbed banks because "that's where the money is," but if he wanted someone to manage his money, he'd probably drive past his local branch and go to where the talent is instead.

Your current advisors. Some sudden wealth recipients already have a tax person, financial advisor, or attorney they know or work with. This can give them the false sense of security that they already have a team in place to help them, when this is usually not the case. It's tough because sudden wealth can create anxiety and alienation, so it can feel good to see familiar faces. The problem with using existing advisors is that they are usually not experts in sudden wealth and do not have the knowledge or skills to handle the complexity of your situation. In fact, it's better when a sudden wealth recipient doesn't have any advisory relationships because it forces them to find them. Part of your job is to start thinking of yourself differently. Pre-money, the financial advisor who helped you set up your IRA or sold you a life insurance policy may have been a good fit for your needs at that time, but post sudden wealth, you're playing at a whole different level. Your advisors need to match that level. Your friendly tax professional who does your 1040 tax return may have been perfect for your needs before sudden wealth, but there is very little chance she/he will know how to minimize your AMT after paying attorney fees.

Friends and family. What happens if you receive sudden wealth and your brother-in-law is an attorney or your best friend is a CPA? Doesn't it make sense to work with people you trust and to support friends and family? Absolutely, but not at the expense of working with someone who may not have the experience or skills to best serve you. Good intentions do not save taxes or protect your assets. It can be very difficult to say "no, thank you" to friends and family. I've seen situations where clients could not bring themselves to say no and suffered greatly as a result. I've also seen situations where the client did say no and their relationships suffered greatly. There are no easy answers. "Sudden Wealth Principle 5: Manage Relationships" will provide you with more insight and tools to help you deal with friend/family advisors who want to work with you but who are not qualified. For now, focus on the fact that you need and deserve the best advice you can get, wherever it may come from, and that the more financially sound you are, the better you are able to help your friends and family.

Referrals. After a sudden wealth event, become used to receiving unsolicited advice and hearing, "You have to talk to my guy," from just about everyone. And although referrals can be invaluable for finding a good restaurant or knowing what movie to see, when it comes to finding highly specialized experts, it's unlikely you'll find advisors with the necessary experience from a referral.

So where should you look? A good place to start your search is through association websites. For example, you can go on the CFP® website at to search for advisors who specialize in "sudden wealth management" by zip code. You can use the Lawyer Information and Information Service online tool (americanbar.org) provided by the American Bar Association to connect to your local chapter and be referred to an attorney. The American Institute of CPAs offers a "Find a CPA" tool (aicpa.org) as a way to start your search.

One strategy is to find one member of your triad – the attorney, CPA, or financial advisor – and then tap into their connections to find the remaining members of your team. The idea is that if you find a great sudden wealth attorney, for example, they will have other sudden wealth professionals in their network they can refer to you.

Get Help Evaluating An Advisor

Having trouble finding an advisor or concerned you won't be able to adequately evaluate them? Hire a consultant to do the research and screen potential advisors. For an hourly or flat fee, they will determine your needs and then provide you with possible candidates. Make sure they are not also compensated by the advisors they screen.

I have put together an informal resource of sudden wealth advisors (CPAs, attorneys, financial advisors) across the country. It is by no means exhaustive, but it might provide you with a good starting point. Go to suddenwealthsolution.com to start your sudden wealth advisor search.

THE BEST OR THE CLOSEST ADVISOR?

One of the most frequent complaints I hear from sudden wealth recipients is that they can't find qualified sudden wealth advisors near them. This is a valid complaint because it is a real problem. If you live in a big city, such as Los Angeles, Chicago, or New York, you should have no problem finding well-qualified advisors. But what if you don't live in a big city? Should you sacrifice qualifications for proximity? If it were me, this is an easy decision I would make without any hesitation . . . I would always go for the very best and most qualified, regardless of how close (or far) they were from me. In fact, my personal CPA and attorney are in a different city from me. I want to know I'm working with the best, not the closest. When in doubt, err on the side of experience, even if that requires a different zip code, area code, or even time zone. What would you rather say, "I have the best advisor in the country, but I wish he were closer?" or "I have an advisor in town I can see whenever I want, I just wish he were more qualified?"

If you decide to work with an advisor who's not in your backyard, set your expectations early on. I suggest having an initial face-to-face meeting. In most cases, the burden should be on the advisor to travel to you. If you prefer in-person meetings, determine how often you expect your advisor to meet with you (e.g., once a year, twice a year). Some advisors won't travel to meet with clients while others will travel freely. Either way, it's better to have this conversation at the beginning of the relationship so you can find the best fit.

It's become easier and easier to have a long-distance advisor relationship. Email, phone conferencing, web meetings, and other tools make it less important to sit at a conference room table – especially once the plan is in place and you are in Stage 3. I have clients in the four corners of the United States and in between. If you can't find qualified advisors in your area, don't be too concerned about lack of communication. If you find the right advisor, communication – regardless of where they are – shouldn't be an issue.

Now that you have a team of experts looking out for your best interests, you will want to make sure you are looking out for your own best interests. Old and ineffective money beliefs and behaviors that could undermine your sudden wealth success may need to be replaced. It's time to upgrade your money beliefs . . .

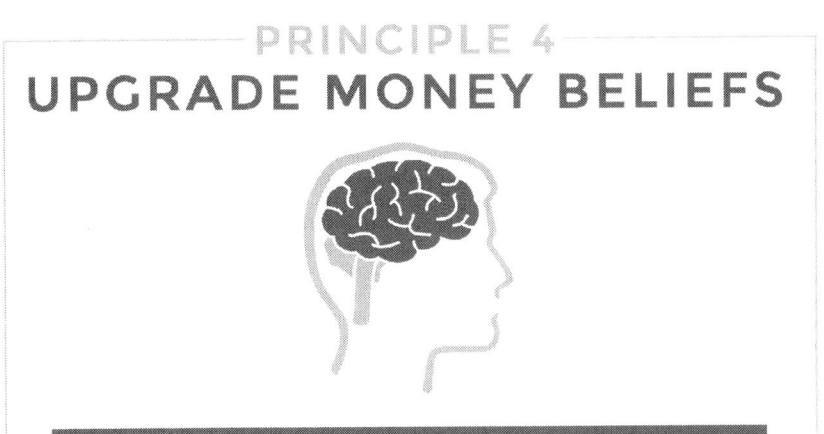

UPGRADE MONEY BELIEFS

Discard limiting money beliefs that will undermine your success.

When some people hear "upgrade money beliefs," their eyes glaze over. I fully understand that reaction. In addition to a master's degree in financial services, I also have a master's degree in psychology. During this program, I learned a lot of theories about human behavior and how we interact with the world. Most of them were rubbish – far too complicated and impractical. I'm only interested in what works. The truth is, we all have money beliefs, and many of us have limiting money beliefs. This just means our view of money is such that it can make acquiring it, saving it, and managing it more difficult than it needs to be. The goal of this chapter is not to spout pop-psychology, but to think about how we think about money. And if you find you are thinking about or using money in a way that is not helpful, you'll learn a few strategies to think about money differently – practical tools to help you manage your sudden wealth more effectively.

Surprising to most, sudden wealth is not about the money. It's more mental and less financial than most people realize. The problems that can arise as a result of sudden wealth rarely are the result of the money; they are almost always psychological, emotional, and relational. If you can "get your head on straight" as one client quipped, you can eliminate many of the potential problems of sudden wealth.

Why do your thoughts and beliefs about money play such an important role? At its essence, sudden wealth – money – is just a tool. It has no inherent value. Its value is what it can provide. Money is potential and possibilities. And because money can be used for many purposes, its value and meaning lies within each of us. For example, money can be used to travel and see the world, giving it the value of adventure, learning, and excitement. Money can also be used to control friends and family, giving it the value of power and significance. How you value money dictates the decisions you make saving, spending, managing, and investing it. A good relationship with money can ensure good decisions, which leads to being able to use money to create a better life. A poor relationship with money – one in which you are plagued with limiting money beliefs – can create unnecessary anxiety, relationship problems, and can lead to quickly spending the money and ending up broke in a short period of time. It's not about the money.

Sudden Wealth Principle 4 focuses on learning about and overcoming limiting money beliefs. Even if you have taken control, slowed down, and have the best advisors in the world on your team, if you don't identify and upgrade your money beliefs, you will quickly undermine your advisors, isolate yourself from friends/family, and make bad decisions until you run out of money. This may sound harsh, but it's reality. I've seen this time and time again over the past two decades. It's not about the money.

The thief in the night who strips you of your sudden wealth doesn't climb through a window and rob you, the thief in the night is in your head. Sudden wealth recipients rarely go bankrupt because they didn't have the best advisors or because they paid too much tax or didn't invest responsibly. They can't help themselves. They make a series of bad financial decisions over and over and over, even when they know better. It's not about the money.

How can you make sure you don't become your own worst enemy? Start by understanding your limiting beliefs, then seek healthier alternatives. This chapter will show you how.

5 STEPS TO UPGRADE YOUR MONEY BELIEFS

1. **Identify your top needs.** Understand how your top two human needs and the vehicles you use to meet them determine your decisions and, ultimately, the quality of your life.

2. **Avoid the Monopoly money phenomenon.** Not all money is created equally. How you receive your sudden wealth plays a big role in how you value the money. How you value the sudden wealth will shape how you manage it.

3. **Drop your money baggage.** The source of your sudden wealth can be neutral (e.g., lottery) or negative (e.g., inheritance from an abusive father). If negative, this "money baggage" can lead to poor financial decisions and reckless behaviors.

4. **Eliminate negative money scripts.** Negative money scripts are typically unconscious beliefs about money developed in childhood that drive poor adult financial behaviors.

5. **Expand your financial comfort zone.** We all have a financial comfort zone – the emotional financial home where we feel most secure and confident in our decisions and abilities – but sudden wealth can thrust us into a radically different financial neighborhood where we feel out of place and unsure.

STEP 1: IDENTIFY YOUR TOP NEEDS

Why do we do what we do? This has been a question that has fascinated me since I took an introductory psychology course in high school when I was 15 years old. Psychologists and researchers have plenty of theories on why we do what we do, and I've studied many of them. But there is one theory that has risen to the top and has helped me understand not only my behavior, but that of others. This theory, called Human Needs Psychology, provides a lens through which you can decipher behavior and not only understand why we do what we do, but also predict what we'll do in the future. It is the most accurate method I've discovered for assessing what drives another person.

Human Needs Psychology is a theory of human behavior developed by famed family therapist, Cloé Madanes, and strategic interventionist, Anthony Robbins. The premise behind Human Needs Psychology is simple. There are six needs every human being on this planet shares. So even though we may be separated by wealth, race, religion, or geography, we all have the same six fundamental needs – they are universal. No more, no less.

For clients who have experienced sudden wealth, they've found it helpful to understand their needs and how they fulfill them. Although we all share the same six needs, it is our top two needs that most influence our decisions and behavior. These are needs, not hopes, wants, or desires. We are compelled to fulfill all of our needs, but our top two needs exert the most influence. Our top two constantly pull at us and we'll make decisions to satisfy these needs – sometimes at the expense of our other needs, relationships, and even our finances.

The better you understand the six needs and can recognize your top two, the more conscious you will become of why you've made some of the decisions you've made. This understanding of what drives you can also help you better evaluate future decisions.

The six needs, according to Human Needs Psychology, are:

1. **Certainty.** The need for stability, security, comfort, and to feel confident that you can avoid pain and gain pleasure. Avoiding pain and uncertainty is key. High Certainty people will avoid risks and plan carefully for the future. They are predictable, seek control, and prefer work that is stable rather than work that is challenging. Because they focus on stability, they may seem unenthusiastic and even boring. Their strengths are their organization, reliability, and dependability.

2. **Uncertainty/Variety.** The need for change, new stimuli, the unknown, and to exercise our physical and emotional range – they need the excitement that comes from variety and many interests. Others see them as dynamic, entertaining, and fun to be around. High Uncertainty people can be involved in too many things at once, bouncing from one experience to the next. They may even put themselves at risk physically, emotionally, and financially. They dislike habits and routines. Boredom is anathema and will be avoided at all costs.

3. **Significance.** The need to feel important, special, unique, and wanted. High Significance people believe that happiness comes from feeling respected and for people to look up to them. They may work hard at being different or taking the leadership role. They often work hard, have high standards for themselves, and are relentless in accomplishing their goals, but because they constantly need to feel important in the eyes of others, they can seem arrogant and full of themselves. They are often disciplined, competitive, and can be perfectionists.

4. **Love/Connection.** The need to belong and to feel closeness with someone or something. High Love/Connection people are generous to those they love and can be very protective of them. They are often nurturing, responsible, supportive, and helpful, but this can come at a cost. Some will repress their own needs and be unable to say "no" to others. In their desire to feel love and meet the needs of others, they can become intrusive without realizing it. They will do whatever it takes to not disappoint others and to feel dispensable or unappreciated, making rejection difficult to deal with.

5. **Growth.** The need to expand, learn, and grow. High Growth people feel the need to develop themselves intellectually, emotionally, physically, and/or spiritually. They love to learn and to challenge themselves. They can become detached, unwilling to share, and may undervalue relationships but, at the same time, are respectful of others. They are typically thoughtful, calm, and dependable. Others may look up to them as a model of self-improvement, although High Growth people don't do it for the respect of others, they do it for the respect of themselves.

6. **Contribution.** The need to give beyond oneself and to support others. High Contribution people believe that their life is incomplete unless they are contributing to others or to a cause. Even though they care for others, they may neglect taking care of themselves or even the ones closest to them. Others may resent the time and energy they put into the cause. Their strengths are their compassion for helping others, bravery, persistence, and generosity. They are often outgoing and enthusiastic, but can become confrontational and angry in the face of unfairness or injustice.

Can you see how the decisions of one sudden wealth recipient who values Love/Connection and Contribution may be quite different from someone else who values Uncertainty/Variety and Significance? It's important to point out that one need is not necessarily better than another – each need has value and we all must fulfill all six needs – but you can begin to see how we might make vastly different decisions based on the needs that drive us.

WHAT ARE YOUR TOP TWO NEEDS?

There are a few different ways to determine your top two needs. First, it can be as simple as reading the list above and choosing the two that seem most important. For some, two of the six needs will fly off the page and feel right. If you're not sure which two are most important, you can take a brief online assessment at , which will provide you with an analysis of all six needs and will identify which two are most important to you.

FOCUS ON THE STRENGTHS AND AVOID THE CHALLENGES OF YOUR TOP NEEDS

Sudden wealth creates stress. It will test your limits. As you've seen, each need has its own strengths, which you'll want to focus on, as well as its own challenges, which you'll want to avoid. It's going to be difficult to change your top needs. It's better to focus on your strengths, and to be aware of your challenges and shift things to minimize them from becoming problems.

Need: Certainty

Sudden Wealth Strengths: You seek an organized and stable life. For someone who values Certainty, it can feel like their world is turned upside down because they lose control and there is a good deal of uncertainty about their finances and even what their life will be like. If your top Need is Certainty, "Sudden Wealth Principle 2: Slow Down" is key. Don't become caught up in the excitement. Slow everything down. Create rituals and routines. Take your time before making decisions. Create stability wherever you can. Stick to your pre-money schedule as much as possible. You excel at planning for the future, so work with your advisors to create stability by holding regularly scheduled phone calls. Keep all of your questions in one place so you can go down the list with them. Try not to focus on the uncertainty of the new situation, but on the stability and security the sudden wealth can provide.

Sudden Wealth Challenges: When you don't know what is going to happen next, this creates uncertainty and stress. In an attempt to control your situation, you may try to control the people around you. Be the passenger on the specifics and let your advisors do what they do best. High Certainty sudden wealth recipients will often want to avoid new people and experiences, making it hard for them to find or work with their advisors. If practical, take your time getting to know them – go out to lunch and get to know them on a personal level. You are sensitive to danger and experience fear easily. This can protect you from bad situations, but it can also paralyze you from hiring advisors, listening to their advice, and making decisions. Tell your advisors they can best work with you by helping you counter your doubts and fears in realistic ways.

Need: Uncertainty/Variety

Sudden Wealth Strengths: You will get a thrill from the excitement, uniqueness, and ever changing experiences and demands of sudden wealth. You will be challenged emotionally and intellectually . . . and you'll love it. You may see the experience as an adventure. You'll have boundless energy and a focus on what to do next. You also like meeting new people and can work well with people of all ages and walks of life. These are all wonderful traits before and after receiving sudden wealth.

Sudden Wealth Challenges: High Uncertainty/Variety people can be too trusting of others, which can lead to being taken advantage of. You'll want to make sure you do your due diligence on the advisors you hire. Verify everything and don't take anyone at their word. In your pursuit of excitement and what's next, you may grow bored with the tax, legal, and financial details required of you right now. Schedule short meetings with your advisors when possible. Don't try to power through a long meeting; insist on short breaks throughout so you can get up, walk around, and clear your head. You can become defensive when you think others are trying to control your schedule or your life. Your advisors can best work with you by understanding your need for the big picture, tackling issues in small bursts, and not hijacking your life or calendar.

Need: Significance

Sudden Wealth Strengths: There are few things that are more unique or special than sudden wealth. You may relish the situation of being the most important person in the room. You probably aren't shy and have no problem being heard. Some sudden wealth recipients take a backseat to their advisors and their plan, but not you. You appreciate taking a leadership role and are not afraid of risk or confrontation. This can be a great boon to you.

Sudden Wealth Challenges: High Significance people bristle at the slightest criticism or at being told what to do. You want to lead, not follow. But even though you may be the big man on campus, your advisors know more than you and will want to give you advice. If you view their advice as condescending or belittling, you may react negatively. A better perspective to take is that because you are so important, you are able to hire the best people in the world to advise you. You are not a follower, you were the leader who hired them. They work for you. Your advisors can best support you by letting you be the driver on the big issues, and when they need you to be the passenger, to remind you that you've told them where you want to go and they are just helping you get there.

Need: Love/Connection

Sudden Wealth Strengths: Most who have a strong need for Love/Connection are good listeners who can relate well to people of all ages and backgrounds. You will feel connected by being part of a "team" so you may enjoy working with your advisors. You are friendly, open, and expressive, which are all strong traits for handling sudden wealth.

Sudden Wealth Challenges: It may be difficult for you to identify or focus on your own needs. This can make it challenging when planning your future and making decisions. Add to this that high Love/Connection people seek acceptance and approval and have difficulty saying "no," and what you have is someone who may go along with what their advisory team suggests when it's not in their best interest. It's important to shift the focus to yourself, but this can feel selfish and foreign. Your advisors can best support you by helping you outline your goals and needs clearly. They should also slow you down if they find you are too focused on others at your own expense.

Need: Growth

Sudden Wealth Strengths: Sudden wealth can be an ideal opportunity for someone who values Growth. This experience is a chance for you to develop new skills, learn new things, and be challenged emotionally and intellectually. Sudden wealth requires great personal growth, so if approached correctly, the high Growth person can shine. You may also appreciate facts and details, which are in high supply before and after a sudden wealth event. The issue that plagues many sudden wealth recipients, and often those who value Significance, is that they accumulate material possessions. You, on the other hand, do not put high value on material possessions. You are more interested in experiences.

Sudden Wealth Challenges: The Growth-oriented person is self-focused. They are most interested in their own personal growth and development. They can be seen as detached, impersonal, and are heavily self-reliant. Add to this that you set careful limits on your time and privacy, and you can see how in the flurry of Stage 2, you can feel overly burdened and taxed with meetings and highly personal questions and decisions you must make as part of a team. Advisors can best support you by allowing you to ask lots of questions, explaining things in detail, and being conscious of your need for space and privacy.

Need: Contribution

Sudden Wealth Strengths: You are highly energetic, especially when thinking about or helping others. You can have a strong sense of purpose and mission in life that may direct your decisions and help when it comes to planning your sudden wealth. You aren't shy about what you believe and what you want to do. Your advisors will know exactly what you want to do with your sudden wealth.

Sudden Wealth Challenges: You can be too outwardly focused – helping people across the world while neglecting your needs and those around you. This can become a problem when you want to give money away before thinking it through fully. You may interpret your advisor's lack of enthusiastic support for all your causes as an affront to you, some kind of personal jab at who you are, when, in fact, they may be focused on your needs more than you are. One way to look at this differently is to realize that the more you can focus, at least temporarily, on your own needs, the better position you will be in to help others. It's the same rationale for why flight attendants encourage us to "put on your own oxygen mask before helping your child." Your advisors can best support you by asking about your beliefs and the causes you support, while gently encouraging you to also focus on your own needs.

HOW DO YOU MEET YOUR NEEDS?

Vehicles are the actions, beliefs, and behaviors we use to meet our needs. The need is the destination – the place at which you want to arrive and experience. The vehicle is how you get there. Your top two needs create the pull, but the vehicles we choose and the rules we create determine what we'll do with our sudden wealth and our life. Here's an example of how the vehicles we choose shape our actions. If a sudden wealth recipient values Significance as his top need, he wants to feel important, wanted, and special. At this point, we can't predict what he'll do with the money - he will use it in a way he thinks will meet his need for Significance. To quench his desire for feeling important, wanted, and special, he could take his sudden wealth and buy a new house, a Rolex, and a Ferrari. These purchases give him the ability to show off, and to flaunt his wealth in an effort to say, "Look at how important and special I am!" Or he could meet his need for Significance with an entirely different vehicle. He may instead donate a considerable sum to a charity and relish in the attention and feeling of importance and significance his big check provides. Same need, different vehicle, different life.

Why It's So Hard To Change

Why do we do what we do, even when it is destructive? We may smoke or eat too much when we know we shouldn't, but we do it anyway. Why? Needs drive our behavior. If we consistently engage in a thought or behavior, it is because it satisfies one or more of our needs. Not so sure? Choose an activity you love to do (or can't stop doing even though you know you should) and rate 1-10 how much it meets each need. You'll find that it will meet your top two or three needs to a high level. You won't change your behavior, even if you want to, unless you find an alternative way to meet that need.

It's important to differentiate between needs and vehicles. Having money is not a need. Driving a Rolls Royce is not a need. Taking your family on a European cruise is not a need. Paying for your nephew's college tuition is not a need. Finishing your degree is not a need. Sitting on the board of a non-profit is not a need. Remember, there are only six needs (i.e., Certainty, Uncertainty, Significance, Love/Connection, Growth, and Contribution). All of the aforementioned items are not needs, but vehicles – things we think will fulfill one or more of our needs.

When you have more money than you've ever had before, you can suddenly afford new and sometimes expensive ways to meet your needs. For example, someone who places their need for Certainty above all others may choose to meet their need for security and safety by building a fortress, hiring 24/7 guards, and arming themselves, while another will forego all of those things and put all of their sudden wealth in a bank account instead. Again, same need but different vehicles to satisfy it.

To best manage sudden wealth, it's critical to know the difference. Once you do, you can look at how you view your money and how you spend your money differently. You may feel a pull to buy a large house (the vehicle) you cannot afford, but if you can dig a little deeper to discover the need you are trying to fill, you may find a more positive and less financially damaging vehicle for meeting the need.

POSITIVE VEHICLES VERSUS NEGATIVE VEHICLES

Needs are neutral, but vehicles are not – they can be positive or negative. Vehicles that are positive are good for you, your loved ones, the world and people around you, and are sustainable. Using all of your sudden wealth to invest in your family and friends' business ventures may meet your need for Significance, Contribution, or Love/Connection, and it may be good for your family and friends, but it is not sustainable or good for you.

Vehicles that are negative are those that are not good for you, friends/family, the world around you, or are not sustainable. For example, I had a client who had a need for Uncertainty. Although there are a million different ways to meet this need, her vehicle was online shopping. She experienced a thrill searching different websites, selecting different items, and opening the box when it came in the mail. Shopping was her vehicle, but she did it to such an extent that it was jeopardizing her finances. This was clearly not good for her, her family who she supported, and was not sustainable.

Two people may have the same need for Contribution, but meet that need in very different ways. As an extreme example, Anthony Robbins has talked about two completely different groups of people who seemingly share nothing in common . . . the September 11, 2001 terrorists who flew their planes into the World Trade Center buildings and the firefighters who rushed into the buildings after they were hit. One was a group of murderers looking to take innocent lives and the other was a group of heroes looking to save lives. Through the lens of Human Needs Psychology, the terrorists met their need for Contribution (however skewed it was) by sacrificing their lives for the greater good of their cause whereas the firefighters met their need for Contribution by risking, and ultimately sacrificing, their lives in an attempt to save the lives of strangers. The terrorists' vehicle for meeting their need was murder. The firefighters' vehicle for meeting their need was risking their lives to save others.

REPLACING NEGATIVE VEHICLES WITH POSITIVE VEHICLES

The needs themselves are neutral, but vehicles can be positive or negative. The vehicles we choose can serve the greater good and create rich and full lives for ourselves and our loved ones, or they can be destructive to ourselves and others.

The goal is not to replace or rearrange your needs (although placing more emphasis on the needs of Growth and Contribution may be ideal), but to identify the vehicles you use to meet your needs and to replace those that are negative or neutral with those that are positive.

Money can create new opportunities to satisfy our needs. The more money you have, the greater the number and magnitude of the vehicles you can use. Your needs don't change overnight, but your ability to meet them does. In fact, because sudden wealth can create anxiety, many sudden wealth recipients find that they cling more tightly to their needs. If someone's top need was Certainty (i.e., stability, security) and they win the lottery, they will often pursue Certainty to an even greater degree after the win.

The danger of sudden wealth is that the rapid influx of money makes certain vehicles that were not feasible suddenly doable. If you're making $30,000 a year salary, there are limits to how you can meet your needs, but if your bank account balance is $15 million, the vehicles that weren't in reach are now easily accessible.

People will violate their own values and morals to meet their needs. They will overeat, do drugs, cheat on their spouse, gamble, and spend their child's education fund in order to even temporarily satiate their needs. You can't get rid of your needs, but you can improve how you choose to meet them, the vehicles you select, and that is the good news. If you seek Significance and discover your vehicle is overspending on material objects so you look important, there are an unlimited number of other ways you can fulfill the need for Significance that are less damaging to your finances. No one is asking you to change what you want, but simply how you get what you want. Embrace the need, but change the vehicle. Here's how…

1. **Get clear on your top two needs.** The best way to determine which needs you value most is to take the brief online assessment here: .

2. **Determine vehicles.** What were you doing pre-sudden wealth to meet these needs? Make a list of your thoughts and behaviors that used to fill your top two needs.

3. **Categorize as positive or negative.** Go through your list of vehicles and separate them into two categories (1) Positive – those that are good for you or others, and are sustainable and (2) Negative – those that are not good for you or others, and are not sustainable.

4. **Crowd out negative vehicles with positive vehicles.** Crowding out is popular in dieting, where the focus is less on eliminating bad foods and more on eating good foods so you are less hungry to eat the bad ones. The same principle works here, too. Many people use a combination of positive and negative vehicles to meet their top needs. Instead of reinventing the wheel, consider slowing down your negative vehicles while spending more energy on the positive vehicles you are already using to meet your needs. When you spend more time meeting your needs in a positive way, you'll crowd out the negative because you'll have less time and energy for them.

5. **Brainstorm new positive vehicles.** Look at the list of negative vehicles and brainstorm ways you can still fulfill your most important needs in a way that is less destructive. Ask yourself what experience(s) can occur to meet the need in a new way. What has to happen for you to feel you have _____ (your top needs) at a high level? Make sure your new vehicle is under your control. It's hard to consistently meet your needs if the vehicle you choose is controlled by someone or something else.

6. **Experiment with new vehicles.** Look at your list of new positive vehicles and try them. Some will work and others won't. Test different vehicles until one clicks. As a good friend of mine likes to say: Seek progress, not perfection.

Here's an example of how this works in the real world. A client's top two needs were Significance and Uncertainty. After receiving sudden wealth, he found his thirst for these two needs was insatiable. In his need for looking important and being respected, he began investing in start-ups his friends and family members were beginning. He'd get the thrill of thinking about different companies and ideas while also being the guy with the money who could call the shots. It satisfied both of his needs on a high level. Investing in small growth companies can be part of a legitimate investment strategy, but investing in risky start-ups so you can look important and because it provides variety are not good reasons. He was close to investing several hundred thousand dollars in a restaurant his brother begged him to fund, even though neither he nor his brother had any experience in the restaurant business. By going through the process of identifying his needs and looking at what was driving his interest in financing his family's ventures, for the first time, he saw his real motivation. He was also able to create new vehicles that still provided him with Significance and Variety but that were better for him and were also sustainable. One of the vehicles we tested was setting aside a small amount of "mad money" to which he could use to invest in small public technology companies. This gave him the excitement of investing in businesses and the prestige when his stock picks turned out well. It was also an amount of money he could easily afford to lose without damaging his finances.

Once you understand the need driving your behavior, the vehicles are limitless. This is but one example of the creative ways you can replace a negative vehicle with a positive vehicle. Other clients have done extraordinary shifts in the way they meet their needs – from self-destructive behaviors that were ruining their lives to new ones that radically changed their lives for the better.

STEP 2: AVOID THE MONOPOLY MONEY PHENOMENON

Have you heard the story of the newlyweds in Vegas? A man and his bride travel to Vegas to get married. They have very little money. They have so little, in fact, that after a small service at a chapel off the Strip, a cheap bottle of wine, and a buffet dinner, the man reaches into his pocket and pulls out the last $5 to his name. Feeling lucky, he tucks his new wife into bed and tells her he's going to try his luck at the slots. He takes the elevator to the casino floor and finds himself lost in a sea of machines. He slips his $5 into one and pulls the lever. Bells ring and lights flash. We have a winner. The floor manager congratulates him on winning $65,000. Feeling euphoric, he stuffed his lucky $5 bill in his pocket and took the rest of his win in chips.

The excitement of the spinning roulette wheel grabs his attention and he places his entire stack on red. Winner! Then black. Winner! What luck! Over the course of the evening, he grows $5 into $10 million. Just before sunrise, he places all $10 million of his chips on red. The balls spins, jumps, rolls, and lands . . . on black. Exhausted and now without chips, he makes his way back to his hotel room just as his bride wakes up. "How did you do?" she asks. "Not bad," as he pulls the $5 from his pocket. "I broke even."

I've always loved this fable. It painfully illustrates how not all money is created equally. A dollar won is not the same as a dollar earned, and this is a critically important concept for sudden wealth recipients to appreciate. If they do not, they can squander their sudden wealth just like the groom in the story.

Our Vegas gambler obviously isn't playing with a full deck. You and I would never be so cavalier with $10 million. Money is money, right? You know a dollar in your left hand is worth exactly the same as a dollar in your right hand. You know a dollar in your wallet is worth the same as a dollar in your bank account. You also know a dollar you earned from a hard day at work is worth the same as a dollar you win or find on the ground. Not so fast...

Maybe you can't relate to the Vegas gambler, but have you ever found money? Did you cherish this money and protect it with the same zeal as you would have if you had earned it or, because it was a "gift," did you find yourself spending it on things you might not otherwise have? If so, you are not alone. A sudden wealth client won the lottery only because he found $20 and used it to buy $20 worth of tickets. When I asked him if he would have bought the tickets if he didn't find the money, he looked at me as if I were a moron and responded with, "Of course not! Do you think I'm crazy?"

Regardless of the source of the money, logically, we know the value is the same, but somehow, a dollar we earn is "worth" more than the dollar we find. Research shows that those who won money in a radio contest were more likely to spend the money than those who earned it by working overtime[7]. Psychologists and behavior economists have coined a term for our tendency to value money differently. They call it "mental accounting," and as a sudden wealth recipient, you need to understand how this limiting money belief can cloud your judgment and ability to make good financial decisions.

Mental accounting describes our tendency to treat money differently, depending on its source. Sudden wealth recipients who fail to appreciate the real effects of mental accounting can suffer enormous consequences – the money that came overnight can disappear just as quickly. A good deal of my work as a sudden wealth advisor is helping clients avoid valuing money they receive from lottery winnings, lawsuits, inheritances, or other sudden wealth events as less than money they earn through their labor.

It's important to note that even if you didn't win your sudden wealth in a lottery, it did come to you overnight. Because it is such a large amount, it can feel "found" or even unearned. One client who received a large settlement check called it "funny money," even though he lost a family member and spent years battling for justice. Clients who have lost close family members and received an inheritance have told me that logically, they know that, but they couldn't help but view a bank statement with all of the digits as anything but "Monopoly money." Whether you have won the lottery, received an inheritance, been issued a judgment/settlement, signed a sports/entertainment contract, exercised stock options, or sold your business, if you think of this money differently or somehow worth less than your savings or money you've earned, the consequences can be enormous and dramatic.

Mental accounting applies to all of us, not just sudden wealth recipients and gamblers. A study referenced in the book, *The Social Meaning of Money* by Vivian Zelizer, illustrates how Oslo prostitutes created a "divided economy." Money they received from welfare, health benefits, and other legal income was "carefully budgeted, spent for the 'straight life', to pay rent and bills." Money earned from prostitution was viewed as less worthy, and as a result, was spent very differently. This money was "quickly squandered on 'going out,' drugs, alcohol, and clothes." The conclusion? "Dirty money burns a hole in your pocket and has to be used quickly."

There are theories on why we value anticipated and earned money over unanticipated and unearned money. For example, psychologist Hal Arkes in "The Psychology of Windfall Gains[8]," concludes windfall money may be deposited into a special "windfall" or "fun money" account, thereby segregating it from earned money. Or just as damaging, the sudden wealth recipient may not put it in any account other than a checking account. Here, the money remains uncommitted and available for "extravagant, frivolous, or speculative use."

HOW TO VALUE SUDDEN WEALTH

Regardless of why we become stuck thinking about sudden wealth differently from other money, the bigger question is how we can avoid this. How can we put more value, weight, and gravitas on sudden wealth, making its value on par with the money we earn and the money in our retirement accounts? How can you avoid minimizing the value of your sudden wealth?

1. **Become aware.** Want to view sudden wealth on par with earned money? Sometimes it's as easy as simply becoming conscious of our tendency to put more weight on money we've "earned" and less weight on money we've "found." After having this conversation with clients, I often see a shift in how clients will talk about their sudden wealth and their plans for it. The degree of their mental shift is often a function of how undervalued they viewed their sudden wealth. They may lament earlier decisions of how they spent their money in light of their newfound perspective. Some have even laughed at how illogically they viewed their money, but nevertheless are grateful of their new understanding and appreciation.

2. **Get perspective.** This is an exercise that blows minds. Calculate how many hours you would have to work to earn the sudden wealth. For some, it would take hundreds of years. Or the next time you are about to make a purchase, calculate how many hours you would have to work to buy it. Then ask yourself if you'd really spend the money if you had to earn it. To get perspective, consider living vicariously through others by giving money to those with nothing to see how much they value it.

   I have a non-profit that supports orphans and disadvantaged kids. When I visited our project in Vietnam, one of our girls had a heart defect and was going to die. The cost for heart surgery? Just $400. Talk about putting the value of money into perspective! (We paid for her surgery and she's a happy and healthy girl today.)

3. **Create a play money account.** When all else fails, embrace mental accounting! Take a small amount of your sudden wealth, an amount you can risk losing, and put it into a separate account earmarked as "mad money." Put the rest of your sudden wealth in different accounts. If you want to undervalue your money, at least put a cap on what you'll undervalue.

The consequences of valuing "found" money differently than "earned" money can be dramatic. Sudden wealth recipients are inclined to take more risks with found money, give it away more freely, and spend it faster and more lavishly. Even if the sudden wealth isn't found money, such as a lottery win, any sudden wealth event can skew how you value the money. All sudden wealth recipients are at risk for de-valuing their windfall, even those who have suffered a great deal and "earned" the money.

To avoid this, follow the tips above and slow things down. Grow into your wealth. Make only those decisions you have to make and hit the pause button on major purchases and life decisions.

STEP 3: DROP YOUR MONEY BAGGAGE

Sudden wealth can become collateral damage, and it's entirely understandable. This is particularly true when the sudden wealth comes from inheritance, lawsuits, and divorce. These events can create so much anguish and anger, it is easy to project these emotions onto the money. You receive an inheritance from an uncle who abused you. You lose a child and get a settlement check. You endure a bitter divorce and get half of the business. It's only natural that the money you receive can feel tainted.

It's akin to the "fruit of the poisonous tree" doctrine in law. If the money is tainted, then anything gained from the money is tainted as well. If you enjoy what the money provides (e.g., travel, new car), does that make you an accomplice? If you use the money to better your life, are you implicitly condoning the source of the money? One client asked, "How can I feel grateful for this blood money?"

Because the money is so inexorably tied to intense emotions, for many sudden wealth recipients, this is the most difficult limiting money belief to overcome. It can take a great deal of time, patience, and work to separate the sudden wealth from the source of the sudden wealth.

How we are wired makes this process difficult. We have two issues holding us back. First, as much as we like to think we are rational and logical, humans are quite irrational and illogical. We are emotional creatures. Remember the triune brain? The sliver of our brain responsible for logic and analysis is often hijacked by the more dominant, automatic, and emotional parts of our brain. Second, we habitually define cause-and-effect relationships when none exist. This has been a key to our survival, but also creates whacky beliefs and behaviors. Put these two tendencies together and what you have is a formula that makes it difficult for some sudden wealth recipients to have a healthy relationship with their money.

The danger in not being able to separate the message from the messenger – in this case the sudden wealth from the source of the sudden wealth – goes back to Sudden Wealth Principle 1. Sudden wealth is, or at least can be, an opportunity. It can mean security and a better life for you and your loved ones. It can mean not having to work at a job you don't love. It can give you the freedom to pursue a deeper calling. It can mean helping others. But it won't mean any of these things if the anger or guilt from the source of the sudden wealth causes you to punish the money.

What are a few signs that you may be punishing your sudden wealth? People will often keep the tainted money in a separate account. The thought of co-mingling the dirty money with their other funds can disturb or even disgust them. They attempt to keep it at a distance – sometimes at a different bank from their other money. They are psychologically and physically trying to get away from it. They will avoid conversations about it with their spouse and advisors. They may refer to it as "that money" and tell their financial advisors it is off limits. They may avoid important tax, legal, and financial decisions. They may stuff unopened monthly statements in a drawer or shred them. The money is linked to pain. The less they have to think about the money, the less they have to re-visit the pain. They do all of this, but they know they are being irrational. I've had clients look me in the eye with tears streaming down their face and tell me they know they shouldn't feel this way, but that they can't help it.

Creating distance from the sudden wealth is common, but usually not harmful. A more dangerous situation is when the sudden wealth recipient punishes the money. This happens when they recklessly spend or give away the money. The faster they are freed from the money, the faster they are freed from the pain. This is all well and good, but in the end, they'll have no money and will still have the pain. It's a noble goal, but carelessly spending the money can lead to further guilt and pain.

In the end, using money to heal an emotional pain doesn't work. Advisors often won't appreciate the power of money baggage. They view the money as just that, money, and the everything else as everything else. They can't understand why the client would leave millions in a bank account earning nothing when they could put it in a money market account and at least earn something. They can't understand why the client refuses to talk about the money or why they fail to show up to meetings and miss scheduled phone calls. They'll use logic and rational explanations to try to get through to the client, but, of course, these fall on deaf ears. If I'm working with an advisor who is having trouble understanding the client's behavior, I'll pose the following scenario.

Imagine you discover an artifact from Nazi Germany in your basement. This artifact is verified as having been used to torture and kill children and babies. You can sell the piece or you can donate it to the Holocaust Memorial Museum in Washington, DC. Does this give you pause? Can you see how you may look at this money differently? What might you be thinking while lying in a hammock in Hawaii on a vacation that was paid for with the proceeds? Would you feel you were somehow benefiting from the atrocities? There is no right or wrong answer, but it provides a glimpse into the power the source of the money can have.

As nice as it would be to separate the inheritance from the father who abused your mother, it can take work. Here are a few strategies that can help...

1. **Create new meaning.** It's up to you how you will view the money. There are an unlimited number of ways to view the lawsuit judgment that results from your spouse's death. Ultimately, the one you choose will shape your decisions. The best interpretation is the one that creates the best life for you – whatever that may be.

2. **Create cause.** Many people who have experienced a tragedy build their life's mission around helping others who have suffered. It can be empowering to make a stand and to use some or even all of the sudden wealth to further this mission. It's a way of flipping the meaning. Rather than be burdened by the money, they use it in a way that unburdens others. It releases them from the guilt of personally benefiting from the money. Instead, they use the blood money to heal others, and in the process, themselves. This is what Beckie Brown did in the aftermath of her son's death – she founded Mothers Against Drunk Driving. Work with your advisors closely and don't make any big decisions until you've considered all the options. For example, a client who initially wanted to give several million dollars in settlement proceeds to a children's hospital after her daughter died, upon reflection and after working with her advisors, determined she could quit her job and start a small charity to support families who lost a child. By pausing, she allowed her knee-jerk reaction to get rid of the money to be replaced with a sustainable plan focused on her new life mission. In the end, you may decide to give the money away, but give yourself the time to consider all your options.

3.   **Separate the money from the source.** With an inheritance or a lawsuit that comes from death or serious injury, the money that comes can feel like a payoff – a trade of life for money, where the value of the life is reflected in the numbers on the check. If I spend this money, it means I accept the value they gave to my loved one. Naturally, sudden wealth recipients can recoil at the thought of being bought or compensated for a loved one dying. The greater the degree they associate the inheritance or settlement with the value of their loved one, the less likely they are to make good financial decisions. Sometimes, the sudden wealth recipient will flip the cause and effect relationship in their head. They'll view the money as the cause of the death or injury. The goal is to disconnect the money from the death by looking at them as two separate events. Mourn the death, but not the money.

4.   **Align the money with a mission.** In Sudden Wealth Principle 8, you will learn how to use the sudden wealth to create a better life for you and others. For many sudden wealth recipients, they are able to re-create, or maybe create for the first time, a mission for their lives. The new mission may be to get behind a cause you believe in or it may not. Regardless of how you define your mission, you can overcome the limiting money baggage belief if you are able to focus on how the money will help you pursue and achieve your mission – you're turning the money you previously viewed as "bad" into a tool for good.

5.   **Focus on the future.** I've seen situations where sudden wealth recipients have neglected to provide the basics for their family because they didn't want to use "that money." No one wins in this situation. The more you can focus on the future, on your loved ones who are still here, the better it will be for you and for them. How can you use this money to best support those you love?

If you've lost a loved one and are having trouble coping, a few pages in a book are not going to be sufficient. Consider talking to a licensed therapist before you make any big decisions regarding your money. To find a therapist who specializes in these issues, go to sudden-wealthsolution.com. Clients who have reacted quickly and without thinking through the consequences often report having to deal with two losses. The loss of a loved one and the loss, and accompanying guilt about making poor decisions, of the money.

STEP 4: ELIMINATE NEGATIVE MONEY SCRIPTS

The term "money scripts" was coined by psychologists Brad Klontz and Ted Klontz to describe our core beliefs about money that drive our financial behaviors. Think of money scripts as apps that work behind the scenes but that influence (and sometimes control) how we think about money and make financial decisions. Just as a fish doesn't experience water because it's part of its existence, we are often unconscious of our money scripts and their influence.

Money scripts are often developed in childhood, passed down from generation to generation within families and cultures, and usually contain only partial truths. Money scripts can be developed over time (e.g., from hearing your parents talk about money), from a cultural financial flashpoint (e.g., the Great Depression), or from the result of a single but emotionally charged, dramatic, or traumatic personal or family financial flashpoint (e.g., parental abandonment, being evicted and having to sleep in the family car). Money scripts forged under these conditions can become resistant to change even when they are self-destructive. The good news is the research shows that once a person's money script(s) is identified – that is, taken off auto-pilot – the app running in the background can be observed, challenged, and changed.

If you have a negative money application running in the background, maybe from an event decades earlier that has shaped how you think about and interact with money, your sudden wealth can be like fuel to a fire. For example, one of the money scripts discussed below is Money Avoidance. This describes someone who believes money is bad and that they don't deserve it. Can you see how this unconscious belief that money is bad can interfere with good financial decisions after a sudden wealth event?

THE 3 MONEY SCRIPTS

Research by Brad Klontz, Sonya L. Britt, Jennifer Mentzer, and Ted Klontz has identified three money scripts associated with poor financial health: Money Avoidance, Money Worship, and Money Status. The following descriptions are those of the researchers.

MONEY AVOIDANCE

Individuals who score high on money avoidance believe that money is bad or that they do not deserve money. For the money avoider, money is seen as a source of fear, anxiety, or disgust. Money avoiders have a negative association with money, believe that people of wealth are greedy and corrupt, and believe there is virtue in living with less money. At the same time, money avoiders are likely to hold the conflicting beliefs that having more money could end their problems and improve their self-worth and social status. As such, they may vacillate between the extremes of holding great contempt for money and people of wealth and placing too much value on the role of money in their own life satisfaction.

Money avoiders may sabotage their financial success or give money away in an unconscious effort to have as little as possible, while at the same time, they may be working excessive hours in an effort to make money. Not surprisingly, money avoidance is associated with poor financial health. Money avoiders tend to have less money and lower net worth. Money avoidance is associated with increased risk of overspending and compulsive buying, sacrificing one's financial well-being for the sake of others, financial dependence on others, hoarding, avoiding looking at one's bank statements, trying to forget about one's financial situation, and having trouble sticking to a budget.

MONEY WORSHIP

At their core, money worshipers are convinced that the key to happiness and the solution to all of their problems is to have more money. At the same time, they believe that one can never have enough money and they will never really be able to afford the things they want in life. The tension between believing that more money and things will make one happier and the sense that one will never have enough money can result in chronic overspending in an attempt to buy happiness. Money worshipers are more likely to have lower income, lower net worth, and be trapped in a cycle of revolving credit card debt. Money worshipers are also more likely to spend compulsively, hoard possessions, put work ahead of their family relationships, try to ignore or forget about their financial situation, give money to others even though they can't afford it, and be financially dependent on others.

MONEY STATUS

People who hold money status scripts see net worth and self-worth as being synonymous. They may pretend to have more money than they do, and, as a result, are at risk of overspending in an effort to give people the impression that they are financially successful.

They believe that if they live a virtuous life, the universe will take care of their financial needs, and that people are only as successful as the amount of money they earn. They have lower net worth, lower income, and tend to grow up in families with a lower socioeconomic status. People with money status beliefs are more likely to be compulsive spenders, be dependent on others financially, and lie to their spouses about their spending. Holding the money status script is also predictive of pathological gambling, indicating individuals may gamble in an attempt to win large sums of money to prove their worth to themselves and others.

OVERCOMING LIMITING MONEY SCRIPTS

IDENTIFY YOUR MONEY SCRIPTS

Did you find yourself nodding along as you read any of the negative Money Script descriptions above? Take the brief online assessment at suddenwealthsolution.com to determine how you score on each of the money scripts.

TAKE AN INVENTORY OF YOUR BELIEFS AROUND MONEY

What was your earliest memory around money? What is your happiest money memory? How about your most painful money experience? What were you taught about the wealthy and the poor? How were your parents around money? Which money beliefs do you think they have? Why?

WORK ON A MONEY SCRIPT LOG

Dr. Brad Klontz recommends a money script log as a way to get insight into your thoughts and beliefs around money. He suggests sudden wealth recipients answer the following:

1. **What was the trigger?** Identify the situation, event, or emotion that prompted the negative money behavior.

2. **What went through your mind?** Focus on what you were thinking before the negative money behavior.

3. **What was your impulse?** What actions did your thoughts compel you to take?

4. **What did you do?** What did you ultimately do?

The money script log creates a bread trail you can follow to the source of your money behaviors. You overcome, or at least interrupt, the automatic money scripts when you use the money log because it forces you to pause and analyze each step in the process. You can insert questions between the impulse of wanting to do something and actually doing it. For example, you can ask yourself, "Is there something else I can do right now that will make me feel better?", "What are the consequences if I do this?", or "Is it really worth it?"

Money Scripts are similar to all of the limiting money beliefs discussed in this chapter. Becoming conscious of the belief may be enough for you to shift your thinking and to create more empowering money beliefs. But for others, knowing they have a problem isn't the same as having a solution. More may be needed. If you've identified your Money Script but you still can't change your beliefs and negative behaviors around money, you should seek outside help. Find a financial therapist or coach here: .

STEP 5: EXPAND YOUR FINANCIAL COMFORT ZONE

The idea of a financial comfort zone may be one of the most important ideas for transforming sudden wealth into lasting wealth. I've talked to clients about their financial comfort zone for almost two decades, and others – notably Brad and Ted Klontz in their book *Mind Over Money* – have written extensively on what I consider to be one of the most pervasive limiting money belief for sudden wealth recipients.

What is your financial comfort zone? This might give you some insight. At an exclusive and posh five-star restaurant, do you feel more at ease and comfortable (a) parking the cars, (b) working as a waiter, (c) dining as a guest, or (d) owning the restaurant? Not what would you prefer, but where you would feel most at "home" and comfortable?

Your beliefs about, and comfort around, money are much more nuanced than this, but your answer, at least in part, reflects your financial comfort zone. Think of someone's financial comfort zone as a balloon. The financial comfort zones of some sudden wealth recipients are more flexible – they can expand beyond their normal range to adopt new beliefs and to meet new challenges. These people can adapt more quickly to the sudden wealth experience and undergo less uncertainty and anxiety. On the other hand, sudden wealth recipients who are less flexible and who have more rigid boundaries have difficulty expanding their financial comfort zone. Instead, as they are thrust into sudden wealth, they are placed outside their comfort zone. Once outside their comfort zone, they may begin to sabotage their sudden wealth in an attempt to fall back into their financial comfort zone, which is what I call Sudden Wealth Regression.

Sudden Wealth Regression is the result of cognitive dissonance – a term psychologists use to describe the unsettling feeling when our beliefs or behaviors conflict with a belief that is integral to our self-identity. Cognitive dissonance can have a powerful influence on our behaviors. If you believe all rich people are selfish, and because of a windfall you are now worth $12 million, what does that make you? You'll either need to change your belief about rich people or dump the $12 million.

Sudden Wealth Regression

When we have difficulty losing weight, doctors call it set point theory. When the stock market rises from its lows and falls from its highs, statisticians call it reversion to the mean. When our body's internal environment remains stable despite changes in the external surroundings, biologists call this homeostasis. In the aftermath of a windfall, it's called Sudden Wealth Regression.

Regression means to return to a former state, and this is exactly what happens in Sudden Wealth Regression. The sudden wealth recipient experiences intense stress and uncertainty that has pushed them outside their financial comfort zone. They feel a real or perceived social isolation, ostracism, or relational conflict from their family and/or friends as a result of their new financial status. In an attempt to feel less anxiety and to feel the comfort and acceptance of their pre-sudden wealth life, they knowingly or unknowingly sabotage their finances in anticipation of or after a sudden wealth event. As one sudden wealth recipient remarked, "My life before sudden wealth wasn't perfect, but at least I had friends to commiserate with."

You may feel a pull from family and friends to stay within your familiar financial comfort zone. The tug you feel to stay put may be under the surface or it may be overt. Sudden wealth clients routinely complain about hearing back-handed comments about the "rich" or about how they are now the "man." They may feel pressure to do more. One client lamented, "At Thanksgiving, my family made it clear this would be the best Christmas they've ever had."

Sudden Wealth Regression is a desperate attempt to get back to the way things were by self-sabotaging their finances and undermining their advisors. Common Sudden Wealth Regression behaviors include giving too much of their money away, making bad investment decisions, taking too much risk, not following the advice of their advisors, avoiding discussions about their finances, undervaluing their true wealth, and spending it carelessly and recklessly.

These behaviors may be an attempt to actually spend down their money to pre-sudden wealth levels or they may engage in these antics to show others they won't be affected by money and that they're still "one of them."

The limiting money belief is not about the fact that we have a financial comfort zone– we all do. Nor is it that we have boxed ourselves into a financial comfort zone based on flawed money beliefs. Our limiting money belief is that we cannot re-define them and that our beliefs cannot be changed. We limit ourselves when we think we are stuck with whatever money beliefs and behaviors we have today. That somehow, our comfort around money and finances is fixed or somehow pre-ordained and inflexible. This, thankfully, is simply not true.

HOW WE CREATE OUR FINANCIAL COMFORT ZONE

We think of ourselves as individualists and as charting our own course, but to a great extent, we are a product of our environment. According to social scientist and Harvard professor Nicholas Christakis, our social networks can exert a hidden and powerful influence that shapes our thoughts, attitudes, and beliefs. We adopt the characteristics of the group. We may sound like them, dress like them, and even vote like them. Heck, we may even weigh the same as them! Christakis' research shows that if your friend is obese, you have a 57% greater chance of being obese, and if your closest friend is obese, you have a 171% greater chance of being obese. The influence of our social network doesn't stop with friends, but it spreads from friends to friends of friends – people you may never have met may be influencing you. Christakis quips, "Humans are copycats, and we copy each other in all kinds of ways."

Fascinating to be sure, but what does this have to with sudden wealth? Our financial comfort zone is not created from deliberate and conscious planning, but more of an indoctrination of our environment.

It is this social environment that shapes not just our shape, but our beliefs about money and our financial values. Our financial comfort zone, what we consider normal and acceptable money beliefs and behaviors, come from the socioeconomic class of our early years, the beliefs of our family of origin, and our current social class and the friends who comprise it.

The money beliefs we inherited may include how we define rich and poor, what we consider to be a good income, beliefs about what it takes to get ahead financially, whether money should be used to buy things or experiences, how we view debt, how much one should show off their wealth, and whether money should be talked about or kept private. These money beliefs create the boundaries of what we consider acceptable or not, which directly influences our decisions. Should we buy or rent? Is debt anathema or simply the cost of enjoying life? Should you flaunt your new money or keep it private?

If you grew up poor, you may have learned that the rich are selfish or that you have to lie, cheat, and steal to become wealthy. You and your buddies may joke about "working for the man," that the people with money rig the system, or that people with money are out of touch with reality and don't care about anyone but themselves. On the other hand, if you grew up with money, you may think the poor are lazy or are always looking for a handout.

Wealthism?

In her dissertation "The Experience of Inherited Wealth," Joanie Bronfman coined the term "wealthism" to describe the "actions or attitudes that dehumanize or objectify wealthy people, simply because they are wealthy." To avoid being stereotyped or resented, some sudden wealth recipients try to conceal their wealth.

Whether you grew up rich or poor, we all have a financial comfort zone that feels right – there is certainty and a sense of security. It's painful to expand beyond our financial comfort zone because it is foreign. We don't understand the rules or values. We are residents in a land we don't understand. We feel uncomfortable. One client said she felt "like a phony" and as if she were "playing a part in a movie." When we stretch beyond our comfort zone, not just financially but any comfort zone, we naturally want to sink back to a place where we feel more confident and where we feel like we fit in. Slow and easy transitions are the work of gradual wealth, but sudden wealth forces us to confront change overnight.

Staying within our financial comfort zone is a powerful force. As soon as we push against its boundaries, we can start to feel anxiety and discomfort. Try this experiment. Cross your arms. Which arm is on top? Now cross your arms with the other arm on top. For most people, it feels awkward and uncomfortable. Now go back to folding your arms the way you naturally do. Doesn't it feel good?

If we can become befuddled just by folding our arms differently, imagine how easily our world can be turned upside down when we are thrust into a new situation that can be at odds with our natural financial comfort zone.

EXPANDING YOUR FINANCIAL COMFORT ZONE

The limiting belief you must successfully overcome is that your current financial comfort zone cannot be expanded.

The truth is that your financial home is flexible and that no matter how you grew up or what money beliefs and values you inherited from family and friends, you can learn and grow into a new financial comfort zone more commensurate with the socioeconomic level resulting from your sudden wealth.

When you push someone beyond their comfort zone, they can either grow into their new circumstances or they can resist the change and try to stay in the confines of their comfort zone. The unfit person who joins a gym for the first time is pushed beyond their comfort zone. They may push past their fears and continue to go to the gym, even though it is uncomfortable and foreign, or they can quit and revert back to their old habits.

How can you gradually expand your financial comfort zone?

BECOME AWARE OF YOUR MONEY BELIEFS

Like the rest of the limiting money beliefs in this chapter, awareness may be the cure for many. Start by becoming aware of your beliefs.

1. How do you define rich and poor?

2. If you meet someone who is rich, how do you view them?

3. What's your reaction when you meet someone with a large diamond ring or expensive watch?

4. Who would you trust more, your gardener or a CEO?

5. Is money meant to be acquired or enjoyed?

6. What does financial independence mean to you?

7. Are poor people just unlucky?

8. Are budgets only for the rich or only for the poor?

9. Does money create stress or alleviate stress?

10. Is the love of money the root of all evil?

TRACE THE SOURCE

Like Money Scripts discussed earlier, the source of our money beliefs and financial comfort zone can be traced back to their source. Although it's not essential, it can provide insight into why you think the way you do.

HOW DO YOUR BELIEFS LIMIT YOU?

Identify the money beliefs that restrict your financial comfort zone. How have these beliefs held you back? What damage has your financial comfort zone had on your finances and your life? If you continue to hold these beliefs and cling to your financial comfort zone, how will this negatively impact your sudden wealth? For example, if your belief is that all attorneys are money grubbing and dishonest, how will this belief hurt your sudden wealth? Maybe you won't hire an attorney, will only hire your attorney friend who is not qualified to help you, or will not trust or take the advice of any attorney you do hire. Without good legal counsel, is it possible you will pay a lot more in taxes and put your sudden wealth in jeopardy?

CHALLENGE LIMITING BELIEFS

What is not true about your limiting beliefs? Can you find exceptions? If your belief is that all attorneys are money grubbing and dishonest, have you ever met one who wasn't? Start to chip away at your general and global beliefs by finding exceptions. Rich people are selfish? Really? All rich people? You may conclude that some attorneys are dishonest and only care about money, but surely you can find an attorney who really cares about her clients (and if you haven't, I can certainly introduce you to one!).

CREATE NEW BELIEFS THAT EXPAND YOUR FINANCIAL COMFORT ZONE

As you chip away at your limiting money beliefs, you can allow room for your financial comfort zone to expand by creating new money beliefs. What are positive money beliefs that can replace your negative money beliefs and expand your financial comfort zone? Look at each negative belief and create an alternative. What would be a better belief that doesn't straightjacket you but allows you freedom to think bigger?

All limiting money beliefs are dangerous to your financial well-being. If they are not identified and upgraded, they can subtly influence your thoughts and behaviors. You may do things that "feel" right and give you comfort, but that are highly irrational and counterproductive to your overall well-being. Your limiting money beliefs can impact not only your finances, but also your relationships.

MANAGE RELATIONSHIPS

How to keep your most important relationships.

Money changes people. You might not want to think money can change your relationships with friends and family, but most sudden wealth recipients experience some change to their relationships. The changes may be positive or negative, but it's certainly some kind of change. Those who are candid about how their windfall has affected their relationships will lament that since their sudden wealth, they have lost friends or grown distant from friends and/or family. They may blame themselves or others, but they will agree that the money negatively impacted relationships that were important to them. It's noble to think you'll be the same guy who was $55,000 in debt when your bank account now shows $15 million. It's noble, but it's not realistic. It's also disingenuous to think your friends and family won't change either. They will.

Sudden wealth recipients will often complain that their friends or family weren't there for them when they needed them the most or that they put too much pressure on them. Their friends and family will complain that they didn't have time for them and that the money changed the sudden wealth recipient. Sudden wealth recipients who come to curse the money don't do it because they had too many meetings with their advisors or felt overwhelmed, they curse the sudden wealth because they view it as causing their divorce, losing friends, and becoming estranged from family. This is why sudden wealth gets a bad rap. And unfortunately, sudden wealth has the power to permanently damage our closest relationships.

The truth is that sudden wealth changes everyone, but this doesn't mean your relationships are doomed. When you think of relationships, "manage" probably isn't the first word to come to mind. Others, such as "build," "enjoy," or "maintain" are probably more common. But if you want to keep the relationships that are important to you, you need to "manage" and take responsibility for them.

One of the keys to happiness is having good relationships. In fact, it may be the key to happiness. Robert Putnam, a professor at Harvard University, who has been a consultant to the past three U.S. presidents, boldly states, "The strongest predictors of happiness by far are our social relationships." The goal of Sudden Wealth Principle 5 is to keep your relationships healthy and strong. Your sudden wealth doesn't have to be a divider. You may be able to create stronger and better relationships with friends and family, but to do this, we first have to examine the challenges a windfall can create on our relationships and learn how to successfully navigate through them.

CHALLENGES OF SUDDEN WEALTH TO OUR RELATIONSHIPS

Managing the tax, legal, and financial decisions of sudden wealth can seem simple compared to navigating the intricacies of relationships, misunderstandings, expectations, and hurt feelings. There are rules to managing wealth, but there aren't rules for managing relationships. Need to resolve a tax issue? No problem, with a bit of research and the right IRS form. Need to resolve a relationship issue? Good luck with that. Need to protect your assets? There are plenty of legal precedents and best practices to follow. Need to protect your relationships? Again, good luck with that.

How would you handle these awkward situations?

- You want to move to a larger house in a better community, but you're worried about how your friends will react.

- You get together for dinner with a group of friends and the bill comes. Do you pay?

- Your sister invites you out to dinner at a restaurant that serves mediocre but inexpensive food. You'd rather go to a better restaurant. Do you suggest a new restaurant and offer to pay?

- Your brother asked for financial help to pay for your nephew's braces, but you declined. It's your nephew's birthday and you are uncomfortable pulling into their driveway in your new $130,000 Mercedes. Do you park down the street?

- Your father tells you he was laid off from work. He doesn't ask for help, but do you offer? Would he be insulted if you gave him money? Would he be insulted if you didn't?

- You and a friend have been talking about climbing Mt. Kilimanjaro for years, and now you have the time and money. Do you go without your friend? Do you invite him but not offer to pay? Do you go without telling him?

- You're holding a swanky black tie party at your house with new and old friends, but your old friends don't have tuxedos and they don't have the money to rent them. Do you pay? Do you tell them to come dressed however they want? Do you not invite them?

- You buy a larger and safer car for your family. Your friend has driven your daughter to school every morning for the past six years in a small car that is not as safe as your new SUV. Do you tell your friend you don't want her to drive your daughter anymore? Do you tell her why? Or do you let her drive her even though you know her car is not as safe?

- You loaned money to your brother so he could start a company, but now your sister is asking for a loan to pay off credit card debt. You don't want to loan her the money, but do you do it anyway?

- You're dating someone new and you want to take a vacation with them to Paris, but you know they don't have the money to go. Do you pay?

- You and your buddies are planning a bachelor party in Vegas for a friend. You're all pitching in, but you'll be staying at a dump. Do you get a room at a better hotel, stay in the dump, or pay for everyone to stay at a better place?

- You happily agreed to pay the college tuition for your niece, but word got out and you are asked if you can pay the college tuition for your brother-in-law's daughter. Do you pay?

- Your sister-in-law overdosed and needs drug rehabilitation treatment, but the $35,000 monthly expense is more than anyone else in the family can afford. You could pay it but it would put stress on your finances. What do you do?

Were these scenarios a breeze to answer or did you get hung up on any of them? These are not fiction. Every single one of these has occurred to sudden wealth recipients – and often more than one and more than once! There are no right or wrong answers, but that just adds to the difficulty.

SUDDEN WEALTH RELATIONSHIP CHALLENGES

Expecting change and anticipating challenges is the first and best thing you can do. The following are several issues sudden wealth recipients face in their relationships:

STRESS

One of the most common complaints following sudden wealth is that people just don't understand the stress and pressures. Instantly, you are responsible for a large sum of money, maybe more money than you've made in total over the course of your entire career, and it's all on you. "I just don't want to screw it up," is something I've heard more than a few times. The money can provide freedom, but for many, it feels like an impossible weight on their shoulders. You have to find good advisors, but who can you trust? Are they looking out for your best interests? Are they really the best? These and a hundred other tax, legal, and financial decisions swirl around your head and must be made. Stressful? That's an understatement!

The intense stress may make it difficult for you to sleep, and you may have trouble eating. As we've seen in the last chapter, sudden wealth can bring up all kinds of emotions, depending on where the money came from. All of these factors can put you in a negative mood and/or cause you to have less patience with friends and family. Adding to this, others may only look at the money as an opportunity and may not appreciate the stress and emotions you are feeling. The people who you are closest to and who should understand you the best can feel like strangers.

Research shows that our need for affiliation and social interaction appears to be particularly strong when we are under stress, but our friends and family may not know what to do or may have their own issues around your sudden wealth and may not be able to support you. This creates distance and can damage the relationship.

ISOLATION

Sudden wealth makes you different. If you're going about your life and then overnight you receive a windfall, this sets in motion a series of events that create change. You and your family/friends need to adapt to this change. If you or they don't, you can feel a disconnection, or at the extreme, isolation.

Humans are social creatures. We long to be part of a group – a community. Regardless of where we live in the world, or even when we lived, humans form tight-knit relationships. We have a strong motivational drive to form and maintain caring interpersonal relationships. Psychologist Abraham Maslow and others have suggested that the need for love and belongingness is a fundamental human motivation. And it's not just because we enjoy the company of others. We do it to survive. There is strength in numbers. There is weakness is singularity.

Social psychological research confirms our strong desire for acceptance. Most human anxieties appear to reflect concerns over social exclusion. In fact, social rejection can lead to a number of adverse psychological consequences such as loneliness, depression, low self-esteem, and aggression. Standing out may work for Lady Gaga, but most of us desire to fit in. We are wired to conform and to be part of the herd. On the savannah, if you're not part of the herd, you're lunch. Our need for acceptance can push us into doing all kinds of things, such as conforming to peer pressure or complying with the demands of others. And for many of the two million teens who attempt suicide each year, feeling disconnected and shunned by their peers plays a significant role in their decision to take their own life[9].

Growing up, one of my favorite shows was *Cheers*. We want the comfort, security, and respect of our own group of misfits. You want a place "where everybody knows your name." There is power in being part of a herd and in feeling connected. Research shows that even people who dislike their job will continue to work if they like their co-workers.

ENVY

"It's easy for a friend to be there for you when you are struggling, but a true friend is there for you when you are succeeding, too."

It is highly probable that one or more of your friends and/or family members will experience envy as a result of your sudden wealth. It's human nature and it's quite common, although most won't admit it. Instead, the green-eyed monster may be bubbling under the surface but you may not even know it. Or, their envy may seep out through a comment that causes you to pause or escalate into a full blown confrontation.

A lot of this depends on how you received your windfall. Sudden wealth from the lottery or an inheritance from a distant relative may engender more envy than money that comes from a long and hard lawsuit battle or divorce. Many are conflicted, they feel guilty for feeling envy but they can't help it and don't know what to do.

CHANGE IN POWER

Every relationship has a certain dynamic to it, a set of rules and expectations, that create the environment for the relationship. In family relationships, there can also be a power structure, like between father and son or big brother and little sister. This power structure creates additional rules about what can and cannot be said and what is and is not acceptable in the relationship. This power dynamic doesn't just exist between family members. It occurs most visibly in boss/employee relationships, but it can often occur in friendships. Even though we'd like to think there is parity with friends, this isn't always the case. The power structure we have with family and friends isn't necessarily good or bad, it just is. But money can change the dynamics in a relationship, and a lot of money can radically change the dynamics.

The most extreme example of this was recounted to me by an attorney. His client was a woman in an abusive relationship. Her husband was an alcoholic and would beat her and yell at their young daughter. The woman wanted to leave for years, but she had no job or resources. She was afraid she'd be on the streets with her child and be in even more danger. She felt powerless and hopeless . . . until one day, she discovered she was getting a $45,000 inheritance. It was not a huge sum, but it was enough to immediately change the power structure. Overnight, she went from being the weak one to being the one in control and with the power. She moved out with her child and never looked back.

A more common example of how money can create a power shift is among siblings. You're the baby in the family and big brother and sisters have always treated you as such. Maybe they went to law school and have successful careers, while it's been harder for you financially. Post sudden wealth, you have a nicer car, bigger house, and more freedom to travel. You may not think anything's changed, but they may see their power and influence evaporate overnight and may react – positively or negatively.

SUDDEN WEALTH EXPERIENCE

Sudden wealth can really turn relationships on their head. It was a difficult transition for us, with plenty of hurt feelings to go around. I went from a traditional stay at home mom to cofounder of a NASDAQ traded environmental company with revenues in excess of $125 million in 18 months. I went from earning no money to earning more money than my husband and banking millions all in a very short time frame. Frankly, it was a shock to my husband. He never saw that coming! We have been together a total of 25 years. Everything we thought would happen as young adults in our early 20s has been turned on its head. But you know what, it's also been fun and we learned that we can get through all kinds of stresses-unexpected blessings (like money), deaths, and jealousy. You name it, we have survived it. The moral of the story is get ready for choppy waters but remember, money just makes you more of who you are. Hopefully you married well and things just get better as a result of the new found wealth. After we worked through the hurt feelings, I now view him as my biggest advocate and he sees me as a super accomplished woman. He says if I ever left or died, that'd be it for him because no other woman can compare. That makes a girl feel good.

~ Joyce Bone, President of Blamtastic

CHANGING DYNAMICS OF YOUR RELATIONSHIPS

Your friends and family may be happy for you, and at the same time, may feel they cannot relate to you in the same way as they did before the sudden wealth. Imagine the employee who used to hang around the water cooler and gossip about management with his co-workers. What happens if he gets a promotion and now is management? Surely he will feel discomfort in his new role just as surely as his co-workers will look at him differently. He's moved up, but his buddies haven't. Friday Happy Hour will be different – maybe better and maybe worse – but definitely different. The new manager may pine for the old days when he was "one of the guys" and a trusted confidant instead of "management."

We frequently take short-lived excursions to a new socioeconomic class – maybe a fancy dinner or exclusive resort – but what happens when you move from one socioeconomic class to another overnight? What happens when we enter a socioeconomic class we used to denounce? As one client asked, "What am I supposed to do when one day, I am deriding the 1% with my friends and the next day, I am the 1%?"

We receive a significant amount of social rewards from work. For a lot of people, this is their primary (maybe even exclusive) source of social interaction. Work is where your friends are and where everyone knows your name. If your sudden wealth was large enough that you could quit your job, you have an amazing opportunity where you can do something different with your life. The challenge of leaving your job is that you are also leaving your friends – the people you spend more time with than your spouse or children. No more water cooler gossip, lunchroom talk of the previous night's TV shows, Friday night Happy Hour, or Christmas parties. Gone. Would most people give up their daily chitchat with work acquaintances for the security of knowing they would never have to worry about being fired or laid off? You bet. But don't underestimate how much you will miss the familiarity and camaraderie of your work friendships.

Even if you can't quit your job, sudden wealth can still impact your relationships at work. If you've been able to keep your windfall private, very little will change. Sure, you might have a little more swagger resulting from the confidence and security of knowing you have a large bank account balance, but your co-workers will be none the wiser. However, if your co-workers know of your good fortune, the dynamics at work can change dramatically. It can be a little more than awkward when you and your buddies complain about salary freezes over a beer and then you drive off in your new Porsche.

Your family and friends may look at you differently. Instead of being "one of us," you are now "one of them." In response, some sudden wealth recipients isolate themselves, preferring to avoid friends and family rather than have to deal with the questions or even criticism.

> *"Two nations between whom there is no intercourse and no sympathy; who are as ignorant of each other's habits, thoughts, and feelings, as if they were dwellers in different zones, or inhabitants of different planets. The rich and the poor."*
>
> ~ Benjamin Disraeli, from his book, *Sybil, or The Two Nations*

FRIENDS AND FAMILY CAN FEEL LEFT OUT

Either money changes you, your friends/family, or both. Some sudden wealth recipients will stick the money in an account, not tell anyone, and go about life as if they never received it. This is common with young trust fund kids, many of who have negative beliefs about money that make it difficult for them to accept their new wealth and integrate the money into their life. And if their friends don't have money, many are fearful of how they will be perceived by their peers, so they keep it a secret. They might be ashamed of the money, while at the same time, longing to use it to better their life.

FRIENDS FEEL STUCK BECAUSE THEY DON'T HAVE MONEY

Sudden wealth provides freedom and opportunity. You now may have the ability to do all of the things you've always wanted to do. But although you may have the time and the money, your friends/family do not. You'd love to take an Alaskan cruise, but who can go with you? Your friends can't get the time off of work, and even if they could, they can't afford to spend $5,000 when they're already having trouble making ends meet.

RESTRICTED CONVERSATIONS

One of the hallmarks of a close relationship with a friend or family member is that you can talk about anything. Although some topics might be off limits to casual friends, it is liberating to be able to talk about anything with those who are closest to you. Clients will lament that after sudden wealth, they don't feel they can talk to their friends about anything. The money has complicated their relationship and they don't feel the freedom to confess, vent, or share certain things they once could.

If you know your friend was laid off or is having trouble financially, can you talk to them about your money problems? Will you feel comfortable talking to a friend about how you're having trouble sleeping at night because of the stress your sudden wealth has created? The last time you bought a new Honda, it may have been a source of great pride and excitement for you, but will you gush over your new Tesla when you know your friend can barely afford their mortgage? Or will your sister hold back on telling you about her money problems because she doesn't want you to feel guilty about your financial success?

These may be small things, but when you've had the freedom to talk about anything and now find you must censor yourself (or your friends/family must censor what they say to you), it can be hard to accept; it can create a wedge in a relationship.

ABANDONMENT

If you move to a new neighborhood, join the local country club, or start to travel more, you will be around new people and chances are, you will make new friends. This is, of course, natural and to be expected. However, your old friends may not see this so clearly. You may not have the same time or attention for them like you used to, they may perceive your new friends as just another way you are trying to shed your old life, and everything in it, including them, for something better. This can create hurt feelings and conflict. Your old friends may disparage your new friends and make it difficult for you to do things as a group. This can put you in the uncomfortable position of having to take sides on something you view as immature and childish, but it's not. At least it doesn't feel that way to your old friends.

One friend of a sudden wealth recipient said, "I felt like I wasn't good enough anymore. We'd been friends for 12 years, our kids grew up together, but then she gets some money and abandons her old life and her old friends." But this wasn't the perspective of the sudden wealth recipient, who explained, "I wasn't trying to abandon anyone. I love my old friends and my new friends. Why do I need to choose between the two?"

OUT OF TOUCH

Money doesn't fix everything, but it does upgrade our problems. We still have the same level of worry and stress, but now we stress about different things. We exchange our worry about how we're going to pay for our child's college tuition for how our investments are performing. Instead of a sleepless night stressing about the company's new round of layoffs, we may have a sleepless night stressing about the hardwood floors being installed.

Sudden wealth doesn't increase or decrease the amount of stress, worry, and anxiety someone experiences. If someone was a frequent worrier before the money, they will find things to worry about after the money. In most (but not all) cases, the stress doesn't magically disappear, it just shifts. Would you rather worry about the inconvenience of new hardwood floors being installed or being laid off? Even though money creates quality problems – problems most people would love to have – for the sudden wealth recipient, they still experience them as problems and these problems create stress.

The danger to your relationships occurs when your friends and family think the money has made you out of touch with the "real" problems of the world. As one sudden wealth friend related, "I was going through a divorce and was struggling with how my kids and I were going to survive. It was the worst time in my life. I unloaded on my friend and I think she understood, but then she starts talking to me about how stressed she was over a holiday party she was throwing at her house. A party?! Really? She just didn't get it."

HOW TO KEEP AND GROW YOUR RELATIONSHIPS

GO SLOW

The stress of sudden wealth can make even the most even keeled and grounded person a little frazzled. It can take a few days or even a few months to really settle in and to hit your stride. Until then, go slowly. Read and re-read "Sudden Wealth Principle 2: Slow Down." Follow the stress reduction tips as much as you can – eat better, sleep more, and exercise.

PHONE A FRIEND

When it comes to your relationships, I've found it is best to have one or two confidants. If you have more than this, there can be too many "cooks in the kitchen." This is a highly emotional and stressful time, and although you need the support from loved ones, you don't want to become overwhelmed with support, advice, and questions. You can either keep your sudden wealth private from others or you can proactively reach out to close friends and family with an email or message.

PROACTIVE COMMUNICATION

Public relations experts always tell their clients to "get in front of the story." This means you proactively get your message, the message you want, out before you get questions and the story gets a life of its own. Here's how you can get in front of your story and for your friends and family to not feel neglected or left out: (1) Give them a brief summary (no details needed) of your situation, (2) Let them know you will be less available while you sort everything out, and (3) That as soon as you can come up for a breath, you will update them. That's it. Could you still receive unsolicited advice and questions? Sure, but just stick to your message.

DON'T CHECK OUT

Resist the temptation to check out. Isolating yourself is rarely a good move. Your friends and family can provide support. Early on, when things are most stressful and when you need the most support, reach out to one or two friends who are the most supportive. If your closest friends are creating the most discomfort, and this can be the case, find other friends/family who can provide you the support you need. Once things settle down for you, then you can reconnect with your other friends.

CONFESS YOUR FEARS

This can be a powerful strategy that can prevent relationship issues before they happen. It's as simple as expressing your fears and what you want to avoid before there are any problems. This is most effective when the sudden wealth is new and hasn't had a chance to create any relationship issues. You can write a letter/email or gather your friends/family together and share with them your fears – that you've done research on sudden wealth and that it is common to have relationship growing pains. Discuss how other sudden wealth recipients lost best friends and family members because of the challenges windfalls can create (e.g., hurt feelings, envy, distance, perceived inequity, etc.) and that you never want your relationships to suffer. This simple (but not necessarily easy) conversation can deflate many of the relationship problems before they become problems. It's amazing how shining light on a potential problem and sharing your feelings and fears can prevent them from becoming an issue.

GET IT OUT IN THE OPEN

What's the only thing worse than having an uncomfortable conversation with a friend or family member? Not having the conversation. No one looks forward to sitting their best friend down and asking them if they think different of you because of the money. But if you don't and the negative feelings linger, it can damage a relationship for which you care deeply. It's better to have a difficult talk and to get everything out in the open, than it is to let these things fester until you're both angry at each other.

BE CAREFUL NOT TO CONFORM

Your desire to fit in may lead you to do all kinds of irrational things, such as giving your money away, throwing big parties, or promising to help friends and family members financially. You may end up doing these things, but give yourself and your advisors time to determine what you can afford. Don't do them just to minimize the pressure, guilt, or other emotions you are feeling.

FOCUS ON WHAT YOU WANT

The mistake most people make when they are hoping for change is to focus on what they don't want, but there are two problems with this. First, it can feel like an attack to be told that what you are doing/saying is wrong. This can escalate the conversation into an argument and a debate. Second, it's not instructive. Paint the picture of what you want so there is a clear objective. It's much easier to hit the target when you know where it is than knowing where it isn't.

WATCH YOUR RELATIONSHIP RULES

Your relationship rules determine what has to happen for you to feel good about your relationships. Rules are 'if-then' triggers we create so we know when a need has been met. For example, you may have a rule for love that requires never arguing, being told every day that you are beautiful, enjoying the same activities, and being able to talk about your feelings without being judged. If these things occur, then you feel love. If only two or three of these occur, you won't feel love. Our rules run in the background. Without even knowing it, we have a checklist that is being compared against our interactions. Check off enough items and we're satisfied. Miss one and there's a problem.

The rules you create control your happiness and your relationships. If you set rules for your relationships that are impossible for friends and family to meet, you will be disappointed. It's not about artificially setting the bar low. It's about understanding what our rules for relationships are and determining if the rules are valid and healthy.

The first step is taking an inventory of your relationship rules. What has to happen for you to feel good about your relationships with your friends and family? Most people's rules start with "If you were a good friend/family member you would…" Figure out the right combination that unlocks relationship happiness for you. Now get ready to make some changes. Look for rules that are difficult to accomplish and/or not under your control and then come up with better rules. For example, if your relationship rule is that your friends should understand your needs and that they should reach out to you without asking for support, you are setting yourself up for failure. Your friends can't read your mind and anticipate your needs. If you expect them to, you will be constantly disappointed. Unreasonable relationship rules can lead you to act desperately or selfishly. Make your relationship rules easy to achieve and under your control.

ASSUME THE BEST INTENTIONS

The poison that can kill a relationship is assuming bad intentions. When you think the worst about someone, it can start a chain reaction of hurt feelings and bad behavior that can tarnish even the best relationships. For example, if a friend didn't send flowers after your mother passed away and your interpretation was that she doesn't care enough about you, what other negative thoughts could this lead to? How will you interact with her if your assumption is she doesn't care about you? Negative assumptions put you on a downward spiral.

Instead, take the high road. Give them the benefit of the doubt and assume the best intentions. Maybe your friend cares deeply about you, but when she heard of your mother's passing, it reminded her of her own mother's passing. Maybe instead of sending flowers, she made you something. If these were the thoughts going through your mind, how would your interaction with your friend change?

There are a million reasons why someone could do something. Instead of assuming the worst, assume the best in your family and friends.

FOCUS ON OTHERS

Sudden wealth can be all encompassing. It takes a tremendous amount of time and energy to effectively deal with everything. But your friends and family have their own lives, issues, and challenges they are facing, too. During the early stages of sudden wealth, the focus is going to be on you. You'll put in a lot of mental energy working with your advisors and thinking about this new chapter in your life. So much so, it can be easy to forget about the needs of your friends and family. Effectively responding to sudden wealth can be demanding and exhausting, but make room for those who are closest to you. Shift some of the attention and focus to them by asking them about their lives and developments.

GET NEW FRIENDS

Don't be afraid to make new friends. For some, sudden wealth can be isolating. Old friends and family members may not understand the pressures. They may not have the time or money to do the things you can now do, such as travel. Get around others who understand your position. One client once remarked, "It is so liberating to be around others with money so you don't have hide your wealth or worry that you'll be asked for a loan." Even though not everyone with money can appreciate the unique challenges of sudden wealth, new relationships won't have the baggage the old ones do. The same client confessed, "Sometimes when I'm around my old friends or with family, I feel like a fraud. Like they are judging me for something I did wrong. Like no matter what I do, they are watching my every move."

Go to and consider attending one of our retreats with other sudden wealth recipients where you can share your story, successes, and challenges.

KEEP YOUR PROBLEMS IN PERSPECTIVE

This cannot be repeated often enough: keep your quality problems in perspective. There's no doubt you are going through a stressful time with lots of ups and downs. It's understandable you will be stressed and that you'll have many new things to worry about. Sudden wealth is also an opportunity. It's easy to become hung up on the challenges you are facing and to lose perspective on the problems your friends and family may be facing. Be thankful you've been able to upgrade some of your problems, but don't forget your friends and family still have their old problems.

Sudden wealth changes people. It will change you and it will change your friends and family. It's hard to avoid this. The goal is for everyone to come out the other side with as little permanent damage as possible.

How many times are we told that "It takes two to tango"? How many times have we said, "You need to meet me halfway" or, "I'll do my part if you do yours"? Intuitively, it makes sense that if each person pulls their weight, the relationship will work, but intuition is wrong. The best and strongest relationships are when each person takes 100% responsibility for making it work. They don't wait for the other person.

If your relationships matter, take full responsibility for doing what it takes to keep them strong. Feeling slighted by a family member because they didn't call you to congratulate you on your win? Take responsibility for the relationship and reach out to them – especially during the early stages of sudden wealth when everyone is adjusting to the situation.

Most sudden wealth recipients experience some relationship growing pains, but with a little insight, patience, and compassion, everyone can adjust to the changes smoothly and have better, stronger relationships as a result. I think the biggest takeaway is to not let mole-hills turn into mountains. My rule is that if something happens once, I let it go. If it happens twice, I address it. It's not all about you. Your friends and family have their own issues and challenges. If you have an encounter where you sense some weirdness about your sudden wealth, let it go. Everyone can have a bad day. But if it happens again, call attention to it. It's communication 101, but focus on how whatever they said or did makes you feel. No need to cast blame or criticize. The more you can share what you're experiencing without attacking them, the better the chance they will understand your point of view.

But there comes a time when you have to say no to even your closest friends and family members.

PRINCIPLE 6
SAY NO

Learn strategies to reduce the onslaught of money requests.

No. So simple. So short. Why is it so difficult to say?

There are few guarantees in life. We know about death and taxes, but we can add one more: If you've received sudden wealth, you will be hit up for money . . . and probably often. Everyone from friends and family to strangers and charities will ask for money. They'll ask for loans, investments, gifts, and donations. They'll ask, and then they'll ask some more.

This is the dark side of sudden wealth. This is the aspect of sudden wealth that those who've never experienced it will never understand. The requests can be unrelenting and they can start before the ink dries on your check. It can leave even the most caring and compassionate person hardened and a little jaded.

There's nothing you can do to avoid these money requests, but there are ways you can deal with them that will make it easier for you and for the people asking. If you follow the guidelines in this chapter, you will learn strategies for saying no that will empower you. You'll have more confidence because you'll have tools and a proven system to say "no, thanks" that minimizes hurt feelings.

"I didn't know what to say, so I said okay," said one defeated sudden wealth recipient. This will not be your fate, however. The element of surprise is what takes people off guard. Rule number one is to expect the desperate calls, emotional emails, heartfelt letters, frantic texts, and in-person pleas for help. They will come from the people you'd never expect and from people you don't even know. They will come when you least expect it and when you are least prepared. Don't delude yourself by thinking it won't happen to you. It will. Expect it and you won't be caught off guard.

> *"It is commonly observed that a sudden wealth, like a prize drawn in a lottery or a large request to a poor family, does not permanently enrich. They have served no apprenticeship to wealth, and with the rapid wealth come rapid claims which they do not know how to deny, and the treasure is quickly dissipated."*
>
> ~ Ralph Waldo Emerson

Sometimes, this is easier said than done. Years ago, when I was helping an investor find private equity companies in which to invest, I received a rather peculiar business pitch. A gentleman (and I'm using that term loosely) sent me a business plan in which he described his idea for making money by capitalizing on a unique talent – he could hang items from a certain appendage below his belt. And he didn't leave anything to the imagination. In addition to the compelling copy in the business plan, he submitted several photos of items dangling from said appendage. Think *X Factor*, but in this case, XXX Factor.

To prepare yourself for the ridiculous and ludicrous requests you may receive, humor can go a long way. My favorite movie is *The Jerk* with Steve Martin. It's been my favorite since I first saw it as a child. Steve Martin's character — an unsophisticated half-wit – receives sudden wealth after inventing a device for eyeglasses. In one memorable scene, a priest shows a film "of a great ugliness" that is spreading in his country . . . cat juggling! Its absurdity can be a great reminder of what you can expect. After I've shared this clip, clients have reported that it's made them chuckle when they are being pitched something. "It's all just juggling cats," joked one client.

Turning Money Requests Into A Game You Can Win

Have you ever been so engrossed in a song or audiobook while driving that you actually hoped for red lights? Instead of worrying about being hit up for money, embrace it. For some clients who feel paralyzed and who avoid social and family situations in fear they will be cornered and asked for money, we turn it into a game. We make a guess at the number of requests they will get at an event or even each week and see who comes closest.

DON'T BLAME THEM FOR ASKING

In the last chapter, I talked about the importance of assuming the best intentions in others. It's especially true when friends and family are asking for money. To avoid becoming hard and jaded, it helps to understand their perspective.

As has already been discussed throughout this book, friends and family do not understand the pressures of sudden wealth. They do not realize the stress you are facing or the decisions required of you, and they certainly won't understand the timing. They just don't get it. The impression from those on the outside is that sudden wealth is all fun and games. Of course, you know that not to be true. It's hard work and it takes effort, diligence, and focus. But again, they don't get it and that's okay. You probably didn't either until you experienced it.

Those on the outside typically overestimate how much money sudden wealth recipients actually have. In the case of lottery wins, lawsuit judgments, stock options, or business sales, when the financials are made public, people become stuck on the headline number but fail to account for legal contingency payments, expenses, advisor fees, taxes, and paying off debts. They see the $50 million lottery win, but don't realize that the lump sum payment may only be $30 million, of which half goes to taxes. In their minds, the $50 million headline sticks even though the winner may actually only end up with $6 million after paying off debts, taxes, expenses, funding your children's college education, and buying a new home and cars. There's no doubt $6 million is a lot of money, but can you see how it would be easier for your brother-in-law to ask you to make a $1 million investment in a company he's starting if he thought you were worth $50 million rather than $6 million?

Your friends and family may be struggling. They might see you as the white knight who will rescue them. They may think you're their last resort. Desperate people do desperate things, the least of which is to ask for money. They may also think that if you knew how much they were struggling, you would want to help them. They may even tell themselves that if the roles were reversed, they would help you. Whether you are their last hope or if they really would help you if the roles were reversed doesn't matter. It's important at this point to simply appreciate where they are coming from. If you're not willing to empathize, it can sour even the strongest relationship.

HOW TO HANDLE MONEY REQUESTS

Over the years, my clients have told me one of the most stressful and uncomfortable things about sudden wealth is being asked for money by friends, family, and strangers. This is the one area that they've said never becomes easier. In fact, many sudden wealth recipients say that it actually becomes worse over time – like a snowball that builds in size and momentum as it rolls down a hill, where more people ask for more and more.

Early in my career, I saw the stress and unhappiness this was causing my clients. They had so much good happening to them, but these requests would turn their lives upside down. If they said yes, but really didn't want to help or couldn't afford to, they'd be angry with themselves. If they said no, they'd feel guilty. The fear of always being asked and the pressure of saying no strained their relationships – sometimes to the point where they became resentful and distrusting of the people around them.

But over the years, I've developed a few strategies that help put the client back in control, and a system that actually reduces the number of money requests. So instead of getting hit up more and more, if you follow the system, you will have fewer people asking you for money over time.

SUDDEN WEALTH EXPERIENCE

My husband and I embarked on an entrepreneurial journey out of law school. In 1997, we purchased a domain name for $100 and started an online legal document filing service in the living room of our apartment, where we worked night and day to grow the business. After some years of growth, we owned a business that was grossing over $1 million in sales every month. In 2005, we sold the business to Intuit for $20 million. Here are our top three tips for new sudden wealth recipients:

1. Be more selective in who you associate with. I never knew I had so many uncles until I sold the business. They come out of the wood work.

2. Be leery of the overnight rushers who literally tell you how much they love you after a nano second of meeting you because I can tell you, they just want to somehow get you to invest in them or lend them cash.

3. Keep your friends close, but keep your enemies closer.

~ Nellie Akalp, CEO of Corpnet, Incorporated

Let's look at how a brother and sister who receive a large inheritance handle requests for money. Reactive Rich does what so many sudden wealth recipients do when it comes to money requests – he reacts. Each request is different and each response is different. Sometimes, Rich says yes on the spot, but other times, he says he's not sure. Sometimes, he uses a written loan agreement, but other times, he loans the money on a handshake. Sometimes, he charges interest, but other times, he doesn't. Sometimes, he runs it by his advisors, but most of the time, he doesn't. Sometimes, he gets a receipt for his donation, but sometimes, he doesn't. Sometimes, he asks for a business plan before making an investment, but other times, he doesn't. Sometimes, he helps his niece with her college tuition, but other times, he doesn't. Rich is inconsistent and reacts to each request based on how he's feeling and who is making the request. Because of this, Rich and his finances are a mess. He's stressed and never knows what to say or how to respond. His finances are dwindling and he doesn't even know where his money has gone. The same friends and family ask him for money multiple times, hoping they'll catch him in a good mood. Word spreads and more distant family members and new acquaintances ask him for money. Poor Rich.

Rich's sister, Consistent Carrie, does things differently. Regardless of who is asking for money or for how much they are asking, she never makes a decision on the spot. She always tells the person she's not sure and that she'll have to get back to them. She doesn't rely on her gut to make decisions. Instead, all money requests are run by her advisors. She doesn't get caught up in the drama or the emotions. She uses her advisors to act as her surrogate. They ask the tough questions about the loan or the investment. Carrie and her advisors require documentation and paperwork for every loan, investment, and donation she makes.

The most significant difference between Reactive Rich and Consistent Carrie is that Carrie has developed and follows a formalized process for handling money requests. This gives her control and confidence. Regardless of who is making the request, the amount, or the type (e.g., gift, loan, investment, donation), she follows the same steps. This gives Carrie confidence and puts her in control.

Why go through the trouble of creating a formalized process to money requests? Here are the benefits:

1. **It trains people.** One of the great benefits of a formalized process is that it provides structure to something that often lacks any. This structure is the process and the system you follow. By doing the same thing every time, you train friends and family on how you expect the money

request to be delivered, how long it will take, and what information and documentation you require.

2. **Slows things down.** Slowing things down is a recurring theme throughout this book. Thoughtful analysis and a measured approach typically lead to more informed and better decisions – especially during the chaos that can ensue around a sudden wealth event. A formalized approach to money requests guarantees there will be no quick decisions that are later regretted.

3. **Puts you in control.** Don't forget the golden rule. She who has the gold makes the rules. Friends, family, and strangers will use high pressure sales tactics or will try to steamroll you with figures or appeal to your emotions with a gut-wrenching story. Many sudden wealth recipients have said that people, even friends and family, will try to take advantage of them by trying to dominate or take control. The process puts you in control, regardless of their agenda.

4. **Fewer repeat requests.** Once someone goes through this process, they may be less inclined to ask you for money again. Or at the least, if they ask for money, they'll know what to expect.

5. **Disconnect personal from financial.** By having a system in place, it takes the pressure off of you – especially when you want to say no. The more you can make the process a business transaction rather than a personal transaction, the less tension and awkwardness you'll experience. And by using a third-party – your advisors – you are taking the weight off of yourself. As one client told me, "I love it. You can be the bad guy!"

6. **Weed out a lot of people.** Friends and family who think getting money from you will be a slam dunk will quickly realize it is a slow, methodical process that requires more than just a familiar face and sad story or clever pitch. The money request process isn't a slam dunk. It takes time, interviews with your advisors, and paperwork. Your buddy with a new concept for a restaurant but without a business plan or financial projections isn't going to make it far, regardless of how novel or great his idea is. Making your family, friends, and strangers talk to advisors alone is enough to discourage some people. After clients get

pitched, I rarely get the call from the friend or family member. Apparently, the money is just not worth talking to me!

7. **Better for your friends and family.** The formalized process doesn't just benefit you, it is also good for the people asking for money. Not only will they know what to expect, the process makes it more businesslike. The questions your advisors ask and the documentation they will require will make it better for your friends and family. For example, your brother-in-law may have a good idea for a new iPhone app, but he may not have created any financial projections. If it's compelling, your advisors can help him think through the business. Additionally, it creates consistency so your friends/family know what to expect. For example, if you've been hit-or-miss in helping your niece with her college tuition, it can be uncomfortable for your sister to have to ask you each semester. The formalized process creates consistency, which is good for everyone.

8. **Better financially for you.** How much can you afford to donate? Does it help you more from a tax perspective to donate this year or next? Is this a good investment? What interest rate makes sense for you to charge? The process is designed to protect your financial interests.

9. **Better records.** By requiring loan agreements, verification of tax-exempt status with non-profits, obtaining donation receipts, investment paperwork, etc., you are in a much better position to take advantage of tax deductions on donations, bad loans, and worthless securities as well as better able to coordinate these gifts and assets with your estate plan.

10. **Greater accountability.** The process highlights the responsibilities of each party and holds them accountable. If you agree to pay your niece's tuition each semester, you will be held accountable for this. Alerts will be scheduled when the tuition is due and paperwork will be in place to make the payments. Your brother who borrowed money to pay off his credit card debt will also be held accountable to make his monthly principal and interest payment to you – or better yet, your advisors. Late payment? There's no wondering what you should do. It's already been discussed and agreed to in the loan agreement.

FORMALIZED MONEY REQUEST PROCESS – THE RULES

RULE #1 – NEVER SAY YES

This is a simple rule, but if you make exceptions, it can come back to bite you. The rule is that you cannot agree or commit to providing a loan, investment, gift, or donation to anyone on the spot. If you don't want to provide the money and you are comfortable saying no, then by all means, make it clear you have no interest. If you are pitched an investment that sounds interesting or you are asked for a loan from a friend and you are uncomfortable saying no, delay the decision. Never commit on the spot, regardless of how urgent they make it seem. You always have a night to think it over, and if they claim they need to know right away, tell them you're not making a decision on the spot. If they continue to pressure you, then tell them no thanks.

Truthiness

When in doubt, lie. This advice is not the making of a Hallmark greeting card or children's fable, but when it comes to sudden wealth, not being 100% honest can serve you well. For sudden wealth recipients who expect to be pressured by friends and family and who aren't comfortable saying no, I suggest they tell those wanting a piece of the windfall that they have less than they actually do and that there are many tax and legal restrictions on getting access to it. For clients who take the lump sum payment in a lottery win or lawsuit settlement, it's fine to tell others they are living on a fixed monthly annuity payment. It's none of their business, but too often, your windfall becomes their business whether you want it to or not. A little fiction can go a long way to protect your finances.

RULE #2 – CREATE A CANNED RESPONSE

Your sister pulls you aside at a family gathering and tells you little Johnny really would like to go to guitar camp but that they've been struggling financially because her husband was laid off. She tells you how gifted Johnny is and how it's not that much money and how it's an opportunity of a lifetime for him and asks if you have the $5,000 for tuition. Your mind races as you fumble for your words. "Uh, well, it does sound like a great camp and Johnny is really talented, and uh…"

and before you know it, you've agreed to give her $5,000. It doesn't have to be this way, though.

No one likes to be pressured and made to feel uncomfortable. The best tool I've found to give clients confidence is for them to come up with a standard canned response they can use whenever they are asked for money. No matter what the situation or the request, you can have a thoughtful reply that you've memorized and practiced, which you can deliver without thinking or fumbling for words. The response I recommend is:

> *"I can't give you an answer this moment, but let me talk to my advisors and we'll get back to you with more questions."*

The advantages of this approach are threefold. First, it takes pressure off of you in the moment by giving you more time to decide. A lot of sudden wealth has been frittered away because of making bad decisions on the spot. Second, it sets the precedent that you are thoughtful with your money and will not be cornered into a decision, no matter how small the money request. Third, you are shifting the decision making power off of yourself and on to your advisors, as well as opening the door to have your advisors respond on your behalf, which many sudden wealth recipients find to be a big relief. To feel comfortable with this response, practice it over and over and over. You want it to flow off your lips without thought. It should feel effortless. Role play various scenarios with your advisors so you can become comfortable with delivering your response.

Many clients are initially doubtful, though. They say, "It looks great on paper and even sounds good to say it, but it won't be enough. They won't let it go so easily. They'll keep talking to me and asking questions." All quite possible . . . and likely. The first time you respond with this canned response, they may not even hear you or acknowledge it. That's okay. You simply repeat it.

> *"Again, thank you for asking, but I can't give you an answer at this moment. Let me talk to my advisors, and we'll get back to you with more questions."*

Still pressured? They want an answer now? They want to give you more details? Simply repeat what you've said. Don't change your message. Repeat your canned response verbatim each time they want an answer or want to pitch you further. You don't have to provide an explanation or any details as to who your advisors are or when you'll be getting back to them. They are coming to you for help. It's your game and you make the rules. If they want to play, they need to follow them.

Clients have said that this memorized phrase is like having armor and that it gives them confidence to go into any situation and not be worried about being asked for money. One client, who had just come into sudden wealth, was so petrified about going to a family dinner and being hit up for money that she wasn't going to attend. After creating her canned response and rehearsing it several times, she transformed into a different person. She was no longer worried or insecure. In fact, she said she couldn't wait for the dinner so she could use her response for real.

RULE #3 – USE YOUR ADVISORS

If you like being the guy or gal who tells people no, then by all means, do it. On the other hand, if you don't want to be in the position of telling friends and family that you can't help them, use your advisors. Almost all of my clients use me this way, and I encourage it. Why? It takes a lot of the pressure off you. Let your advisor get the information and ask the tough questions. Let them negotiate the details. Let them say no. It allows you to avoid confrontation and makes your advisors the bad guys.

I recommend using your financial advisor as the initial go-to person. They usually have a broader knowledge base for which they can analyze different requests, and they are more in tune with your financial situation and ability to make donations, loans, or investments. Added bonus: it will be cheaper for you. Attorneys and CPAs typically charge by the hour, but most financial advisors do not.

Pro Tip

Discuss with your financial/legal professional exactly how you will respond to solicitations – and then stick to it. It's often best to refer all solicitations directly to your advisors, so they can be the "bad guy," not you. Remember that many of those solicitations will come from friends or family, not strangers. It's okay to say "no." It's also okay to say, "I need to discuss that with my financial planner/lawyer."

~ John Hagerty, Virginia Lottery

RULE #4 – SEND A CANNED NOTE

For highly publicized sudden wealth events such as a lottery, sports/entertainment contract, stock options, or some lawsuits, your friends and family will be all over you with advice and questions. To avoid much of this, I've found a successful solution that is both direct and caring. Send this email/letter to your friends and family:

"Thank you for reaching out to me. As you can imagine, life has been crazy for me lately. I'm sorry that I haven't been able to get back to you, but I want you to know I appreciate our relationship. I'm working with my advisory team. Once I'm able to come up for air, I will give you an update. At this point, I don't need any advice or suggestions, but if this changes, I will let you know. Again, thank you for your understanding while I sort everything out. I look forward to being able to catch up with you soon."

RULE #5 – USE THE MONEY REQUEST TOOL

To better formalize the review process, I created an online form for money requests at suddenwealthsolution.com. The form contains a series of detailed questions the requestor must complete and submit. The advantage of using the form – at least initially – is that it asks a lot of important questions and can be a big time saver by providing a good overview of the request and the requestor. To help you stay out of the process, have your advisor email the link to the form to the person asking you for money. The completed form can then be emailed directly to the advisor for his review. Your advisor can then have a conversation with you about the request and can go back to the requestor with more questions.

RULE #6 – ASK ME ONCE, IT'S FINE. ASK ME TWICE, WE HAVE A PROBLEM.

Friends, family, and strangers will ask you for money. If you have a relationship rule that says, "Someone who cares about me will never ask for money," then you will perpetually be disappointed. Over the years, I've raised the threshold for becoming upset. I created a better rule:

Ask me whatever you want and I won't be upset. If I decline and you ask me again, we have a problem.

It's one thing for a friend or family member to reach out to you for help. If you give it careful consideration but decline, it needs to end there. If they continue to ask, you and/or your advisors need to make it clear that they've crossed a line and that further requests will jeopardize your relationship. Clients have told me this is harsh and that they couldn't imagine having this conversation with close friends or family members. I agree. It's not an easy conversation to have, but it is an important one. Here's why. It tells them you care enough about your relationship that you do not want it damaged. It tells them what you are willing to accept and what you are not. It sets the operating rules and gives them the choice to decide whether they value your relationship or your money more. If they want to ruin the relationship, it's on them.

To make the process more formalized, some sudden wealth recipients have created a written document that outlines each step in the process, who is involved, timelines, etc., which they share with friends and family after being asked for money. Documenting your process isn't required, but if your sudden wealth was made public and you are receiving a lot of requests from strangers, it's an effective strategy for handling numerous requests, setting expectations, and getting everyone on the same page.

Sudden wealth isn't all about saying no. There will be some family and friends you want to help, but before you start writing checks, the next Sudden Wealth Principle will show you how to help the right way.

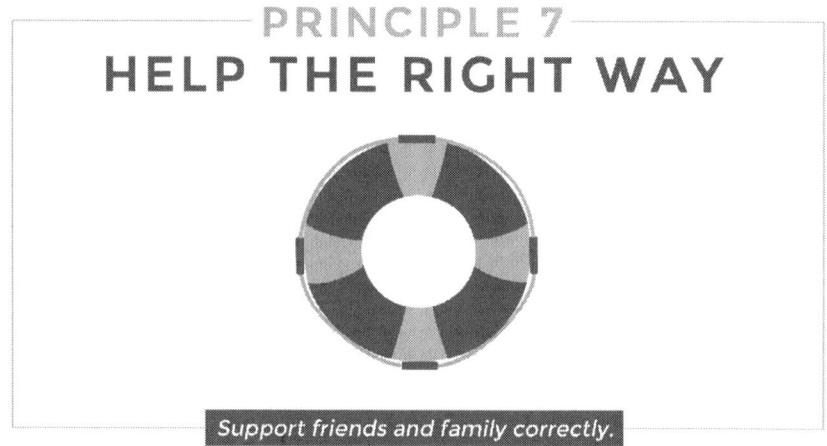

PRINCIPLE 7
HELP THE RIGHT WAY

Support friends and family correctly.

Many sudden wealth recipients want to use their new wealth to help their family and close friends, but just as many are unsure of the best way to help. Should you send a check? Take everyone on a trip? Agree to pay their mortgage? Buy each a new car? How much is too much? There are lots of questions and usually not enough clear answers.

When it comes to helping family and friends, it's not all smiles and sunshine. If you go about this the wrong way, it can ruin relationships and create a great deal of pain for yourself. You've learned to say no, but what about those times when it makes sense to help friends and family members financially? There's a right and wrong way to say yes. This is a delicate area that requires planning and clear communication. Here is what NOT to do…

1. **Making promises too quickly.** In the frenzy of the moment, many sudden wealth recipients have reported being so excited and thankful that they spontaneously make promises to friends and family. They may blurt out that they will pay off their parents' mortgage, buy a sibling a new car, pay off a nephew's student loans, or invest in a college buddy's restaurant. One of two things will happen. You'll either follow through on your promises or you won't. If you don't have as much money as you thought you would, your heart may be bigger than your bank account. At that point, you may have to retract your promises or feel pressure and resentment if you make them anyway. There is absolutely nothing to be gained from making promises too early. It's a lose-lose situation. If you can't resist in the heat of the moment, make a generic statement that you will do your best to help, but don't make specific promises to anyone.

2. **Giving money without talking to advisors.** Talk to your advisors about how much you can afford to give. Also, there may be creative tax advantages in how you give. If you rush into writing checks, you may miss out on these strategies. For example, is it better to make a loan to a friend to help his business or is it better to make a loan (or buy shares) in the company directly? Talk to your advisors so they can structure the deal that will benefit you and your friend/family most.

3. **Using money to control others.** Sudden wealth can put you in the driver's seat of your life, but don't fall into the trap of thinking you can use your money to control friends and family. I see this most often when parents of adult children try to use their money to reward certain behaviors and punish others. For example, a parent will undermine the relationship with a new boyfriend by not inviting him on a family cruise. Don't do it. It will end badly for you and for your relationships.

4. **Helping when it hurts.** I'm reluctant to share horror stories of sudden wealth clients who were made to feel guilty and pressured into helping because many of them you just wouldn't believe. We've all heard the stories of how acquaintances from years past come out of nowhere to ask for help, and although these encounters can be uncomfortable, the situations that have really upset my clients have not come from distant strangers or long-lost "friends," but from the people closest to them. It's easier to blow off a Facebook request for money from a grade school friend than it is an uncle in your living room. If you are giving money to avoid feeling bad, something is not right. You should only give money when it feels good.

5. **Giving money unequally.** One common source of relationship discord is when one person finds out you're doing a lot more for someone else. Some sudden wealth recipients scoff at this recommendation and hold the opinion that they should be happy receiving any help, even if it is uneven. And even though that is true, if you are trying to use the money to create a better life for yourself and others, if you can avoid tension, it's better for everyone. If you're not able or willing to help equally, just make sure you articulate this and don't try to hide it.

Here are a few ideas for how some sudden wealth recipients have been able to help others create a better life while avoiding some of the common relationship landmines:

WHO'S IN YOUR LIFEBOAT?

Imagine you're on the *Titanic* with everyone you know. The ship is going down but you have a lifeboat that holds a limited number of people. If you try to take too many, your little lifeboat will sink and you and everyone you know will sink with it. Who do you take on the lifeboat?

Likewise, you may want to use your sudden wealth to help everyone, but if you help too many or too much, you can sink your own finances. You need to determine who's in your lifeboat and who's not – who you are willing to help financially and who you aren't.

The people you bring into your lifeboat are the people you would help even if it means you would hurt yourself. When I first started working with sudden wealth recipients, I would try to use logic and numbers to talk clients out of helping beyond what they could afford, but time and time again, they would do it anyway. I realized that there were certain friends or family members each client was willing to help to the end, regardless of what I said. This became clear when a client who had just helped pay for drug rehab for her young grandson poignantly asked, "What would you have done?" I had to admit I would have helped, too. It was a good lesson for young Robert to learn and one I have not forgotten.

If a client will risk their own financial solvency to help a handful of people in their life, then we better do everything we can to plan for the worst and support those few people in a way that not only helps them but also minimizes the financial damage to the client. Rather than fight it and be surprised each time, I now help them plan for it.

Start by creating a family tree. On top should be your oldest living relatives. Then work your way down to yourself, siblings, nieces and nephews, in-laws, grandchildren, unborn children, etc. Do something similar with your friends. At this point, the goal is to create a visual of the people in your world, whether you want to help them or not.

Once you have a snapshot of your social universe, you can begin to think about who you want to assist. If it's helpful, you can begin to classify people as:

1. **Musts.** These are the family and friends who you absolutely want to help in some way, big or small.

2. **Maybes.** These people you'd consider helping if financially feasible, but not at the expense of helping the friends and family in the Must category.

3. **Misses.** Lastly, even though you may love these people dearly, they are not people you are willing to help financially.

I've had sudden wealth clients who have helped college friends before parents. It's not my job to make judgments about who should or should not be helped, and if at all possible, you shouldn't judge yourself for making anyone a Must or a Miss. It's your choice. Feel good about it.

Once you and your advisors determine how much you can afford to help, you can modify who is on your list and/or how much help you are willing to provide. The benefit of this exercise is the awareness it creates regarding your priorities. Life becomes much more clear when you know who you want to help, how much you can afford to help, and who you can say no to. Knowledge is power, and when you receive requests for money that fall outside of your lifeboat, you don't have to second guess yourself each time.

Gifting Can Be Taxing

Did you know that you have to pay tax if you give too much? Most people don't realize that we have a "gift tax." You are allowed to gift an annual amount each year without tax, but above that, you may have to pay gift taxes. Work with your CPA and financial advisor to ensure you are helping the right way by taking advantage of the annual gift tax exclusion.

INVESTMENT OPPORTUNITY FUND

One strategy to help the people in your lifeboat is to create an investment opportunity fund. An investment opportunity fund is an investment account that you've contributed money into. This fund represents the maximum amount of money you are willing and/or able to give. For some, this is a private foundation, but it can be any account. The money in the account is invested in traditional investments such as stocks and bonds and/or in private businesses or ventures, or loans to support friends and family. As the investments produce a return, the growth is put back into the account so additional giving is possible. If managed well, the opportunity fund can grow over time and allows for ongoing giving rather than one-time gifts. If it's not managed well, the account and giving dries up. This aligns your interests with the receiver's interests. You can even recruit friends, family members, and advisors to sit on the investment committee and review each proposal. This helps to keep the pressure of saying yes or no off of you and more in the hands of the people with the most to gain and lose.

Another related strategy to align interests even more closely when making loans or investments in friend's/family's businesses is to create individual opportunity funds. If the loan is repaid or if the investment performs well, the money stays in an account earmarked for them for future loans/investments or for helping their children pay for college, etc. Your brother-in-law may think twice about asking you for money on a longshot business venture when he knows his children's college education hangs in the balance.

ANNUAL GIVING PERCENTAGE

If you've ever asked for charitable donations from a company, you've seen this strategy first hand. Limit the amount of money you will give each year to a fixed dollar amount, percent of your portfolio, or to a percentage of the growth in your portfolio. Once you've allocated the maximum amount of giving in a year, you are done. This has the benefit of taking the pressure off of you for saying not now and lets people know there are clear parameters about what you are willing and not willing to do. One of the goals when it comes to giving and helping is to set clear expectations. The more ambiguity there is about how much you'll give, when you'll give, and who you'll help will only cause more people to ask for more money. Be like a company and make the process clear and inflexible.

HURDLE RATE

Instead of committing to a set dollar amount for charity/helping each year, I favor a more fluid approach. One method that again aligns the interests of those you help along with your own is to set aside an amount of profit you make in your personal investment portfolio above a hurdle rate up to a certain cap. For example, if you have $10 million invested and you make 2% more than your target growth rate for the year, you would have made an additional $200,000 above your target. If the maximum you want to give in any year – your cap – is $50,000, you would be able to do that.

If your investments don't do well in a year, you may not be able to give. When friends and family know this is your strategy for helping, they may be less inclined to pitch you on a risky investment scheme. This sounds more complicated than it is, but your advisors can help you calculate your hurdle rate and how much you can give each year.

KEEP SOME DRY POWDER

In investing, it's always a good idea to have some cash – or what financiers call "dry powder" – in case you see a good investment opportunity. It's also good to have dry powder to help for the unexpected emergencies that often occur. If you've already given all you can afford for the year by June, what happens when you get an urgent plea for help in August? Keep an emergency reserve, not just for yourself, but for those in your lifeboat.

MAKE IT CLEAR

Seek clarity when it comes to helping/giving to friends or family. The temporary discomfort of discussing the details is much better than the potential long-term damage to relationships that can result from not being clear. What should you make clear? If you are going to do a one-time loan, investment, or gift, make it known that this is it. Too often, the friends and family of a sudden wealth recipient think the money will keep flowing into new loans, new investments, and new gifts. If you're not willing to do more, let them know. And don't be surprised if they change their mind for what they need the money. I've seen several situations where an initial request for an investment into a business was quickly changed once they realized this was the last or only help they'd get. Can't-lose investments suddenly don't look so guaranteed when everything is riding on it.

Give To Receive

Structured properly, a Charitable Lead Annuity Trust (CLAT) can create a large income tax deduction. These trusts have been around since the 1970s and are popular among the very wealthy. Users contribute money to a trust and determine a certain amount that will be withdrawn and sent to a charity. The remaining assets come back to you after a certain time period — the longer the time period, the larger the deduction. For example, a 20-year term may provide you with nearly a 90 percent deduction, while a 10-year term will provide a 47 percent deduction. This is a worthwhile strategy to consider because you can receive a large upfront deduction, and then at the end of 10 or 20 years, you get all of the assets back.

If you are helping, it means the person is in your lifeboat. Clearly you care about them and want to see them succeed. Help them best help themselves by letting them know what you are and are not willing to do. What will be best for them? If they know they have only one shot, they may think harder about asking you for help and may force them to dig deep to try to find the best way you can help them.

A client said it best: "It's like a roll of toilet paper. When there's a big roll, you don't think much about it, but when it's running low, you start to think a whole lot more about how best you're going to use each square." Give them a roll and tell them they better make the most of it.

DISTINGUISH BETWEEN CHARITY AND INVESTMENT

One of the questions I always ask my clients who want to give money to family or a friend is if it is an investment or charity. If you understand the difference, you can set expectations up front and avoid relationship issues down the road.

For example, a client wanted to give money to his brother-in-law to help him with his struggling business. In this case, the client could afford it and he wanted to do it. But was it charity or an investment?

An investment is where you anticipate making a return. You invest $100,000 and you think it will grow to $125,000. An investment can lose money, but your expectation is to see some growth. The criteria for an investment are numerous. An investment requires a calculated assessment of the risks and the potential reward. It requires due diligence and contracts. The motivation for an investment is to make a profit. On the other hand, the motivation for charity is to make a difference. Charity has no such expectation for profit. Charity is simply a gift where you don't expect a return on your money or your money returned.

The client needed help with his business, and despite his brother-in-law's intentions, this was not an investment. If the client went into this transaction thinking it was an investment, he would have been disappointed. Once he realized that it was a terrible investment but a wonderful way to make a difference in his sister's life, the decision became easy. When he communicated his desire to make a gift, it took all of the pressure off his brother-in-law and sister. They didn't feel the need to perform, quickly pay the money back, or worry about awkward silences and tension when the families got together.

Don't delude yourself or your advisors into thinking that you are making an investment when you are really making a gift. They often look the same, but they are not. An investment is an asset that becomes part of your balance sheet and your net-worth. A gift is an expense. Call it for what it is and everyone will be better off.

TEACH A MAN TO FISH

One of the best ways to help the right way is to not just give them a quick fix, but to provide them with the skills and tools to create a better life for themselves. The greatest financial asset they have is not their house, 401(k), or even their current job. Their greatest financial asset is themselves — the skills, education, and experience they have. Their "human capital" is much more important and valuable than their investment capital in the long run.

Why is this so important for sudden wealth recipients? It follows the truth behind the saying, "Give a man a fish and you feed him for a day. Teach a man to fish and you've fed him for a lifetime." It's common to try to fix the symptom but neglect the cause. For example, your newly unemployed sister may ask you to help pay her mortgage, and because she's in your lifeboat, you may not hesitate. But if you want to help your sister the right way, you need to look beyond the surface. Maybe she is unemployed because she doesn't have the right kinds of skills or has difficulty getting along with others. Maybe she is in a low skilled industry with low pay and high turnover and even with a job, she has trouble making her mortgage. Dig deeper and see how you can truly help – not just today, but for the rest of her life.

When you invest in others, you are making a deposit that will pay them dividends for life. Instead of paying off your nephew's credit card debt, what if you paid for him to attend a personal finance seminar to learn how to manage his finances better? And after that class, you could pay for him to finish his degree or get an advanced designation at a local community college? There is power when you invest in others. For example, one night class can earn a 100,000% return on the tuition. How is that possible? If your nephew currently makes $15 an hour as an administrative assistant, how much more would someone pay him per hour if he could also maintain the company's website and make minor changes to it when necessary? What if he learned how to use QuickBooks? What if he learned how to set up and run the company's blog? Would he be worth $16 an hour? Maybe $17 an hour? A $100 class at the local community college can earn him an additional $4,000 a year for the rest of his career.

Focus less on the immediate need and start to think about what will best benefit them in the long term. What skills can they learn that will make them more valuable? When you invest in others, it's good for them and it's good for you.

When You Should Consider A Donor Advised Fund

If you want to give to charity and take advantage of a nice tax deduction but do not want the administrative hassle of running your own private foundation, look into a donor advised fund. Here you receive a federal income tax deduction up to 50% of adjusted gross income in the year you make the deposit, so it may make sense to do this in the year of your sudden wealth event when you have a spike in income. Once the money is in the donor advised fund, you can then make recommended grants for which charities you would like the money to go. Donor advised funds are great in a time pinch because you get the immediate tax deduction, but you can take your time deciding to which charities you want to contribute.

COVER THE BASES

The people you've identified as being in your lifeboat – the ones you would help even if it would damage your own finances – require special planning. If, at the end of the day, you are the one writing the check to get them out of a jam, then you should proactively help them prevent the jam. Minimizing or avoiding the jam not only helps them, but it also ultimately helps you. As they say, an ounce of prevention is worth a pound of cure.

If you can afford it (work with your financial advisor to determine this), consider getting low-cost catastrophic health insurance for each person in your lifeboat who doesn't have it. Why? I've seen too many sudden wealth recipients scramble to write large checks to cover medical expenses because their friend/family had no health insurance. Medical procedures can cost hundreds of thousands of dollars. If anyone in your lifeboat doesn't have insurance, you'll be on the hook. This is a huge liability just waiting to happen, so instead, spend a few hundred dollars a month on a high deductible plan to give them the health protection they need and the financial protection you need.

Another growing issue is the rising costs of taking care of parents. Skilled nursing can easily top six figures a year. For an extended stay in a facility, it can decimate even the most solid financial plan. If you can afford it, it may be better for you and for your parents to buy a long-term care insurance policy. This will give them the peace of mind knowing they won't receive substandard care and you will have low cost protection if they require an extended stay.

BUY AN ANNUITY

If you have the desire to help, and only if you can afford it, consider buying an annuity for each person in your lifeboat. The advantage over writing everyone a single check is that an annuity provides them with income for life. Because the money doesn't come all at once, an annuity protects them from financial mismanagement. The steady stream of income they receive also protects you from having to write additional checks if they make bad financial decisions.

Annuities are also highly customizable. Each person can be guaranteed a different monthly amount, and you can start the income immediately for some, but delay it for others. Work with your CPA and financial advisor on gift tax consequences to determine if it makes more sense for each person to be the owner of their annuity or for you to be the owner.

In a perfect world, you would be able to provide as much financial help as you wanted to as many people as you wanted. There would be an unlimited amount of resources you could use to give everyone what they wanted. Unfortunately, you do not have enough money to help all the people who need it. There will always be more need than money.

I've worked with clients who were worth over $500 million, and even they didn't have enough to help all the people they wanted. Remember, no matter how much sudden wealth you have received, it is not enough. You'll have to say no.

Sudden wealth recipients who have a strong need for contribution and/or those who feel guilty that they have money when others do not should be the most careful. I've seen people give and give and give until there was nothing left to give. One client described their family and friends as sponges. "They will suck every last drop out of you if you let them," he said. Your friends and family may not know any better, but you and your advisors should.

When sudden wealth recipients finally understand this, they describe it as feeling like a weight has been lifted off of their chest. You can't help everyone, but for those you can, help them the right way. Keep the ideas in this chapter in mind and discuss them with your advisors to see which ones will work best for you. And although sudden wealth can be an opportunity to help others, it's also an opportunity for you to create a better life.

CREATE A BETTER LIFE

Use the money to create the best life possible.

Despite the stress and challenges of sudden wealth, you can use this opportunity to create a better life for yourself and for others. You cannot leave it to chance, however. It takes introspection and effort to create meaningful and lasting fulfillment. I've discovered an interesting phenomenon by working with sudden wealth recipients. Many sudden wealth recipients will hold one of these two polar opposite views:

1. Money will be the <u>solution</u> to all of my problems.

2. Money will be <u>source</u> of all my problems.

This dichotomous and extreme view of money is unhealthy. It affords too much power to money while disempowering the individual. Those who view money as their savior sit back and expect happiness to happen, but happiness doesn't just happen. You have to know what makes you tick and what you value. Happiness takes work. Those who view money as a problem don't make the most of their sudden wealth. Their fear of money prevents them from creating a better life.

And really, who can blame someone for having either of these views? We live in a culture that worships money and the shiny things it can purchase. A common misconception – especially by those who had very little money before their sudden wealth – is that a large bank account balance creates happiness. But is this true? My experience working with sudden wealth recipients tells me no.

There's no doubting a large bank account balance can help to alleviate financial stress and create feelings of empowerment and security. You can walk down the street with a sense of confidence just knowing you have money in the bank, but simply having money isn't enough to produce lasting happiness or a sense of joy or fulfillment. And this is a big shock for many sudden wealth recipients. They have money –

often more than they had ever dreamed – but they don't feel as much happiness as they want.

We also live in a culture that demonizes money and those who have it. If you do an Internet search for "sudden wealth," one of the top results will be "Sudden Wealth Syndrome." Sudden Wealth Syndrome is the ominous sounding term that describes the maladies some people experience after a windfall – guilt, isolation, and fear. Some authors and professionals talk about sudden wealth as if it were a life sentence of misery.

The truth is somewhere between these two extremes – sudden wealth upgrades, but doesn't eliminate our problems. Sudden wealth can be an opportunity to improve your life. If you worship money, it will use you. If you castigate money, you won't use it. You need to have a healthy understanding for what money can do and how to use it most effectively. It takes work. You can use your sudden wealth to create a better life, but it takes a conscious and active effort.

For all of the stress and often pain over a loss (e.g., death, divorce, injury) associated with sudden wealth, there is no doubt money can be used to create a better life for you and those you care about. A better life doesn't mean a perfect life, however. I've worked with sudden wealth recipients whose lives were permanently scarred. Money was not going to solve all of their problems or bring back a loved one. Fortunately, there are best practices for how to use money and there is a process you can follow to help you get clarity on what you value. This Sudden Wealth Principle will provide you with tools to create the best life possible, but first you have to avoid the challenges of sudden wealth happiness...

Grief And Sudden Wealth

Sudden wealth obtained through the death of a loved one, a divorce, a lawsuit settlement, or even a business sale can be traumatic. There is a natural grieving process, but sometimes, the sudden wealth can interfere. You can become so caught up in working with your advisors and handling the sudden wealth that you don't properly grieve. It's also common for people to spend feverishly on stuff to dull the pain of the loss. As we've seen, because of our lizard brain, we are quite bad at making good long-term decisions when we are under stress. It's better to address only the most critical tax, legal, and financial issues and then put everything else on hold while you work through your grief. There's no need to do anything with it until you get to a place where you can think clearly. The money will be there.

CHALLENGES TO SUDDEN WEALTH HAPPINESS

UPGRADING

Our commercial culture is based on planned obsolescence. Samsung's tagline is "The next big thing is here," but it's not. The next big thing is always just around the corner and just after you buy today's big thing. We live in an upgrade culture, where what we have is inferior to what you could have. Apple does a masterful job at making their new product seem so much better than their old product, even when there are few improvements or differences. In fact, they put on day-long events to show off the latest upgrades to their gadgets. As a friend joked, "True happiness is the time between buying the latest iPhone and when they upgrade it." As soon as the next Mercedes S class is released, which is usually even before the smell fades in the one you just bought, you start to think a little less of yours.

Marketers create an artificial need by making the new version seem so much better than the existing version. In doing so, they help to make us think less of what we already have and create the urge to upgrade. The problem is that all of these upgrades cost a lot of money. We can ruin a perfectly good financial plan by always having to have the best. Additionally, we are in a perpetual state of discontent. We are never really happy with what we have and are always looking at what's next. But when you're always looking at what's next, you can't enjoy what you have. This is the real tragedy.

To get off the upgrade treadmill, where you have to run just to stay in place, become aware of the marketing machine and how it makes you feel. Compare what you have with what's next. The differences will be trivial. Be grateful for what you currently have. If you continue to feel the urge, work with your financial advisor and schedule planned upgrades. For example, if you feel the need to get the newest car each year, instead, plan on upgrading every four or five years. This can take the pressure off each year when a new model comes out. Knowing you won't upgrade for several years, you may be less inclined to visit the showroom or read online reviews.

ABUNDANCE

Some sudden wealth recipients buy and do so much after receiving their windfall, they begin to lack appreciation for what they have. Authors of *Happy Money*, Elizabeth Dunn and Michael Norton, write, "Abundance, it turns out, is the enemy of appreciation." The more we are exposed to something, the less impact it makes. "From chocolate bars to luxury cars, habituation represents a fundamental barrier to deriving lasting pleasure from our purchases," they continue. This is one reason many sudden wealth recipients try to fill the void with buying more and doing more. We raise the bar, become accustomed to it, and then look for a bigger and better bang for our buck.

Dunn and Norton write, "At the same time that money increases our happiness by giving us access to all kinds of wonderful things, *knowing* we have access to wonderful things undermines our happiness by reducing our tendency to appreciate life's small joys." This creates a conundrum for sudden wealth recipients. You now have the money and the freedom to experience things, but in doing so, it can decrease your enjoyment.

Fortunately, there are ways to combat the boredom that comes from habituation. There is no compelling research that proves reducing consumption increases happiness, but there is research that shows altering consumption can lead to more enjoyment. Dunn and Norton suggest creating scarcity and turning the pleasures into occasional treats. For example, if you think a Porsche will provide you with a life full of joy and excitement, it won't. Your enjoyment will depreciate faster than the price. But if you only drive the Porsche occasionally, it will retain its luster forever. In practice, you may have a commuter car and a fun weekend car. Figure out how you can create scarcity in other areas and how you can turn things you take for granted into treats. For one client, this means taking a daily ride on his horse. Unlike things that never change, he never gets bored or unappreciative of his horse. You can also consider volunteering or traveling to less affluent countries. Once you stay a few weeks in a place with limited power and indoor plumbing, you will quickly appreciate the simple things in life again.

Dunn says, "We think the best way to be happy is to have lots of everything. But in fact, having less of the things we like best, at least temporarily, can renew our capacity to appreciate them."

COMPARING YOURSELF TO OTHERS

Would you rather earn $75,000 a year when all of your friends earn $50,000 or $100,000 when all of your friends earn $125,000? If you are like the majority of people who answer this question, you'd rather make less as long as you were making more than your friends (i.e., $75,000 instead of $100,000). Why would anyone choose to take such a large pay cut? What's wrong with us? A monkey would know better . . . or would they?

An ingenious study of capuchin monkeys demonstrates just how important relative (as opposed to absolute) differences matter. In the study, two neighboring caged monkeys are rewarded for picking up a rock in their cage and handing it to the researcher. The researcher rewards the first monkey with a cucumber slice, which the monkey happily eats. The researcher cues the second monkey in a separate cage to hand her a rock. This time, the researcher rewards the monkey with a grape – a much better treat than a cucumber – as the first monkey watches this unfold. Now it's the first monkey's turn again. The researcher provides the cue, the monkey selects a rock, hands it the researcher, and waits for his reward. The researcher hands him a cucumber. Flabbergasted, the monkey does something completely unexpected (and absolutely hilarious) . . . the monkey throws the cucumber slice at the researcher! Just a minute earlier, he happily ate the cucumber, but now, in the face of inequity, he angrily hurls the cucumber. This is repeated over and over, and not just with monkeys but with other animals. Welcome to the theory of relative deprivation.

Relative deprivation is the perception of an unfair difference between your situation and that of others. In other words, someone has something you don't and you feel entitled to it as well. But if you receive sudden wealth, wouldn't you be the envy of others? Yes, but only if you stay within your current circle of friends. Typically, after a large windfall, the sudden wealth recipient expands his social connections to include those with even more money than him. For example, someone of average means has friends of average means – some with a little more and some with a little less. Even though everyone wants more money, most people are generally content with their social standing amongst their peers. After a sudden wealth event, it's common to expand your social circle. For example, a person may move to a new neighborhood and join a yacht club. Many of his new peers have more than he does. They talk about sailing and their latest purchases. Even though he always knew the yacht club was filled with million dollar boats, he never felt entitled or pulled to "need" one until those around him had one. With sudden wealth, it's not keeping up with the Joneses, it's more like keeping up with the Rockefellers.

Many athletes go through enormous amounts of money trying to look the part. They grew up with a visual of what "success" looks like, and once they sign their first contract, they buy the latest version. If Joe three lockers down drives to practice in his new Porsche Carrera GT, suddenly your Porsche 911 – a car you'd drooled over just three months earlier – seems mundane. Upward social comparisons can drive some to achieve more, but it can have the negative consequence of creating disparity and feelings of inequity.

Author, Malcolm Gladwell, in his book, *David and Goliath: Underdogs, Misfits, and the Art of Battling Giants*, concludes that relative deprivation applies not only to fast cars and big boats, but also to the perception of our intelligence and skills (watch Gladwell's presentation on this topic at suddenwealthsolution.com). The research indicates that your relative position at your school is more consequential to your postgraduate success than the school from which you graduate. This means it's better to be top in your class from No Name University than it is to be mediocre at Harvard University. Why? We compare ourselves to those around us. If we are brilliant but happen to be in the 50th percentile at Harvard, we think of ourselves as inferior. If we are of average ability but happen to be in the 99th percentile at No Name University, we think of ourselves as geniuses. We take either interpretation with us after we graduate. The "inferior" student does little after graduation while the "genius" takes on the world – this happens even though the Harvard graduate could run circles (intellectually speaking) around the other graduate. Relative position against your peers matters. Being a big fish in a small pond is much better than being a small fish in a big pond.

Trying to keep up with your neighbors is not a recent phenomenon. Economist Thorstein Veblen wrote that the ordinary citizen takes his cue from those wealthier than him and tries to match the "conspicuous consumption" (a term he coined) of the rich. He wrote this in a book not in 1999, but 1899! Regardless of the zip code in which you reside, the car your drive, or the jet you fly in, there is always a slightly better one, newer one, or faster one to which you will aspire. It is in part from this feeling of constant agitation, of never quite feeling comfortable, that we spend more than we should.

Ultimately, when you compare what you have with others and feel pressure to get the next best thing, it devalues what you already have and makes you less happy. A Porsche 911 is one of the best and most beautiful cars in the world, but comparing it to the car in the next parking spot cheapens the joy it provides you. Happiness is not having what you want, it is wanting what you have.

What can you do to not be sucked into the comparison game? Here are a few ideas that have worked with my sudden wealth clients over the years:

1. **Become aware.** As always, being conscious of our tendencies helps. Awareness won't stop us from making these automatic comparisons, but it can give us just enough pause and insight that we don't reflexively react to them. If you find yourself pining for something someone else has, sit with that thought for some time. Don't force the thought out of you, but instead, embrace it. Become curious as to why you suddenly feel the drive to have what they have. Do you want it for yourself or for others? Imagine having it and exploring what feelings you might have. Pleasure or pride? Would you have wanted this pre-sudden wealth? Keep a journal or list of items you want and revisit the list every few weeks. Does the pull to make the purchase decrease over time? Ask your peers if they would buy the same thing again? There is truth to the saying that the happiest day in your life is the day you buy a boat, and the next happiest day in your life is the day you sell your boat.

2. **Play shrink.** Observe your peers and their purchasing behaviors. Is there a jockeying for position within your circle of friends to have the best? To constantly outdo the next person? Watch carefully who buys and does what. If you can withdraw yourself from the pressure to keep up for just a moment, it can be eye opening to see just how much power relative deprivation can have on people as everyone tries to increase their relative position among the group.

3. **Find a smaller pond.** If the pressure to keep up is too strong, consider spending more time with those who have less. Remember, happiness isn't making $100,000 a year. It's making $100,000 when your friends are making $75,000. Spend a little less time at the country club and a little more time at Sam's Club.

4. **Find a better role model.** Just like a fish doesn't know it's in water, when you are surrounded by a culture and peer group that is obsessed with having the next big thing, it can be a challenge to see the environment for what it is. Find someone who's been where you are and has a more

enlightened view. For example, if you are an athlete who is surrounded by other athletes who are tripping over themselves to keep up, find someone older who has been in your shoes and can speak to you about their mistakes. So often, sudden wealth problems are not a money problem, they are a mentor problem. In ambiguous and stressful situations (this perfectly describes sudden wealth), when we don't know what to do, we look to others and model their behavior. If our role models are caught up in the frenzy of keeping up, we'll make the same mistake. Find a better role model and mimic their behavior.

5.   **Be smarter than a monkey.** When all else fails and you still feel the urge to keep up with your peers, watch the Capuchin Monkey video at . Not only will it provide a good laugh, but you may also decide you want to be more mature than a monkey.

6.   **Witness true need.** At least once a year, I travel to a new country. Throughout my travels to Asia, Africa, and South America, I've seen the face of true need – people not concerned about keeping up with their neighbors, but concerned about staying alive. One of the best ways to put your life and desire into perspective is to see how others live. If traveling to third-world countries doesn't interest you, spend a few hours volunteering. When you're surrounded by affluence, it's easy to forget just how fortunate you are. A gentle reminder can make a big difference and can squelch the insatiable desire to keep up.

7.   **Be grateful.** According to research, one of the best ways to become happier is to experience gratitude. Being happy and content with what you have is the ideal prescription for minimizing envy. A simple strategy that has been proven to increase well-being is writing in a gratitude journal each day. It takes less than five minutes and it can help you appreciate what you have and to ground you.

MONEY VIGILANCE

It's a good thing to be careful with your money and to be alert and watchful about how you spend it, but taken to the extreme, money vigilance can undermine your ability to enjoy your sudden wealth. Of the four Money Scripts identified by Brad and Ted Klontz, Money Vigilance is the only one associated with better financial health, higher income, and higher net-worth. These benefits come with a cost. The cost is that those who scored highly with this money belief tended to be more anxious and secretive about their money.

If you are constantly worried about your money – fretting over each purchase and whether you are doing the right thing – you may not fully enjoy your sudden wealth and may overlook the security and other benefits money can provide. Taken to the extreme, sudden wealth recipients who are ultra-protective of their money may either underspend or hoard their money. Even though these behaviors ensure they don't go broke, they almost guarantee they will remain emotionally poor.

To avoid the anxiety Money Vigilance can create, use the money script log discussed in Sudden Wealth Principle 4 as a way to gain insight into your thoughts and beliefs around money. Start by answering the following:

1. **What was the trigger?** Identify the situation, event, or emotion that prompted the negative money behavior.

2. **What went through your mind?** Focus on what you were thinking before the negative money behavior.

3. **What was your impulse?** What actions did your thoughts compel you to take?

4. **What did you do?** What did you ultimately do?

Money vigilance is rooted in an irrational fear of not having enough or losing it all. This can be particularly pronounced for sudden wealth recipients who grew up poor and who quit working. Without earning a steady income, their fears of not having enough can be heightened. If this describes you, work closely with your financial advisor. Let her know your concerns. In these cases, I've found that setting aside cash in an account that the client draws down each month – like a paycheck – can alleviate some of the uncertainty. Also, make sure you stay in constant communication with your advisor and that they show you monthly reports of where you are financially.

Many sudden wealth recipients who are anxious about their money will track their investments and finances daily or even hourly. This is counterproductive and can lead to irrational decisions (e.g., sell on a down day) as well as creating unnecessary stress and anxiety. Make a "date" with your financial advisor once a month to go through your statements and accounts. If you have concerns or questions, write these down in a journal and discuss them at your monthly meeting.

NOT KNOWING WHAT MAKES YOU HAPPY

If the researchers are correct, that almost all of our actions are based on predictions of the emotional consequences of these events and that we are really bad at predicting what will make us happy, this can make for a whole lot of problems – especially for the sudden wealth recipient.

"When we try to predict what will make us happy, we're often wrong," says Daniel Gilbert, a psychology professor at Harvard University. "Researchers all over the world find the same predictable errors, whether the pursuit involves romance, a new car, or a sumptuous meal." We think we know, but we don't. We overestimate the intensity and duration of our emotional reactions to future events. We'll spend money on things, thinking it will give us lasting enjoyment, but it doesn't. The stuff we buy can give us a burst of happiness, but it is usually fleeting. Psychologists call this hedonic adaptation, which describes how we quickly become accustomed to things (good and bad). This explains how the thrill of our new car fades just as fast as the new car smell, or how the once amazing view from your new home becomes hum drum after a couple of months. This can lead to chasing ever newer (and more expensive) things to titillate our senses.

One sudden wealth recipient described it as "trying to catch a rainbow" and another as "scratching an itch that never goes away." But why are we so bad at predicting what will make us happy? There may be a few causes. First, we tend to have a happiness "set-point." Research by psychology professor, Sonja Lyubomirsky, indicates that 50% of our happiness is pre-programmed within us. Think of this 50% as something we cannot change. It's like having a software operating system you cannot upgrade. Tigger will always have a higher happiness set-point than Eeyore.

But what accounts for the remaining 50%? Lyubomirsky's research shows that just 10% of our happiness is influenced by our life circumstances – things such as whether we are rich or poor, married or divorced, with children or childless, healthy or unhealthy, attractive or plain, etc. Yes, just 10%! This is why when good or bad things happen, we can see a spike in happiness, but we'll eventually settle back down to our normal set-point level of happiness. All of the things we tend to think will boost our happiness – new house, sports car, clothes – actually only plays a minor role. This is one reason so many sudden wealth recipients go through their money so quickly. They spend hundreds of thousands, if not millions of dollars, on things that barely move the happiness needle. When that doesn't work, they look for new things to buy. Lyubomirsky writes in her book, *The How of Happiness: A New Approach to Getting the Life You Want*, "We tend to look for happiness in all the wrong places. What we *believe* would make a huge difference in our lives actually, according to scientific research, makes only a small difference."

And the other 40% that dictates our level of happiness? This is the most exciting part, because although we can't change our pre-programmed set-point, and it is difficult to control many of our life circumstances, we can control how we think and what we do. Later in the chapter, you'll learn what researchers have found the happiest people do and think.

Another reason we are bad at predicting what will make us happy is that we overestimate how much impact any event will have on us. We tend to overestimate the degree of happiness we'll feel and the duration for which we'll feel it. We think the new convertible will lead to a dramatic and long-lasting boost in happiness, when, in fact, it only leads to a small and short bump.

To make matters worse, research (and common sense!) shows we don't learn from our "miswanting" as Gilbert calls it. It's a nostalgia bias. "People tend to misremember how happy they were in the past," claims Gilbert. Once the shine begins to fade on our latest purchase, we move on the next thing we are sure will bring us everlasting happiness . . . and then forget that it didn't give us the boost we wanted. Partially at play here is our tendency to remember peak moments and eliminate the more routine ones. We'll recall the thrill of taking our new boat out on the open water for the first time, but we'll forget the drudgery of what it takes to own a boat.

So, what's the solution? Gilbert says, "Don't trust your gut," but instead, suggests one of the best indicators of whether something will make you happy is if it makes me happy. Use other people's experiences. Talk to them or read reviews. Even though we like to think we are unique, Gilbert says we will be 30% to 60% more accurate by asking others rather than imagining it ourselves.

Another option is to become more conscious of what makes you happy and what doesn't. Think back to something you thought would make you really happy, maybe a new watch or putting in a pool in your backyard, and give it a perceived happiness score (1 if you didn't think it would give you very much happiness and 10 if you thought it would bring you a great deal of happiness). Then give yourself a rating for how much happiness it actually provided. If there is a discrepancy, and there likely will be, ask yourself why. Why didn't it live up to your expectations? For new purchases, rate how much happiness you think it will provide and then follow-up a week or two later. Again, why the difference between your imagined future and reality?

My young daughter was obsessed with getting an American Girl doll. Once a week for several months, I asked her to rate how happy she would be if she got the doll. Consistently, she predicted the doll would give her immense happiness – a 10 each time. She worked and saved her money, and after some time, she bought the doll. A week later, she said the doll only provided a 6 on her happiness scale. Now when she is about to make a purchase, I'll remind her of this experience. It's not a panacea, but sometimes, she'll change her mind on a purchase.

This can work for you as well. Before each substantial purchase, do a pre and post assessment. Try to learn from the purchases that didn't provide the boost of happiness you expected and those that did. You won't always bat 1,000, but by being more aware, you'll begin to learn what provides a longer-lasting happiness bump.

Lastly, we tend to think in generalities and gloss over the details. This can be a mistake. Will spending $5,000 on a ski trip to Aspen really boost your happiness? Maybe, but it might not. Instead of jumping your imagination to flying down the slopes, think about all of the small steps needed to get you to the mountain. Having to get up early to catch the flight, the layover, driving on the ice to get to your hotel room, getting all the gear together, sloshing through the cold and wet snow, standing in line, and finally getting on the slopes. For some ski enthusiasts, these are but just trivial steps to an incredible day skiing, but for the less inspired, it can detract from the experience. Considering the "inessential details," as Gilbert calls them, matter. They can help you become a better predictor of what will make you happy.

FILLING THE VOID WITH STUFF

The greatest punishment is not to be stripped of everything you have, but to be given everything you want.

Life is full of gaps between what we have and what we want. We want to take a trip to Italy, but we don't have the money. We'd love to write a children's book, but we don't have the time. We want a 1969

Mustang, but we can't afford it. We want to have a successful retirement, but we don't have enough discretionary income to save. We want to hike the Inca Trail, but we are out of shape. We weigh 154 pounds, but we want to weigh 135 pounds.

With gradual wealth, the financial planning process focuses on identifying where you are, where you want to go, and then building a bridge between the two. At its most basic, it is simply a process of closing the gap between what you have and what you want. For example, if a gradual wealth client wants to have a good retirement, we'd first define what a "good" retirement would look like, see what resources and savings they have today, and figure out how much they need to save and what they need to do to go from where they are currently to where they want to be when they retire. This is what all goal-setting is about – identifying a want and coming up with a strategy to achieve it.

When we desire something, we curse the gap. It can take months or even years of struggle to finally close the gap and achieve our goal. Life would be so much better if only we could snap our fingers and get whatever we wanted, right? Easier? Definitely. But better? Maybe not.

The gap is what fuels effort. The gap is what provides the angst. We'll get up early and stay late at the office. We'll sacrifice today to achieve tomorrow. The gap can provide purpose and meaning. Psychologist, Mihaly Csikszentmihalyi, coined the term "flow" to describe the deep sense of being fully immersed and engrossed in a challenging and mentally stimulating activity. Contrary to expectations, his research indicates, "The great majority of flow experiences are reported when working, not when in leisure[10]." Relaxation is important, but we experience the most joy when we are sufficiently challenged.

Pre-sudden wealth, most people have a set routine in their daily lives, achievable goals, and a general sense of their purpose and meaning of their lives. The alarm clock buzzes, they get ready, drive to work, work for eight to ten hours, drive home, fix dinner, watch TV, and go to bed. It's a predicable schedule that provides a structure to their life. Love or hate their job, it doesn't just answer what they did for the day, it also provides a "why?" to their day. Your identity, who you are and how you see yourself, is grounded, but sudden wealth can disrupt your sense of who you are. The gap is what creates the hunger and the challenge of the hunt – the pursuit and focus to achieve something you don't have.

The Zoo And You

What do animals in captivity have to do with sudden wealth? More than you may think. One of the challenges for zookeepers is to create an environment for the animals that resembles their natural environment and is sufficiently stimulating. Animals have natural instincts to hunt, forage, and mate, but when animals are kept in prolonged captivity and are given everything, they can exhibit "zoochosis" – a term for signs of extreme depression, boredom, and frustration some animals experience in captivity. Animals will work to obtain food even when abundant food is readily available. The inner drive to hunt and achieve – at least in some animals – may be stronger than their need to eat and survive. Jordan reports in the Foundation for Wildlife, "The psychological problems encountered in captive animals are frustration and boredom due to their being prevented from fulfilling inherited biological needs" (Jordan, 2005). The takeaway is that animals aren't the only creatures that can lose their oomph when given everything. Each of us has an inner drive to achieve and need for challenge. If we placate all of our needs and strip away all challenge, we run the risk of experiencing our own version of zoochosis.

But what happens when there is no gap? When there is no distance between what you want and where you are? When there is no struggle? When the hunger is replaced by satiation? When we can do or have anything we want, it can suck the drive from us. I call this Sudden Wealth Stagnation. It is when the wonder of your windfall and new toys turns to weariness, and you grow increasingly bored and despondent. Growing up, I had a friend with a laissez-faire attitude about studying and figuring out what he wanted to do in the world. Why? He was waiting on a large trust fund in his name.

Many sudden wealth recipients experience a "honeymoon" phase after receiving their windfall. The honeymoon phase is when the sudden wealth recipient feels excitement about the possibilities their new money can provide. They may buy new cars and a house, travel, and purchase all the things they ever wanted, such as a jet ski, boat, jewelry, art, and clothes. The honeymoon phase is like Christmas morning for a kid – full of wonder and all the toys they dreamed of. But unlike Christmas, the honeymoon phase doesn't come around just once a year. It can last several weeks or even months. Sudden wealth recipients say this is the most thrilling time of their lives. Anything is possible and anything is attainable. Sounds like fun, right?

But what makes Christmas so special is that it only comes around once a year. If Santa came every night, at some point, you'd have all the toys you ever wanted. With no goals or unmet needs, you would have little to look forward to. This is when the honeymoon phase ends. When the thrill of being able to have whatever you want loses its luster.

At this point, many sudden wealth recipients experience a feeling of emptiness or void. Ironically, even though they are surrounded by everything they ever wanted, they feel like they are missing something. They have it all, but they feel a longing for something. Meaning is the degree to which we feel our lives have value, purpose, and impact. If we no longer feel we are making a difference, contributing, or are having any impact, we can experience a deep dissatisfaction with life. In my counseling work with clients, I've found that no one wants to feel like they just exist. They want to feel they are alive for a reason and that they are making a difference in the world or at least in their world.

What happens next is critical. Some sudden wealth recipients try to fill the void with more stuff. They'll buy more toys and do more in an attempt to experience fulfillment. Paradoxically, the more they try to fill the emptiness, the emptier they feel. So they double down by buying more and doing more in a never-ending loop. These are the sudden wealth recipients who can end up going broke. In fact, some go through all of their sudden wealth and then some – going into debt and having to declare bankruptcy.

But this doesn't have to be your fate. Even though most sudden wealth recipients go through some form of the honeymoon phase, they don't all end up broke. Why? At some point, they realize the path to fulfillment is not filled with stuff. Don't get me wrong, a nice house, cars, trips, and toys can be wonderful things that most sudden wealth recipients enjoy, but these things do nothing to provide meaning and purpose. Although the path can be more difficult, the sudden wealth recipients who resist the urge to fill the void with stuff have the opportunity to find a higher purpose and achieve a deeper sense of meaning than those who experience gradual wealth. Why? Sudden wealth allows you to create a life by design, rather than one by default.

Most of us have become experts at living life by default. We have become passengers instead of drivers. One client remarked, "I've lived my whole life as the passenger interspersed with a few brief moments of taking the wheel." Sudden wealth can give people a second chance. Instead of living a life by default, sudden wealth recipients can live a life by design. The fallacy is that you need a sudden wealth event to shape your life, but anyone of any financial standing can take a bigger leadership role in their life. Sudden wealth helps because it provides freedom and opportunities, but it is by no means necessary to create a life by design.

A life by design takes work. It does, by definition, require effort. You have to know what you want and what you value. You have to know what drives you and what creates lasting fulfillment. These are issues that are highly personal and individual – my ideal life isn't going to look like yours.

Unlike gradual wealth, where the goal is to close the gap between where you are and what you want, the path to meaning and fulfillment with sudden wealth is to create a gap – to create an environment where there is challenge, struggle, and hunger to achieve and grow. This is why I tell clients sudden wealth flips financial planning on its head. Franklin D. Roosevelt had it right when he said, "Happiness lies not in the mere possession of money; it lies in the joy of achievement, in the thrill of creative effort." This doesn't mean you have to go back to work. There are innumerable ways to experience meaning and happiness without clocking in. The following are a few tried and true methods for filling the void:

1. **Philanthropy.** Giving money to a cause has been one of the most common practices of the affluent for millennium. When you have enough to satisfy your needs, it is common to turn to the needs of others. Getting behind a cause (or several) you believe in can give you a sense of meaning and purpose. Seeing your money transform the lives of others can provide the fulfillment another toy cannot. Philanthropy can also provide much needed social interaction and can help to create a new identity. Research shows that it is not just the receiver who benefits, but the acts of giving strongly benefit the giver as well. Researchers call these benefits "giver's glow" and the "helper's high." Benefits can include feeling more energetic and calm, less depressed, and increased feelings of self-worth.

2. **Personal cause.** Many affluent individuals and families over the years have gotten behind a single cause and directed their time, energy, and money into it. In addition to writing checks, many start their own charity or foundation and become involved in the day-to-day management of the

organization. This can become their new "job." Many report that they work longer and harder at this than they ever did when they were working for money because it provides them a greater sense of fulfillment and meaning. "I've never worked as hard in my life as I do now," gushed one sudden wealth recipient. "But I've never felt so good or been so happy to get up in the morning."

Some sudden wealth recipients who experience tragedy through the death of a loved one or injury will take their loss and channel not only their money but their pain into a cause so that they may ease the suffering of others. By starting your own non-profit, you can expose your children to philanthropy and give them an active role in the operations of the organization. This has the added benefit of giving them real world work experience in a safe and comfortable "family business."

3. **Entrepreneurship.** Many sudden wealth recipients who relish in the idea of quitting their jobs can't imagine wanting to work again, but for some, after the honeymoon phase, they become restless and long to be part of something again. But this time, instead of working for the "man," you become the man. Starting your own company can be a fulfilling way to invest your talents and time. For sudden wealth recipients with business experience, such as those who sell their business or those whose wealth comes from stock options, they may tire of their early retirement. Entrepreneurship can offer the best of all worlds – they can experience just as much (if not a lot more) challenge as they grow their business along with the freedom and autonomy of not having a boss.

Starting your own business can provide a sense of excitement and uncertainty that can go missing with sudden wealth. As reported by one sudden wealth recipient, "After I sold my company, I felt a huge hole in my life. For years, I knew exactly who I was and why I needed to get up every morning, but after I cashed out, I drifted aimlessly for a couple of years. I knew I had more to prove to myself and to give to the world. I missed the challenge and the ups and downs, so I started another company. It's been incredibly difficult, and I love every second."

4. **Mentoring.** Some sudden wealth recipients with knowledge and experience who want to give back but don't want to start a company or dive into a cause find fulfillment through mentorship. There are many organizations that pair those who want to help with those who need help. For example, the Big Brother/Sister organization is one of the most popular. Others, such as the non-profit association SCORE, have been connecting retired business leaders with start-ups for almost 50 years.

5. **Hobbies.** One of the biggest complaints of most people is lack of time. They have so much they want to do, but so little opportunity to do it all. A large windfall can change that by allowing you to quit your job, but even if your sudden wealth isn't large enough for you to retire, you can use money to buy yourself time (see below). Many sudden wealth recipients use this new time to engage in old hobbies or participate in new ones that were too time consuming (e.g., golf) or expensive (e.g., race car driving).

6. **Personal growth.** Some sudden wealth recipients turn their attention inward and opt to learn, improve, and expand themselves. They may learn a new language, travel the world, go back to school and get the degree they always wanted, train for an Ironman Triathlon, write a novel, hike across the Himalayas, or immerse themselves in a project . . . or all of these!

The common factor across all of these is that they satisfy our Human Need for Growth and Contribution – the two needs that attribute the most to life-long joy and happiness. If there is one thing research into happiness has determined, it is that our level of happiness quickly adjusts back down after we get a new toy. Not so when we are engaged in the activities just described. Each of these provides meaning and deep and long-lasting spikes in fulfillment. Toys change with time – they break, rust, or become outdated – but these activities change us with time. These things can define who we are and help to create our identity much more than the things we own.

USING SUDDEN WEALTH TO CREATE A BETTER LIFE

Sudden wealth gives you the opportunity to make positive changes in your life. If you don't like the trajectory of your life, your windfall can help you find a better path. But it takes more than money. There are many horror stories of sudden wealth recipients who burn through their money and end up less happy with their lives. But sudden wealth doesn't sentence you to a life of despair either. As I've discussed, sudden wealth is an opportunity and money is just a tool. A powerful tool but still just a tool. You can use money to create a better life for yourself and others. Here is what the research on well-being and nearly two decades of hands-on experience working with sudden wealth recipients has shown me about how to create a better life…

SUDDEN WEALTH EXPERIENCE

I am a pediatric emergency physician who won millions of dollars in the Florida Lotto in 2001. After I won, I naively thought my life was going to be perfect with all that money, but I soon learned that the money did not protect me or my family from life's adversities such as my husband's near-fatal illness and my son's drug addiction.

On the other hand, I embarked on a remarkable journey. I started doing things that I always wanted to do. After another year at my job, I decided to work part-time. I wrote a book, went on a medical mission to the Dominican Republic, started a movie club, traveled to visit family more often, joined book clubs, and created a small foundation for Holocaust survivors. After some time, it "hit" me. I realized that most of the new things I did and the opportunities I took could have been achieved without the Lotto money. In the end, and I can hardly believe it myself, most of the confidence and personal growth I once thought were the result of winning the lottery could have been achieved without all that money. I just didn't recognize it then. I hadn't prioritized like I should have. Only in hindsight did this become clear to me.

~ Dr. Shirley Press, author of *Pressing My Luck : A Doctor's Lottery Journey*

WANT LESS/MORE

Sudden wealth is just one piece of the happiness puzzle. To create a better life, you also need insight into yourself. A powerful tool to help you know what's working and what needs changing in your life is the want more/less inventory.

Simply take a piece of paper and draw a line down the center. Label one column "Want Less" and the other "Want More." List all of the things in your life that you want less of. This can include experiences, chores, feelings, and even people. In the other column, you write all of the things currently in your life that you want more of. Again, this can include experiences, feelings, and people. This simple exercise can help you get clarity over what you like about your life and where changes are needed.

One of the tragedies of sudden wealth is that recipients think everything has to change, but that's not true. Why throw out the baby with the bath water? If it's working, keep doing it. If it's not working, look for something different.

Do this inventory exercise a few times over the course of several weeks and look for items that show up consistently. Work with your advisors to see how your sudden wealth can be used to decrease the items you want less of and to increase the items you want more of. It's a simple exercise, but powerful.

DRUDGERY DESTROYER

"If I didn't have to [fill in the blank], I'd be so much happier!" Turns out you just might be happier. My experience tells me that if you can eliminate the tasks in your life that cause you anxiety, grief, or pain, you will experience more joy – or at least fewer headaches.

This may seem like a trivial suggestion, but if you are able to identify and eliminate many of the things you dislike doing, it can have a profound effect on your mood and level of well-being. Don't believe me? Think about three tasks you despise doing, and imagine a Saturday where you had to do all three of these. How would you feel at the end of the day? Grumpy? On edge? Angry? Probably all three. The things we hate to do can suck the spirit and the joy from us. It can turn an ordinarily calm and rational person into a bitter and indignant person instantly.

For example, I'm usually an easy going person. I like to think of myself as rational, level-headed, and analytical. But give me a home improvement project and the wheels come off the car. Even the thought of a home improvement project quickens my pulse and increases my blood pressure. I despise fixing or putting things together. If I never had to fix anything in my life again, I'd be a happy man.

Maybe fixing things isn't your nemesis. For you, it might be vacuuming, housework, cooking, going to the grocery store, or any number of other things. Sudden wealth gives you the opportunity to minimize or even eliminate the tasks that cause pain.

Don't underestimate the power of eliminating these tasks from your life. Freeing yourself and your soul from these things can be one of the best uses of your money. Start by brainstorming all of the activities that take a ton of your time and/or you don't like doing. If you didn't have to do something, what would it be? Write down everything as it comes to you. You might need several pages for this exercise. Next, once you have a healthy list of unwanted tasks, rank them from the worst to least offenders. Now, depending on what you can afford, you know where to start.

The most common disliked tasks are also the easiest and most cost-effective to hire others to do. Here are several examples:

1. **Paying bills.** There are business management firms or individuals who can provide this service. Be careful, however. There are things you need to do to protect yourself, which are discussed in Sudden Wealth Principle 10.

2. **Managing your investments.** There is no shortage of firms and advisors who would love the opportunity to help you manage your investments. Follow the tips in Sudden Wealth Principle 3 to find the best advisors for your needs.

3. **Mowing the lawn.** Easy to find cheap and plentiful labor.

4. **Cleaning the pool.** Usually inexpensive.

5. **Filing.** Slightly more skilled, but you should be able to find someone cheap. Whenever you are going to have someone come in your house, and especially if they are going to see personal documents, it's important to call references or even run a background check.

6. **Housecleaning.** Again, easy to find cheap and plentiful labor.

7. **Event planning.** There are many options so you will never have to plan another birthday party or family reunion again.

8. **Manual labor.** Perfect for moving furniture, helping you clean the garage, etc.

9. **Cooking.** Whether you can hire a personal chef or subscribe to a food service, if you hate to cook, there are plenty of options for you to eliminate this task from your life.

10. **Babysitting/Childcare.** You should have no problem finding a pool of qualified talent right in your neighborhood.

11. **Decorating.** Some people have the knack and patience for decorating both inside and outside for the holidays, whereas others don't have the time or desire. It's easy to hire individuals or companies to do your holiday lights and decorations.

12. **Handyman.** My favorite. Fortunately, like the other tasks above, there are people you can hire who love to tinker and fix things so you never have to pick up another screwdriver again.

BUY TIME

Time is the great equalizer. Sudden wealth or gradual wealth, we all have the same 168 hours in a week. Money can buy lots of things, but it can't buy you more time . . . or can it? The rich don't have more hours in the week than the poor, but they have more time. If you commute for two hours a day on public transportation and work two jobs just to make ends meet, you still have 168 hours in a week, but you may only have a few hours that are yours. In my last book, *The Other 8 Hours: Maximize Your Free Time to Create New Wealth & Purpose*, I made the case that life happens during the time you are not sleeping or working. It is how you invest the time between when you get off work and go to bed that determines your quality of life, relationships, health, and overall happiness. The poor are in a vicious cycle where they spend so much of their time just surviving that they don't have the time to invest in themselves to help them jump out of the cycle. If you have just a handful of hours a week that are your own, it's hard to go to night school to get the degree, learn a new skill, network, or take care of your health.

As a sudden wealth recipient, you can buy more time. This is one of the best ways to use money to increase your level of happiness.

Elizabeth Dunn, psychology professor and author of *Happy Money: The Science of Smarter Spending*, says, "Anything that fundamentally changes the way you spend your time is good use of money – it's happy money."

When you are thinking about the life you want to create post-sudden wealth, think of how you can create more meaningful time for yourself. Are there tasks you are doing that you can outsource? Err on the side of using your money to buy more time instead of more things. It will have a greater impact on your overall satisfaction.

INVEST IN EXPERIENCES

Do you relish in past purchases or past experiences? Do you cherish things you've bought or things you've done more? When your mind wanders, are you more likely to think of toys you have or trips you've taken? On your deathbed, what memories will make you smile?

Money can be used to either buy material things such as cars, houses, and flat screen TVs, or experiences such as concerts, trips, Broadway shows, or special meals. Research shows that people seem to get more joy from experiences than from material things. As someone who's always preferred to hike through a jungle in a far off place over buying a Rolex, this makes sense to me, but it's not as intuitive for others.

Even if they aren't aware, the reason most people enjoy experiences over things is because experiences are usually shared with others, and if there is one thing (and only one thing!) psychologists agree on, it is that social connections and relationships are the biggest contributor to happiness. As discussed earlier, we become accustomed to things quickly, but not so with experiences. We not only can enjoy the anticipation of an upcoming experience and the experience itself, but experiences also provide what I think of as "happiness capital," which is like a mental happiness account. Once you make a deposit, it continues to provide dividends. Invest in experiences.

Material things lose value over time – financially, of course, but also in terms of the amount of happiness they provide. Experiences, however, increase in value over time. My wife still talks about a childhood vacation she took to Disneyworld with her family. This experience was paid for decades ago but still produces enjoyment today. In fact, I think the emotional value of this trip has increased over time for her. Invest in experiences.

Experiences also help define who we are more than the things we buy. We'll buy a BMW to project an image of who we want to be, but experiences define who we are. Things don't change us, but the right experience can. A trip or a play can change how we look at the world and ourselves. Some sudden wealth recipients focus too much on acquiring things. Material possessions are fine – assuming you can afford them – but you'll get more meaning and enjoyment from experiences. When you think about the life you want to create, don't forget to invest in experiences.

MIRACLE QUESTION

One sudden wealth recipient who was a bit overwhelmed and in awe over his windfall, even after a couple of years, said, "This money is like driving a really fast race car in a residential neighborhood. I know there's so much more I could be doing with it, but I just don't know how." This is often the impression I have when I start working with a sudden wealth client – they know they have a life-changing opportunity in front of them, but they just aren't sure how to make the most of it. This can be an agonizing feeling as they flounder from one thing to the next, hoping they will stumble onto happiness.

The difference between the sudden wealth recipient who makes the most of their windfall by creating the best life possible and those who don't is that they have a vision for what they want their life to look like. They create a life by design instead of a life by default.

To help you create a life by design, start by answering the miracle question:

Suppose that tonight while you sleep, a miracle happens and all of your problems are solved. But because you were asleep when the miracle occurred, you aren't aware that it even happened. When you wake tomorrow morning, how are you going to discover evidence of that miracle? What will you see yourself doing, thinking, or believing about yourself that will tell you a miracle has happened in your life or business?

The miracle question is a standard question in Solution-Focused Therapy, a type of counseling that is short-term and focuses on what you want (i.e., solutions) instead of what you don't want (i.e., problems). How will you answer this question?

If this question is a bit too esoteric, consider an alternative. Fast forward five years from now. What needs to happen for you to feel fulfillment and that you've been able to create the best life possible with the sudden wealth?

Both of these questions force you to think about not just your future self, but your happy future self and what needed to happen for you to feel this happiness. Instead of working toward a goal, these questions assume you already are experiencing everything you want and ask you to work backward. In addition, they help you focus on what you want, rather than what you don't want.

Sudden wealth recipients who spend some time with either or both of these questions usually feel a sense of contentment because they may, maybe for the first time, begin to think about their future and realize that they can use their windfall and control it rather than feel it controls them.

MANTRA

Some sudden wealth recipients appreciate having a money mantra to keep them focused and grounded. A mantra in this sense is not a chant or meditation technique, but something more practical that may help you reconnect to what is most important to you. A money mantra is a simple phrase that describes how you want to think about money. The following are a few examples of money mantras:

1. Money is a tool to help me live my best life.

2. Money is a tool that provides security.

3. Money is a tool that allows me to help others.

4. Money is a tool that lets me help my children.

5. Money is a tool that lets me take care of my family.

The idea is to think about what money means to you. One of the best ways to determine what money really means to you is to answer the question, "What's important about money to me?" and then to continue to drill down with each answer by asking what's important about that to you. For example, clients may answer the question, "What's important about money to you?" with, "It lets me buy things for my family." When asked, "What's important about buying things for your family?", they may respond with, "So I can take care of them." Then they might answer, "What's important about taking care of your family?" with, "So I can give them the life I never had as a child." When asked, "What's important about giving your family the life you never had as a child?," they may respond, "So that they never experience hunger or have to suffer like I did." And finally, they may answer, "What's important about never letting your family go hungry or suffer?" with, "I can die a happy man knowing I've made a difference in their lives and that I've been able to give them the opportunity to create the best life they can."

In this case, the client may realize that money is a tool for making a difference in his family's life and for providing opportunity. Faced with this realization, when contemplating a new boat purchase, he may realize it doesn't serve his greater goal.

The objective of the mantra is not to come up with what sounds good or even what makes the most financial sense. The objective is for you to become as clear as possible on what this sudden wealth means to you so you can control and direct it in a way that services your greater good. Without this awareness and connection between money and purpose, I've seen some sudden wealth recipients invest a lot of money into the wrong things. Share your money mantra with your advisors so they understand what drives you and so they can politely remind you if they see you getting off track.

There is another proven way to increase your own happiness: help others. Study after study shows we get a boost whenever we help others, whether it's someone we know or a total stranger. Because of evolutionary benefits, some scientists have suggested we are predisposed to experience joy from giving. Although not everyone experiences the same level of joy from giving, and some may give even at their own detriment, there is a science to giving that provides the biggest boost of happiness.

In the next Sudden Wealth Principle, you'll learn just how much you have and how much you can help others and yourself…

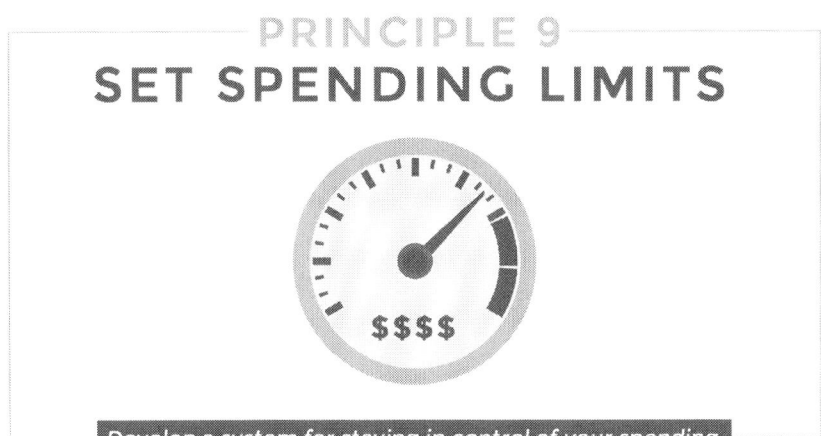

SET SPENDING LIMITS

Develop a system for staying in control of your spending.

If you committed to following just one of the 12 Sudden Wealth Principles, this should be the one. Knowing what you have and what you can spend is the most important. If you can't answer these two questions, you are flying blind. Forget about learning how to create a better life, growing your wealth, or staying on track. If you don't know how much you have, how can you expect to know how much you can afford to spend? And if you don't know how much you can afford to spend, how will you know if the house you are buying is reasonable or if it's going to bankrupt you? How can you enjoy the Caribbean cruise if, in the back of your mind, you don't know if you can afford it?

Fortunately, determining how much you have and how much you can spend is not rocket science. The goal of this chapter is not to make you a professional financial analyst. Your advisors can calculate these numbers for you, but it's important to understand the story behind the numbers.

WHAT IS YOUR SUDDEN WEALTH LEVEL?

There's sudden wealth, and then there's sudden wealth! Your level refers to not just the amount of money you will be receiving, but how this money will impact your life. Your level will determine how dramatically your life can change as a result of the money you are receiving.

LEVEL I SUDDEN WEALTH

Level I sudden wealth is an amount of money that will not materially change your life. It's small enough that it doesn't allow you to buy a new house, quit your job, or change your day-to-day lifestyle.

For example, a $20,000 inheritance wouldn't be enough to have much of an impact on most people's lives. Sure, you could buy a car, get new countertops, or pay off some bills, but your life would go on unaffected by the inheritance.

Most people will experience Level I sudden wealth in their lifetime, either through inheritance or divorce. Although Level I sudden wealth won't change your life, it can still be an excellent opportunity to pay off credit card debt, student loans, use as a down payment on a house, fund college savings accounts, or save for retirement.

Often, Level I sudden wealth doesn't cause some of the anxiety, indecision, and paralysis that larger amounts of money can create. The challenge is that because it is a smaller amount, some people view it as more disposable and are more inclined to spend it freely and without as much consideration, which is a true shame. Level I sudden wealth is an opportunity to improve your life and financial standing. And although it may not have the same gravitas as Level II or Level III sudden wealth, there are techniques and strategies to make the most of this new money.

LEVEL II SUDDEN WEALTH

Level II sudden wealth is an amount of money that can have a big impact on your life, but not so much that you can quit your job. At Level II, you may be able to buy a bigger house, travel more often, pay off all your debts, fully fund college savings accounts for your children, purchase a fancier car, and have more income to spend each month.

If you follow the 12 Sudden Wealth Principles, Level II sudden wealth can be a life-enhancing opportunity that may allow you and/or your spouse to retire early, work part-time, help loved ones, and generally have the means to enjoy life to the fullest. Although most people will experience a Level I sudden wealth event in their life, far fewer will receive a sum of money large enough to qualify for Level II.

After a relatively short transition period, most Level II recipients are able to adjust smoothly to their new situation, because even though they are worth substantially more than they were before the windfall, they are still grounded by the same rules that apply to most of us. That is, they still need to get up to go to work each morning, they still have a limited amount of vacation time, and they still need to save and invest for their future. They are able to incrementally improve their finances and lives, but for the most part, they are still the same people, following the same path and rules their friends and family follow. Although this may not seem significant, there is a gigantic shift between Level II and Level III sudden wealth. The necessity to continue to work makes Level II sudden wealth much different from Level III.

LEVEL III SUDDEN WEALTH

Level III sudden wealth is an amount of money that allows you to quit your job. This may not seem like an important distinction, but it makes Level III sudden wealth a game-changer. The difference between Level II and Level III cannot be overstated. It is as dramatic a difference as precipitation at 33 degrees versus 32 degrees.

Why is not working such an important distinction with Level III sudden wealth? Most people who work will spend more time at their job and with their co-workers than anywhere else and with anyone else. Although certainly not true for everyone, a job can be a source of social connection – we can develop deep friendships with co-workers – and it provides us with purpose. Even if we are not saving lives at our job, it provides routine, structure, and meaning to our day. It makes our weekends and vacations that much more significant. If we stop working, which many Level III sudden wealth recipients decide to do, a space in our days and in our souls can be created that needs to be filled. We may not find our purpose through our work, but our career certainly provides the foundation our days and lives are built upon.

A Level III opportunity can radically change your life by freeing you from a 9-to-5 job and allowing you to develop meaning and purpose outside of a career, but for some people, this search for meaning can be disconcerting.

> *According to a General Social Survey poll, nearly three-quarters of Americans wouldn't quit their jobs, even if a financial windfall enabled them to live in luxury for the rest of their lives.*

Our need to work also makes us "normal" and like everyone else. When we have so much money that we can choose not to work, this puts us in a category not shared by many others. What happens when you have enough money and time to travel but your friends still have limited resources and jobs they go to each day? Again, these are quality problems, but nevertheless, these are issues Level III sudden wealth recipients have to face.

Very few people experience Level III sudden wealth. Those who do, typically receive it from inheritance, lawsuit judgment/settlement, lottery, or a business sale. The 12 Sudden Wealth Principles in this book are written for you. Each and every one of them are vital to helping you make the transition smoothly and for helping you blend what you loved about your pre-money life with your post-sudden wealth life. Your success in navigating this process is directly correlated with how closely you can follow these 12 Sudden Wealth Principles.

So what's your level? Level I is often obvious, but the distinction between Level II and Level III is more nuanced. Half the time, I've found that those at Level II think they are Level III and want to quit their jobs prematurely. This can be a devastating mistake that can have profound financial consequences. The other half of the time, there are those who are Level III who don't truly believe they can quit their jobs. The first group thinks they have more money than they actually do and the second group thinks they have less. In both cases, they don't fully understand their position, but you will…

HOW MUCH DO YOU HAVE?

The technical term for knowing how much you have is your "net worth." The calculation is simply:

Assets - Liabilities = Net Worth

For most people, this is a simple calculation achieved by adding their assets, such as the value of their house, 401(k) account, automobiles, IRAs, bank account, and brokerage accounts, and subtracting their home mortgage, credit card balances, student loans, and other debts they owe. If you own more than you owe, your have a positive net worth. If you owe more than you own, you have a negative net worth.

For sudden wealth recipients, it's often not quite this easy. Why? Taxes. The balance in your bank account may not be all yours. For certain sudden wealth types, including lawsuits, lottery, stock options, sports and entertainment contracts, and the sale of a business, you will almost always owe income taxes on the money you receive.

It's not just family and friends who become fixated on the larger headline figure (discussed in the last chapter). Sudden wealth recipients also commonly focus, or as behavioral finance economists call it, "anchor," on the big number but fail to account for taxes, expenses, fees, and other items that can dramatically reduce the amount of sudden wealth they actually have.

Lots Of Cash But Very Few Assets

Is it possible to have a small net worth but still be wealthy? Yes, this is a common occurrence for lottery winners who choose to or are required to take an annual annuity payment instead of a lump sum payment. For these lottery winners, especially during the first few years, they may have a meager net worth but because they are guaranteed a big check each year, they are wealthy.

Congratulations! You just won a $60 million lottery. But did you really win $60 million? It sure seems like it. The big check you held up at the press conference says $60 million. The newspaper reporting your win reads $60 million. Your friends and family keep talking about $60 million. So $60 million it is. But is it? Sadly, not even close. Here's the breakdown:

A $60,000,000 jackpot equates to $33,500,000 cash. Subtract state tax (assuming NY) of approximately $3 million and federal income tax and Medicare tax of $14 million, and your net worth after tax amount is closer to $17 million.

Again, the goal in this chapter is not to turn you into a financial analyst or tax expert. You pay your advisors for that. The goal is for you to become clear on what you have, not what you think you have. If you're going to anchor a figure, make sure it's $17 million and not $60 million! As one lottery winner confessed, "I was spending like I had $20 million, but I barely had $3 million to my name."

In addition to subtracting taxes, which your advisors can both help to reduce and calculate for you, the headline number also needs to be reduced by all of your debts. Subtract student loans, credit card balances, back taxes, loans to family members, automobile loans, unpaid child and spousal support, and any other debts you owe. What you're left with is how much you actually have. I call this the end of day number. Forget the headline number and focus on this number instead.

Just In Case The Taxman Cometh

Income tax planning is equal parts art and science. Your advisors may take a tax position they think is defendable in an IRS audit, but that is in the gray area of tax regulations. In these situations, I set aside the maximum amount of tax the client may have to pay if they are audited and if the IRS rejects our tax position. For example, we took a well-researched but still debatable tax position for one of my clients, which saved her almost $4 million of tax. Because the IRS could have contested our position and demanded part or all of the $4 million, this money went into a separate account and I didn't include this in her end of day number. Once audited, or when the statute of limitations expires, you can move the money back into your net worth calculation.

But even your net worth can be confusing. What does it mean if you have $10 million? For many sudden wealth recipients, they see their end of day number, but they can't get their head around what it means. If you've been making $50,000 a year and now your bank account shows $10 million, your sudden wealth can seem both overwhelming and also meaningless. One client recalled her sense of confusion: "I knew $22 million was a lot of money, but because it was an amount so outside my ability to relate, I couldn't grasp just how much it was. I mean, I knew it was more than $21 million and less than $23 million, but other than that, I had no comprehension of what it meant."

The danger with big numbers is that they can feel like Monopoly money. If you don't value your sudden wealth, you may be more inclined to squander it. To make your sudden wealth more understandable and relatable, convert it to income. A $10 million net worth is an intangible number on a page, but a $400,000 annual income means something. Even if you were making $50,000 a year and $400,000 seems like a ridiculous income, most sudden wealth recipients can still at least start get their head around this number.

HOW MUCH CAN YOU AFFORD TO SPEND?

Your end of day number is the key ingredient in determining if you can quit your job, buy a new house, travel the world, pay for your children's college, and whether you can afford a new Tesla or a Honda. This number determines how much you can afford to spend.

Once you determine how much money you actually have, you can now calculate how much you can comfortably afford to spend. Seems obvious, but many sudden wealth recipients skip this critical step and go straight to spending their windfall. This is a financially fatal mistake and the quickest way to go through most, or all, of your money. Don't let this happen to you.

Most sudden wealth recipients (and even some advisors) approach this backwards. They add up all of their lifestyle expenses (e.g., mortgage, travel, insurance, entertainment) and then figure out how much they need to withdraw a year to support their lifestyle and cover their expenses.

Buy A Cactus, Not A Fern

Spending $50,000 on a new BMW costs a lot more than spending $50,000 on a family vacation. Why? The luxury car will boost your insurance premiums, maintenance costs, and registration fees, and it requires premium gasoline. Ferns require daily watering, whereas cacti can go a month without H2O. Take into consideration not only the initial cost, but also all of the ongoing costs.

How can you convert your end of day number into income? There has been a tremendous amount of research into "safe withdrawal rates." A safe withdrawal rate is a percentage of your portfolio that you can take each year without much risk of taking too much and spending down your account. For example, let's say you have $1 million in your investment account and you are taking out $150,000 a year to live on. Your withdrawal rate is 15% ($150,000/$1,000,000). Take out $300,000 a year and the withdrawal rate is 30%. The withdrawal rate is significant – it may be the most significant number in this book – because if you take out too much each year, your account will drop from $1 million to $950,000 to $900,000, etc., until you run out of money. As I was explaining this to a client who was having trouble understanding, a smile came over her face as she blurted out, "You don't want to kill the chicken that gives you eggs." Brilliant!

So what is a safe withdrawal rate? Your advisors will be able to help you determine how much you can spend, but the research shows 3% on the low side and 5% on the higher side, depending on the investment allocation and other factors. I typically use a 4% withdrawal rate as a rule-of-thumb. This means you can calculate how much you can comfortably spend each year without spending down your assets by multiplying your end of day number by 4%. For example, if you have $6 million, you can withdraw and spend approximately $240,000 a year ($6 million X 4%). The 4% rate is not a rule set in stone, but if your living expenses require you to withdraw more than 4% a year, this is a red flag. Work closely with your advisors to make sure you are not withdrawing too much and follow Sudden Wealth Principle 12 closely.

WHEN 4% ISN'T ENOUGH

Part of the thrill of sudden wealth is the freedom and options it creates. For someone who had very little time or money, sudden wealth can be the ultimate emancipator. With so many choices, it's important to understand how each decision you make is interrelated with your finances and how it can affect your future options. For example, if you quit your job, this will give you more time to travel, but it may also prevent you from being able to move into the house you really want. Or if you quit and move into the house, you may not be able to afford your children's college expenses. Sometimes, going through one door closes another. This is why it's so important to examine all of your options before making decisions, but thinking through all of the options can cause a headache. The best remedy is to take a step back and examine your priorities. What are the things that really matter most to you?

START WITH THE BIG ROCKS

Imagine a table with a glass jar, several large rocks, a stack of smaller pebbles, and a pile of sand. Your job is to fit as many of the rocks and pebbles and as much sand in the jar as you can. Where do you start? Most people start by dumping in the sand and a few pebbles – leaving the bigger rocks on the table. This is a popular analogy with time management gurus. If you start with the little things, you run out of time for the big (and significant) things in your life. The same holds true for your finances.

Don't misinterpret insignificant for inexpensive – I've seen sudden wealth recipients spend millions of dollars on things they didn't value. The insignificant stuff sucks the air from the room and the money from our accounts when we spend it on things that don't matter. It's better to start with the big rocks, then the pebbles, and if there's still room, the sand.

Find your big rocks by going through the wishlist you've been working on. Ideally, you'll have pages of ideas for what your life might look like and thoughts on what you want to own and experience. Your wishlist is the beginning of your blueprint for your life post-sudden wealth. At this point, and by design, it's a random list of what could be. It's time to give the wishlist more direction.

PRIORITIZE YOUR WISHLIST

> "As you climb the ladder of success,
> be sure it's leaning against the right building."
>
> ~ H. Jackson Brown, Jr.

The first time I took my daughter into a Toys 'R' Us, she was overwhelmed by the options. Everywhere she looked, there was something clamoring for her attention. She had trouble focusing on what she wanted. It wasn't until I narrowed her options that she was able to figure out what she was most interested in.

Figure out your big rocks. Focus on the things that are going to give you lasting fulfillment and be leery of the shiny things that try to distract you. Make 20 copies of your wishlist, and then make a note next to each of the items:

1. **Musts.** These are your high priority items – your big rocks. The things you've determined are most important to you.

2. **Maybes.** These items are important to you, and if feasible, you'd like to make them a reality. These are your pebbles.

3. **Misses.** These are the least important items on your wishlist – the sand. In a perfect world, you'd be able to do these, but they are not priorities.

Remember, slow down. Take your time. It might take you an afternoon or it might take you a few months. You're not looking for a snapshot in time, what you're most interested in now, but what is truly most important to you and will give you the greatest fulfillment. To get the best reading, go through this process once a week for several months. Clients have found that when they go through this process several times, their priorities shift slightly. What was initially a knee-jerk Must (e.g., move to a bigger house), may change to a Maybe once you think about how a move would require a new school for your kids, etc.

If you have a lot of Musts, you can further refine your wishlist by ranking each from one to ten or assigning them a letter grade. How you figure out what is most important is irrelevant, just as long as you do.

Next, have your financial advisor create different scenarios for you, based on your priorities. For example, if your Musts were to quit your job, buy a bigger house, buy your parents a new car, pay for your niece and nephew's college, and spend $40,000 on travel a year, how does this affect your finances? Can you afford it? How much cushion does this leave you? If this requires withdrawing more than 4% from your accounts a year, how does it look if you cut your travel back to $20,000 a year and agree to cover half of the college costs?

Creating your ideal life is like chiseling a perfect sculpture. You start with a big block of stone, and with each decision you make, it takes its shape. As the artist, you have the freedom to sculpt whatever you desire, but with each strike of your hammer to create one shape, you are also making a decision to not make another. If you buy a larger house, it may mean you won't have as much to travel. Unless you have more money than you can spend, sudden wealth is not about having everything you want, it's about having what you want most.

Ultimately, you will find the right mix that works for you and your finances, but don't become too comfortable just yet. Your sudden wealth can be suddenly gone if you don't protect it . . .

PROTECT WEALTH

Learn how to protect your wealth.

There are just a handful of sudden wealth events that create a windfall overnight, but there are an unlimited number of ways for your money to disappear just as suddenly as it came. In my first number one bestselling personal finance book, I called these dangers a "reverse lottery" because of the speed at which you could lose everything. Consider these as threats to your sudden wealth and to your way of life. These threats are constantly lurking and can pop up at any moment. Am I being too dramatic? Do you remember how you felt when you first found out that you would receive sudden wealth? Now imagine how you'd feel if you just found out it was all going to be taken away.

I cannot overstate the importance of this Sudden Wealth Principle. The guidelines in this chapter are often forgotten, ignored, or neglected. If you care at all about your money, you need to be cognizant of the risks and do everything you can to protect your wealth from them.

Threats to your sudden wealth can be internal or external. Internal threats are those over which you have control, such as overspending, giving away too much money, or making bad investments. This chapter deals with external sources – those threats for which you have little or no control.

6 Sudden Wealth Sins

Here are the most common factors that contribute to sudden wealth recipients losing their money:

1. Spend too much

2. Give too much

3. Divorce

4. Invest badly

5. Fraud

6. Lawsuit

See Sudden Wealth Principle 12 for a complete description.

Even though external threats are often sudden and dramatic, you can minimize and even eliminate the top threats to your money by focusing on these four areas with the acronym SAFE:

1.   Separation/Divorce Preservation

2.   Asset Protection

3.   Fraud Prevention

4.   Estate Planning

SEPARATION/DIVORCE PRESERVATION

The statistics on divorce are sobering. Anyone who has experienced a divorce will tell you it is a tumultuous experience where no one wins. Emotions aside, there are few single events that can do more damage to your finances as a separation or divorce. In addition to the legal expenses, which can easily exceed six figures to resolve a contested divorce, it's not only possible but probable that you will lose at least half of your assets to your ex-spouse, as well as be required to make ongoing payments for years to come.

The laws are complex and vary by state, so it's important to work with an experienced family law attorney to help you navigate these issues. It's helpful to think in terms of pre-marriage and post-marriage when looking at how to protect your wealth. There are different tools and strategies available to you before you get married and others once you are already married.

PRE-MARRIAGE

If you are not yet married and want to protect your assets from existing or anticipated sudden wealth, explore these ideas with your legal and financial team:

1. **Co-habitation Agreement.** A client once joked, "The best way to protect yourself from divorce is to never get married!" His advice may protect you from many of the negative financial issues surrounding divorce, but even this extreme position won't protect you from all of the problems. Why? Many states have cohabitation laws or recognize common law marriage. This means that if you live with your partner, even if you never get married, and then separate, you may have some financial liability. Even in states such as California, where common law marriages are not recognized and there are not automatic rights for non-marital cohabitants, there could still be a claim if there was an expressed or implied agreement between the parties.

   What does this mean? It means if you are wealthy, it's highly possible your ex-partner will find an attorney who will argue you made an agreement to provide support, even if you didn't. In other words, even if you are not married, you need to be aware of this threat. One way to protect yourself is to enter into a cohabitation agreement with your partner. A cohabitation agreement is a document that outlines how property, assets, and debt will be divided, as well as how financial support will be handled among other issues.

   If you are living with someone and haven't received the money yet, or even if you have, speak to a family law attorney about the financial risks you face if the relationship dissolves. Find out if a cohabitation agreement makes sense for you.

2. **Prenuptial Agreement.** A prenuptial agreement (often called a "prenup" or a premarital agreement) is an agreement you enter into before marriage that spells out who

owns what, how income earned during the marriage will be treated, whether there will be spousal support, and other issues. Without a prenup, your ex-spouse can be entitled to a large portion of your sudden wealth. The laws are tricky and different in each state, but if you have a properly drafted prenup, it can save you hundreds of thousands or millions of dollars in legal fees, spousal support, and assets.

If you have already received the sudden wealth and are getting married, work with a family law attorney who specializes in prenups. Ideally, you would start working on the prenup at least 90 days before you get married. Prenups are binding agreements with strong case law and precedent, but if yours is to be held up in court, it must be done correctly. This means your partner must have his/her own legal representation and they must have adequate time to review the document. The court needs to see evidence that your partner was not cajoled into signing this the night before the wedding. Prenups are not inexpensive to draft, but they can save you millions of dollars if you divorce.

If you are uncomfortable speaking to your partner about a prenup, talk to your attorney for ideas on broaching the subject or have your attorney facilitate the discussion in a joint meeting.

Prenup 2.0?

If you are looking for extra protection for your assets in a divorce, consider placing some of your assets in a Domestic Asset Protection Trust (see additional information on these advanced asset protection vehicles later in this chapter). A handful of states allow these trusts, but only Nevada (as of this writing) has no "exception creditors," which means no creditors, including spouses, can gain access to the assets. No offense to Nevada, but the good news is that you can take advantage of the Nevada trust laws without having to live in Nevada. Talk to an attorney about this strategy before you get married.

POST-MARRIAGE

What happens if you receive sudden wealth and you are already married? Depending on several factors, there still may be a way to protect this money. The degree to which you can protect your windfall is determined by many issues, including the state in which you live, the source of your sudden wealth (e.g., inheritance, lottery), and the timing of your sudden wealth (e.g., did you sell a business that you started before you married?). A few paragraphs in this book won't do the topic justice, so you will need to work with a family law attorney who specializes in this area.

1. **Separate Property.** In community property states where assets are usually owned 50/50 by each spouse, separate properties are assets that are owned 100% by one spouse, given that he/she acquired it before marriage, by inheritance, as a gift, have their source in separate properties, or whatever is agreed to by the spouses. If your sudden wealth is from inheritance, lawsuit, stock options, or a business sale, you need legal advice on how to keep your windfall as separate property. For example, if you are married and you receive an inheritance from your mother, set up a separate bank or investment account and be careful not to co-mingle the inheritance assets with your joint assets. If you were involved in a lawsuit before you were married and you receive a judgment or it settles after you got married, work closely with an attorney to keep these assets separate. Likewise, if you earned stock options or started a business pre-marriage, but then exercised them or sold the business after you became married, you may be able to separate these assets from your joint assets.

Keep Your Assets Separate

Consider keeping assets separate. Depending on the state in which you live and the source of your windfall, if you deposit the money into a joint account with your spouse, this money could instantly become half theirs. For some, this isn't an issue, but for others, this could pose a problem. For example, if you have children from a previous marriage and commingle an inheritance you receive with your new spouse, your children may receive less than you expect when you pass away. This problem becomes even more damaging if you are contemplating a divorce. Tip: If you don't want your spouse to have ownership of your windfall, talk to an attorney and keep the assets in a separate account.

2. **Postnuptial Agreement.** A postnuptial agreement (commonly called a "postnup" or postmarital agreement) is an agreement that is signed after you are already married. Although prenups can be fairly straightforward, postnups are technical, can take longer, and cost more. This doesn't mean you shouldn't consider one, but it means you need to discuss the facts of your situation with a family law attorney who specializes in drafting these documents. Like a prenup, however, a postnup details what happens in the event of a separation or divorce. A well drafted postnup can save a lot of money in legal fees and can protect at least some of your windfall.

3. **QTIP Trust.** A QTIP Trust is funded when the first spouse passes away. The surviving spouse has access to the assets transferred to the QTIP Trust until she/he dies, but she has no control over the assets at her death. Where the assets are transferred and who gets them is entirely the decision of the first spouse.

    The QTIP Trust is usually used by couples who have children from previous marriages and who want to ensure their spouse benefits from the assets but that their children ultimately receive an inheritance. For example, if John has more assets than his new wife, Mary, John's goal may be to make sure Mary is financially secure while providing his children from his first marriage with an inheritance. If John simply passes all his assets to Mary, she will be financially secure, but there is no stipulation that prevents her from giving the assets to a charity or leaving them to her family upon her death. More specifically, passing all the assets to Mary does not guarantee anything for John's children. If John passes his assets to his children at his death, Mary cannot use the assets to help her remain financially secure. The QTIP trust is designed to help John satisfy both his goals.

    A QTIP Trust works best when the surviving spouse is considerably older than the children who will ultimately receive the assets. Remember, the surviving spouse has access to the QTIP assets until she/he passes away. If your surviving spouse is fairly young, she/he will have access to the funds for a long time and your children might have to wait a long time for their inheritance.

A QTIP trust preserves your assets from a financially unsound spouse or from your ex-spouse's new spouse, if he or she remarries. As an added bonus, A QTIP trust protects against the surviving spouse's creditors (but it doesn't provide protection while both spouses are alive).

A divorce can wipe out 50% or more of your assets overnight. If you are in a relationship, whether married or not, and you are coming into, or have already come into, sudden wealth, talk to an attorney about your options to protect your windfall in the unfortunate case of a separation or divorce. Even if you are uncomfortable with the idea of a prenup or postnup, at least talk to an attorney to discuss which strategies may make sense for you.

ASSET PROTECTION

The numbers are shocking. Every day that your house, car, checking account, and investment accounts are exposed is one more day you are gambling against this type of risk, and the odds are not in your favor. Given these statistics, one of your primary objectives should be to protect your newly acquired sudden wealth.

Too many people use our legal system as their personal lottery. With a baseless claim and a contingency attorney, anyone can sue you. Lawsuits affect people from all walks of life. No one is safe, including "The Godfather of Soul," James Brown. His daughters sued him for more than $1 million, asserting that they should have received royalties on 25 songs they claimed to have helped him write, even though, at the time, they were as young as three years old.

The purpose of asset protection is to safeguard your sudden wealth from lawsuits. Asset protection does not defraud creditors or shield your money from illegal activities. Just as it is someone's legal right to sue, it is your legal right to protect what you have from the countless lawsuits disrupting the lives of so many. Protecting your assets is entirely legal and ethical.

TWO REASONS TO PROTECT ASSETS

You accomplish two things by taking preemptive steps to protect your assets:

1.   **Shield Assets.** You help prevent those shielded assets from being taken in a lawsuit. If you are aware of state and federal laws, you can take advantage of them to bullet-

proof your assets from court judgments. When you work with an attorney who specializes in asset protection strategies, they can take advantage of the laws and will know how to make them work in your favor.

2.   **Discourage Lawsuits.** Asset protection can minimize the chances of being named or involved in a lawsuit in the first place. Imagine two homes of similar size and value. One home has a visible alarm system and one doesn't. Which house will be burglarized? Obviously the house without the visible alarm has a greater chance of being burglarized. The same holds true for your sudden wealth. With an asset protection plan in place, your greatest pre-emptive defense is to inform the other party that the lawsuit will be fruitless because you don't have assets they can reach through a court judgment. This technique is often successfully used by attorneys representing defendants who have taken the extra step to protect their assets.

Although it is difficult to prevent these asset searches, you can quickly squash a plaintiff's hope for success if you have an asset protection plan in place. Most attorneys who work on contingency won't even take a case when there's little chance of financial reward.

Hide And Seek

Many people think that by hiding their assets, they are protected. This is a mistake. Through court appearances, depositions, interrogatories, and subpoenas, it is easy for a litigant and his attorney to uncover all of your assets and evaluate whether you have sufficient resources to make a lawsuit worthwhile. Even prospective litigants can inexpensively hire a professional search firm to locate your assets. "Hiding" your assets is like putting them in a glass box—it just doesn't work.

ASSET PROTECTION STRATEGIES

There are numerous strategies that may be available to you to protect your sudden wealth from lawsuits. This is a technical area of law where it makes sense to work with a specialist. The following are just a few ideas to consider…

UMBRELLA LIABILITY INSURANCE

As I wrote in my first personal finance book, the first line of defense is to have a personal liability insurance policy. A personal liability insurance policy is designed to protect you against judgments from property damage, bodily injury, and personal injury lawsuits. The personal liability policy is sometimes called an "umbrella" liability policy because it sits on top of your automobile and homeowner's insurance policy and covers claims that are either not covered by these policies or that are beyond the limits of these policies.

Umbrella liability insurance starts at $1 million in coverage and goes up from there. A good rule of thumb is to get a policy that is at least $5 million or twice as much as your net worth. For example, if your net worth is $6 million, you'd get $12 million of liability insurance. If your net worth was $2 million, you'd get $5 million of insurance.

Bodily injury and personal injury lawsuits frequently result in multi-million dollar settlements. Umbrella liability insurance is an inexpensive way to safeguard what you've worked so hard to achieve.

IRREVOCABLE TRUSTS

There are two basic forms of trusts—revocable and irrevocable. If you are sued, the type of trust you have becomes extremely significant. Most trusts are "living trusts" established for estate planning purposes. These living trusts, such as "The Smith Family Trust," are typically revocable, meaning those who set it up retain complete control of the trust. They can place assets into the trust, remove assets, change the trust beneficiaries, and even terminate the trust at any time. A revocable trust provides you with complete control and flexibility.

This flexibility has a price. A revocable trust provides very little to no asset protection. If you are sued, your creditors assume your rights. Basically, they stand in your shoes. If you have a bank account, now your creditors have a bank account. If you have a revocable trust and full control of the assets within it, your creditors retain the same full control and access to that trust.

Although you shouldn't count on a revocable trust to protect your assets, there are states that may provide marginal protection. Typically, however, if you transfer property to a trust and retain the ability to either revoke the trust or control the disposition of the trust assets, it will not provide protection.

While a revocable trust provides you with full control, an irrevocable trust restricts control of the trust assets. When you establish an irrevocable trust, you immediately lose control over any assets you place in the trust. You can't terminate the trust, change beneficiaries, or remove assets. The decision is irrevocable. This lack of control is what protects the assets within the irrevocable trust. When your creditor stands in your shoes, he is stuck with the same lack of control — he can't terminate the trust, name himself the beneficiary, or remove the assets.

This protection comes at an obvious cost—you give up control of the assets. They are protected from lawsuits but you no longer have the flexibility or freedom to control them. Depending on the situation, it can make sense to place some assets in one or more types of irrevocable trust.

TYPES OF IRREVOCABLE TRUSTS

There are several types of irrevocable trusts that may make sense to shield your sudden wealth, including these:

1. Spendthrift Trust
2. Asset Protection Trust
3. Charitable Remainder Trust

SPENDTHRIFT TRUST

A spendthrift is defined by the Oxford English Dictionary as "one who spends money recklessly or wastefully." A spendthrift trust is an excellent way to protect assets from creditors and from spendthrift beneficiaries themselves.

When assets are placed in a spendthrift trust, the *income* generated from those assets is available to the beneficiaries, but they cannot access the principal. The beneficiary's creditors also cannot access the principal. Therefore, the principal is fully secure from both the beneficiaries and their creditors. At the beneficiary's death, the assets are transferred to the remainder person beneficiary set up by the grantor of the trust.

Typically, the spendthrift trust is used to ensure a child is cared for financially, but because the child is too young or financially irresponsible, the grantor is unwilling to leave control of the assets to the child. A spendthrift trust is also commonly used to ensure assets are kept within the family in the event of divorce. Parents who want to support their children and pass assets to their grandchildren have several options. If they simply leave the assets directly to their children and the children divorce, it is likely that part or all of the assets will be lost in a divorce settlement. A spendthrift trust is a better option. With a spendthrift trust, the principal passes to the grandchildren, regardless of a divorce or lawsuit.

A spendthrift trust can be either revocable or irrevocable. If the trust is revocable, the assets are protected from the beneficiary's creditors, but not from the grantor's creditors. For example, if you fund a revocable spendthrift trust for your child, your child's creditors can't touch the trust assets, but your creditors can. If the trust is irrevocable, the assets are protected from both your creditors and your beneficiary's creditors.

Are Your Assets At Risk? Take the Threat Matrix Quiz

Any time we work with a new client, we do a threat matrix. This is where we analyze the specific situation of the client and we look for weaknesses—holes in their plan and things that could destroy their finances overnight. We want to know what those weaknesses are so we can create strategies to protect them. Here are a few questions that will help you determine your overall risk:

1. Are you on the board of a company or non-profit?

2. Do you have household help?

3. Do you have a small business you operate as a sole proprietorship?

4. Do you have a small business where you have a partner but have not formed a corporation or LLC?

5. Do you have a child who drives your automobile?

6. Do you or your employees use your automobile in your business?

7. Do you have rental property with tenants?

8. Do you have a boat, jet ski, or motorcycle?

9. Are you an active user of Twitter, Facebook, or other social media?

10. Does your company provide a retirement plan for employees?

You can take the full threat matrix questionnaire
at suddenwealthsolution.com

ASSET PROTECTION TRUST

Can you create a trust, transfer assets into the trust, and name yourself the beneficiary? Prior to 1997, this type of trust was invalid in the United States. In 1997, however, Alaska and Delaware saw an opportunity. Billions of dollars were leaving the United States and being protected in offshore trusts where the grantor was also the beneficiary. To stop the flow of funds going offshore and to attract additional investments, a handful of states have changed their trust laws to legalize the Domestic Asset Protection Trust (DAPT).

This can be a good strategy if you have considerable assets and want to build a fortress around at least part of your portfolio without going offshore. A DAPT is an irrevocable (in other words, you can't change your mind) trust that allows you to be the beneficiary, yet the assets still be protected from your creditors. This may not sound like a big deal but it is. Typically, if you are the beneficiary of a trust, your creditors become beneficiaries and you jeopardize the assets in the trust. Not so in a handful of states including Nevada, South Dakota, Alaska, and Delaware, which provide special laws that can make your assets out of reach of creditors.

Fortunately, you don't have to pack your bags and move to Las Vegas to take advantage of the laws in Nevada as long as you have a co-trustee who lives in the state. Not only can a DAPT protect you from creditors, but it can protect your assets from soon-to-be ex-spouses. Because of this, some clients are using DAPTs in addition to a pre-marital agreement for extra protection.

There's one potential problem with DAPTs. The U.S. Constitution requires each state to recognize judgments in other states. In other words, if you have an Alaska asset protection trust, the assets can be reached if you are sued in another state. This is potentially a serious drawback of the asset protection trust, but the attorneys I work with stand by the asset protection trust as an effective means to shield assets.

Go to suddenwealthsolution.com to read and listen to an hour-long interview on DAPTs I conducted with a Nevada-based trust company.

CHARITABLE REMAINDER TRUST

A charitable remainder trust (CRT) is an excellent estate tax savings tool with tremendous asset protection features. There are several versions of the CRT, but the concept is simple. You gift assets to the CRT. You then select a charitable organization to receive the assets at your death. You are able to invest the assets and are required to receive at least 5% of the CRT every year. Properly drafted, the assets in the trust are entirely protected from your creditors. This type of trust also provides immediate income tax benefits as well as estate tax benefits.

If asset protection is your only goal, however, a CRT is not the right tool. Although it offers bulletproof protection, it is a little extreme to give your assets to charity just to protect them.

When does this kind of trust make sense? As the name implies, there needs to be a *charitable* desire. Rather than will the assets to a charity and risk losing them to creditors during your life, the CRT protects the assets and provides you with at least 5% annually. The CRT ensures that your charitable interests are fulfilled and you have the comfort of knowing the assets are safe from creditors.

A CRT is also useful when you want to protect your assets and support a charity, but also want to leave an estate for your family. In this situation, you gift low basis assets to the CRT and use the required annual distribution of at least 5% to purchase life insurance. At your death, the charity receives the assets in the CRT and your beneficiaries receive the life insurance proceeds—both estate and income tax free.

The CRT is irrevocable. You should never place 100% of your assets in a CRT, but it can be a valuable part of your asset protection plan if you intend to give to a charitable organization in the future.

FAMILY LIMITED PARTNERSHIPS AND LIMITED LIABILITY COMPANIES

Family Limited Partnerships (FLP) and Limited Liability Companies (LLC) will enable you to protect your assets while providing incredible income and estate tax benefits. The majority of states base their laws on the Uniform Limited Partnership Act (ULPA) and the Uniform Limited Liability Company Act (ULLCA). In those states, "charging order" protection is granted to owners of FLPs/LLCs. Their ability to provide protection from charging orders is the primary way FLPs/LLCs protect your assets.

The courts provide a charging order to your creditors following a lawsuit judgment or bankruptcy. The charging order allows your creditors to receive your share of any distribution due to you from a FLP/LLC. For example, if your neighbor breaks his leg walking on your driveway and successfully sues you, he is now a creditor—you owe him money. As a creditor, he has certain legal rights to what you owe him. If you have a FLP/LLC and get a distribution of $125,000 a month from it, the court may grant your neighbor a charging order that will instruct your FLP/LLC to pay him the $125,000 typically due to you every month. He will continue to receive the payment until you have satisfied your debt to him.

The Pros And Cons Of A Series LLC

If you have rental property, or expect to invest in rental property after receiving your sudden wealth, create a business entity, such as an LLC or corporation, to shield your other assets from a disgruntled tenant. By doing this, if your renter sues you for $5 million, they can attack the assets in the entity that holds the real estate, but the rest of your personal assets are protected. Tip: Create a separate business entity for each rental property or consider a Nevada or Delaware Series LLC, which is designed to protect each property within a single LLC. Listen to my interview on Series LLCs at suddenwealthsolution.com.

So far, having an FLP/LLC doesn't seem to offer much protection, but in practice, the charging order is actually weak because of the following protections provided by state law:

1. Creditors are Powerless – When I was in college, I went on a two-week, cross-country bus tour. There were a handful of pre-planned stops, but most of the stops were at the driver's discretion. When on the tour, I was increasingly frustrated as my destination ideas were consistently vetoed. My frustration reached its limit when the other passengers decided we should go to North Carolina instead of Washington D.C. I got off the tour bus in Gatlinburg, Tennessee and went to D.C. myself. For the ten days leading up to my departure from the tour, I was completely powerless. It didn't matter what I did or what I said, there was nothing I could do to change the direction of the tour. This is how creditors must feel when they have a charging order against an FLP/LLC.

An FLP/LLC is run like a totalitarian government, and you are the ruler. A creditor may be granted a charging order, but they have no voting rights in the FLP/LLC. They can't sell the assets, dissolve the FLP/LLC, or decide to make larger distributions. They don't have a say in any decision made by the FLP/LLC. You retain complete control. If your creditor is receiving a payout of $25,000 a month from your FLP/LLC, you could simply vote to cease distributions to yourself and your creditor would be powerless to stop it.

If you needed the monthly distributions but did not want the creditor to receive them, you could vote to cease monthly distributions and instead pay yourself and your spouse a salary for operating the FLP/LLC. Your creditor would then need to file with the courts to have your wages garnished. If they were successful, you could vote to stop paying yourself a salary and start paying a family member not plagued by creditors a salary for operating the FLP/LLC. You could then receive these funds from that family member as a gift.

2. Creditors Pay Your Taxes – FLPs/LLCs are "pass-through" entities. The FLP/LLC doesn't pay taxes; each owner is responsible for paying tax on his/her share of the FLP/LLC income. Even more importantly, the owners are responsible for this tax, even if the income is not distributed. A creditor who receives ownership in the FLP/LLC through a judgment immediately becomes liable for taxes on income from the FLP/LLC.

Frank gets a charging order against your FLP/LLC and can't wait for the checks to start rolling in. A month or two passes and he doesn't receive a distribution. Frank finds out you voted to let the income accumulate in the FLP/LLC and stop monthly distributions. Frank discovers there is nothing he can do. A couple of months later, Frank then receives a tax bill in the mail. Frank owes several hundred thousand dollars in taxes. The income generated in the FLP/LLC would normally be taxable to only the owners of the FLP/LLC, but because Frank obtained a charging order, he is now responsible for paying his share of the income tax even though the income wasn't distributed. To make matters worse for Frank, once he was granted the charging order, he might not be able to relinquish it without the approval of the FLP/LLC owners.

In summary, Frank cannot reach the assets, cannot take distributions, is required to pay tax on income he doesn't receive, and can't get out of this predicament without approval from the owners of the FLP/LLC.

Become A CEO To Shield Your Assets

Create business entities to shield assets. If you have a small business or do part-time work on the side without having a formal business structure such as an LLC or a corporation, you are operating as a sole proprietorship. The "sole" means it's just you, so unlike a partnership, you don't have to worry about a partner's actions . . . but all of your personal assets are at risk if you are sued. Tip: Create a business entity that shields your personal assets from lawsuits against your company.

FRAUD PREVENTION

On December 11, 2008, anyone with an investment or bank account took a collective gasp. It was on this day that Bernie Madoff was arrested by the FBI on suspicion of committing the largest Ponzi scheme in history. Ultimately, thousands of clients were bilked out of billions of dollars. But, unfortunately, Bernie Madoff was not the only advisor stealing from clients. In the days and months that followed Madoff's arrest, hundreds of other Ponzi schemes were exposed.

It seems like a week doesn't go by that I don't see a headline about unscrupulous advisors taking client funds. As a long time viewer of CNBC's television show *American Greed*, I see just how depraved some people can be.

There are numerous ways to lose your money, everything from divorce to spending too much or making bad investments, but fraud is a different animal. It's theft, plain and simple. Although the media reports give the impression that financial fraud runs rampant, its frequency and the degree of damage it creates is far smaller than divorce or some of the other dangers to your assets. Nevertheless, theft does occur, and it can devastate someone's finances overnight.

There are hundreds of different types of financial fraud. Bernie Madoff operated a classic Ponzi scheme, but there are many others. Some types of fraud can wipe out a significant amount of money instantly (e.g., wire fraud) whereas others are more gradual (e.g., skimming). In 2013 alone, there were 67 Ponzi schemes detected, worth nearly $3 billion dollars[12]!

To protect yourself from fraud, you need to look at your areas of exposure. The most common areas of concern for sudden wealth recipients are:

1. Investment advisors
2. Investments
3. Bill paying/Business managers

INVESTMENT ADVISORS

A good investment advisor will know more about you and your finances than almost anyone else in your life. They'll know how much you make, how you spend your money, how much you give to charity, and will often know about relationship issues before others. They'll know your background and who you are as a person. This can make for a deep, intimate, and satisfying relationship – one that can last for decades and is built on trust. It can also lead to abuse.

Warning: Read If You Have Household Help

If you are going to hire household help (e.g., nanny, cleaning people), work with an employment attorney to protect yourself. You will want each person to sign an NDA – non disclosure agreement – to prevent them from sharing personal details about you with others/media. You will also want them to sign employment agreements to protect yourself. Be sure to get Employment Practices Liability Insurance through your homeowner's policy to cover claims against you for sexual harassment or discrimination. Also be sure to run background and credit checks on all of your potential employees. You can download a free sample independent contractor and/or employment agreement at suddenwealthsolution.com.

Crooked investment advisors can use your trust, coupled with their access to your financial accounts, to take advantage of you. Unless systems are in place, they could wire funds out of your account, overcharge you in fees, make investment recommendations into bogus companies, etc. A good rule of thumb is to trust, but verify. Regardless of how long you have known them, if they come to your children's birthday parties, or that they were referred to you by a family member or friend, never let your guard down. Don't blindly trust, verify instead.

You won't be able to eliminate all risk when you work with an advisor. By nature of what they do, they will have access to your accounts and personal data. Consider the following to protect your wealth:

1. **Research your advisor.** The first place to start is by finding the right investment advisor. Closely follow the advice in "Sudden Wealth Principle 3: Get Help" — use the AdvisorFit.com questionnaire, do a background check, and verify if they've ever had any regulatory issues. Your approach to getting an investment advisor should be to hire slow and fire fast. Take your time in finding the right person at the right company. If you sense any issues or wrongdoing, fire fast to avoid damage.

2. **Independent oversight.** Hire an independent accounting firm to reconcile your bank and investment accounts each month. They will track income and withdrawals and make sure there is no "leakage." The independent

accounting firm should not be associated in any way with your advisor or the advisor's firm. Find the accounting firm on your own. Do not request a referral from any of your advisors. The goal is to avoid the risk of collaboration amongst your advisors.

3. **Hire a consultant.** Instead of transferring your assets to an account in which the advisor has control, open a discount brokerage account at Fidelity or Schwab. Your advisor won't have access to this account, so you'll need to be more involved. When your advisor recommends trades or if you need a wire transfer, he won't be able to do this for you. You'll be the only one with access to the account. It's not the best approach for most clients and advisors, but if you are overly concerned, it is a strategy that minimizes investment advisor fraud.

4. **Seek deep pockets.** There are many well qualified solo investment advisors who could provide you with excellent financial advice, but if they work alone or for a small firm without solid financial backing, you may have little recourse if you are defrauded. Work with mid-sized to large firms with hundreds of millions, if not billions, under management. Bigger firms tend to have better financial controls and oversight in place, and if you pursue legal action, a larger firm may have the resources to pay a claim. But don't assume you have to go with the large brokerage firms such as Merrill Lynch or MorganStanley. There are hundreds of independent mid-sized firms with just as much oversight who can pay a claim. What you're trying to avoid is the small firms or one-person shops.

5. **Require phone confirmations on wires.** No money should be wired from your account to an account not in your name without signature and verbal approval from you. This will help prevent unauthorized wires.

6. **Never sign blank forms.** Under no circumstances should you sign blank forms or documents. Some advisors will ask you to do this because it makes their job easier if they need to open new accounts or initiate wires, but do not sign these forms. In fact, after you sign each form, get a photocopy of the form with your signature and/or take a photo of it with your phone. This will help prevent unauthorized wires and transfers from your account.

7. **Separate custodian.** As was discussed in Sudden Wealth Principle 3, your money should be held at a separate and unrelated firm from your investment advisor. Because Bernie Madoff was the investment advisor and held the assets, he was able to withdraw client funds and create fictitious monthly statements. Keep your assets at an unaffiliated company who will send you statements so you can see exactly what is happening in your accounts.

8. **Watch those statements.** Resist the temptation to toss the monthly investment statements into the drawer. Take the time to review the withdrawals and the account activity for suspicious activity.

9. **Verify insurance.** Large custodians will have adequate insurance in place to protect unlawful withdrawals from client accounts. Verify your custodian has this insurance.

10. **Watch those transfers.** If you are switching investment advisors or moving accounts, you will be required to sign an account transfer form. Pay close attention to this form. Verify where the money is being transferred, make sure it is in your name, and make a copy of the paperwork for your records.

11. **Check your checks.** Never sign a blank check and never make a check payable to your investment advisor. If you are making a deposit, make it out to the custodian and not your investment advisor.

Pro Tip

Often times, when people suddenly find themselves in a position of wealth, there comes a change in their visibility profile within society. The way they increased their wealth will sometimes have a direct bearing on the decrease in privacy. For example, a large business sale will usually make local or regional media at a minimum, a lottery win will undoubtedly make the national press and so on. The threats faced by families or individuals who find themselves in unchartered territory include:

I.   Unsophisticated criminals who target clients for financial gain through blackmail, philanthropy, or hardship type stories;

2.   Sophisticated criminals experienced in profiling and targeting the newly wealthy, who, many times, are ill prepared from a security perspective; and

3.   Random/Chance situations that may arise as a result of their lack of understanding in how to conduct themselves.

For example, a recent lottery winner contacted us because now that he was famous, he wanted some help in managing his affairs and taking care of the home. We screened and vetted all household staff. We also analyzed and profiled the family, the home, and their online personas. From this, we built a plan to reduce the risk profile, increase the privacy profile, and to develop contingency situation plans so that moving forward, the family can begin to approach life with a different outlook and better understanding of how to reduce risk.

~ Michael Guidry, President & CEO of The Guidry Group

INVESTMENTS

Investment fraud can be intertwined with investment advisor fraud or it can be separate. For example, if you have a dishonest investment advisor, he may not steal from your accounts directly, but he could recommend an investment that is nothing more than an empty shell of a company, or he can suggest an investment in a company that he or an associate controls. But investment fraud can originate not from the investment advisor, but from a "friend" or someone you meet at a party.

To mitigate investment fraud, stick to publicly traded investments, such as stocks, ETFs, or mutual funds, and avoid investments in, or loans to, private companies or real estate deals. "Sudden Wealth Principle 11: Grow Wealth" will highlight which types of investments you should avoid in more detail, but for now, if you are pitched an investment, have your financial advisor and attorney review the details.

BILL PAYING/BUSINESS MANAGERS

For many sudden wealth recipients, managing their finances and paying bills is a monthly burden they are all too happy to offload onto someone else. Many view it as a tedious and time consuming activity that they put on top of their "do less" list. If this describes you, make sure you protect yourself. Because business managers have more control than investment advisors – they can write checks on your behalf – they require even more oversight and there needs to be greater safeguards in place to protect your wealth.

There are two main risks of fraud when working with a bill payer/business manager. The first is outright theft of your funds. Because they have access to your bank and checking account, they can simply write themselves checks or initiate wires out of your account. Even if you're not paying that much attention, you will likely notice checks paid to them or transfers out of your account. It's hard to mask these transactions for too long. The other risk, and this one can be difficult to detect and can be perpetrated for years, is making relatively small payments to shell companies they own, ordering items with your credit card, opening new lines of credit in your name, and hiring their friends on your behalf and overcharging for services. These are much harder to detect, but with systems in place, you'll be in a much better position to catch these and protect your wealth.

If you have anyone paying your bills – whether it is a business management firm or your bookkeeper – keep these ideas in mind:

1. **Open a separate bank account.** Instead of giving someone complete access to your bank account, you should set up a separate bank and checking account and give them access only to this account. Transfer money into this account each month to cover your monthly expenses and no more. This limits the amount of money your business manager has access to at any one time. If they were to steal your funds, they would be limited to one month's worth of bills.

2. **Use an account aggregation service.** Mint.com is a free service owned by Intuit that aggregates all of your financial accounts (e.g., bank, retirement, brokerage, mortgage, credit cards) into one consolidated view. There are other online companies that provide this service (my clients use 360 WealthView), but Mint.com is good for consumers who don't require a lot of advanced planning. To protect your wealth, set up email/text messages when withdrawals occur over a certain limit you specify. For example, you can be alerted when a check for more than $1,000 or $10,000 is written from your account. This keeps you on top of the activity in your accounts as things happen instead of having to wait for the monthly statement.

3. **Get copies/notifications on all accounts.** When you engage a business management firm to pay your bills, they will contact your vendors and credit card companies and have them send duplicate statements and invoices to them. As long as they are receiving duplicates, this is fine. However, you should confirm that you will also receive copies from the institutions. Why? Don't rely exclusively on the reports your business management firm produces for you. Although they may be easier to read than the bank or credit card statements you receive, you need to look at the original statements to reconcile your accounts.

4. **Limit authority.** When possible, limit the amount of authority you provide your business manager on your bank, investment, and other accounts. When available, give your business manager "inquiry only" access. This allows them to call on your account and ask questions, but won't give them the authority to change your address, open new accounts, or withdraw funds.

5. **Use a separate accounting firm.** Hire a separate accounting firm (many business managers work for accounting firms) or independent consultant to review your accounts, the statements the business manager provides, and double check the numbers each month.

6. **Limit check writing.** Give them check writing authority, but set a limit on the maximum size of the check they can write. This won't prevent them from writing multiple checks to the same payee, but it provides some protection from large single checks/withdrawals.

7. **Eliminate check writing.** You can free yourself from much of the hassle of paying bills while still staying in control by not giving your business manager access to your bank accounts or providing them with check writing authority. Instead, they can prepare a list of the invoices and the checks you need to write each month. This keeps you in full control while lessening the burden of bill paying.

8. **Conduct spot audits.** Either you or your assistant can call vendors randomly to confirm invoices and that bills were paid. If you get a report that a vendor has been paid but the vendor shows you are three months past due, there's a problem.

9. **Protect your credit.** Because business managers know your personal information and have access to your finances, it is possible for them to open credit cards or apply for loans in your name. To minimize this from occurring, consider signing up for a service such as Life-Lock, which freezes your credit and prevents anyone from opening accounts in your name. Also consider using a credit monitoring service. If you get reports that you are past due on payments, you will immediately know there's a problem.

Who's Got Your Back?

We worked with a client who came to us with substantial assets. The family had over $500 million of liquid investments from the sale of a business. The large investment bank who handled the transaction was also managing the assets. The family wanted an additional layer of investment oversight. They were not concerned with fraud, but they wanted another set of eyes reviewing the investments and portfolio decisions. In addition to discovering nearly 40% of their portfolio was invested in mortgage backed securities (this was 2005 and right before the meltdown in mortgage backed securities), the firm was receiving hundreds of thousands of dollars in transaction fees by marking up the bonds they sold to the client. Although this was not illegal or fraudulent, the client had no idea this was happening. If you have substantial assets, it may make sense to hire an independent firm to analyze and monitor your investments, fees, and your investment advisors. Visit wealthdefend.com to learn about *WealthDefend* — a completely independent service that doesn't replace your advisors but instead provides ongoing monitoring of your performance, risk, and asset allocation to make sure you are not falling behind, paying too much in fees, or that your investment advisor doesn't "go rogue" with your hard-earned money.

ESTATE PLANNING

Divorce isn't the only way you can lose 50% of your sudden wealth overnight. Estate taxes can deprive your family and heirs of nearly half of your net worth. As soon as you know you will be coming into sudden wealth, it is time to start a conversation with an estate planning attorney. In addition to the basic estate planning documents, such as a Will, Power of Attorney, and Living Will, you should also consider more advanced estate planning documents to protect your interests and to (legally) minimize estate taxes, including the living trust, family limited partnership, and an irrevocable life insurance trust.

LIVING TRUST

A Living Trust is the most common and basic of the advanced solutions discussed in this chapter. A Living Trust can have many names—Living Trust, revocable Living Trust, family trust, and inter vivos (Latin for "lifetime") trust. Regardless of the different names, a Living Trust is created when you are alive and is revocable —meaning you can modify or terminate it at any time.

A Living Trust has two benefits. It allows you to avoid probate and have greater control of your assets.

WHAT IS PROBATE?

Avoiding probate is a tremendous advantage, but unless you are familiar with the probate court process, you may not fully appreciate this benefit. Probate court is the state court that handles the orderly transfer of your assets according to your wishes as expressed in your will, or if you don't have a will, by the intestate laws of your state.

Not all of your assets need to go through probate. Any accounts that are held jointly with rights of survivorship are automatically transferred to the survivor, bypassing your will and avoiding probate. Transfer on death and payable on death accounts also bypass your will and avoid probate. Although there are things you can do to avoid probate for some of your assets, you won't be able to avoid probate on all of your assets unless you have a trust.

PROBLEMS WITH PROBATE

You may be thinking, "What's so wrong with probate?" Depending on the size of your estate and the laws of your state, the probate process can be time-consuming, difficult to navigate, expensive, and public.

1. Probate is time-consuming. For example, in the state of California, the probate process normally takes over six months and often exceeds a year. What does this mean for your loved ones? They won't have control of your assets until the probate process is completed— again, maybe 12 or 18 months after you pass away. If they need your assets before the probate is complete, they will be locked out. Would you rather give your loved ones full and immediate control of your assets or make them wait months and months?

A long and drawn-out probate process also puts additional stress on your family. Recovering from the death of a loved one is one of the hardest things to experience. Different cultures and people handle this process differently, but dealing with a six-, 12-, or 18-month probate process is not healthy and does not make it any easier for those you care about.

The Living Trust Solution. The Living Trust is like a will on steroids. Like a will, it specifically expresses your wishes but unlike a will, it doesn't require probate to oversee the transfer of your assets.

2. Probate is expensive. If you go through probate, there are certain fees you must pay. State laws vary considerably, but usually, these fees are based on a percentage of your assets going through probate and paying your attorney and the executor (the legal representative of the assets of the deceased in probate). These fees can be high — often $20,000, $30,000, or more.

The Living Trust Solution. Again, all of the assets in your Living Trust bypass probate court. Because your assets don't need to go through probate before they are distributed to your loved ones, you can avoid costly probate fees.

3. Probate is public. Remember, probate is a court proceeding. As a result, once the probate process is completed, the Will and the inventory of estate property is a public record and freely available for anyone to review. If privacy is important to you, a Living Trust is your only solution.

The Living Trust Solution. The initial formation of the Living Trust and the eventual disposition of assets from the trust is completely private. The Living Trust and the assets avoid the public nature of the probate court proceedings.

The bottom line is that if you can avoid probate, you should. Your loved ones will be going through enough without dealing with the bureaucracy, expense, and publicity of probate court.

LIVING TRUSTS OFFER MORE CONTROL OVER ASSETS

The second advantage a Living Trust has over a will is that it allows you to retain more control over your assets, both how and when they are distributed to your heirs. With a Will, once probate is complete, your heirs immediately receive your assets — in most states, children under the age of 18 receive their assets on their 18th birthday.

What's wrong with having your loved ones receive their inheritance immediately? In some circumstances, nothing. For example, if you have older and responsible adult heirs, this might not be much of a concern. However, there are many situations in which using a Living Trust to limit how and when your heirs receive assets makes more sense.

1. Underage children. If you just have a will, a guardian will be appointed over the assets you leave your underage children. The guardian will be responsible for managing these assets and using them for the benefit of the children. On the child's 18th birthday, the guardianship automatically terminates and the children receive full and immediate access to their assets.

It's often a mistake to receive an entire inheritance too quickly. Even the most mature 18-year-old is probably still in high school and unable to best choose how to use an inheritance. For families with underage children, even with a modest estate, I always recommend a Living Trust. What would you have done with thousands of dollars at 18?

In a Living Trust, you set the terms. You decide who is a beneficiary, what they receive, and when they receive it. Don't want Suzie to receive her inheritance until she is 30? You want Billy to receive 5% of his inheritance when he turns 18, 15% when he turns 25, 50% when he turns 30, and 30% when he turns 35? You can make these choices evident with a Living Trust. It's your money, you can control when your heirs receive it.

2. Unmotivated adult children. Even if your children are adults and into their 20s or 30s, you may still want to control when they receive their inheritance. An "unmotivated" child is an ambiguous label that could describe a child who can't hold down a job, dropped out of college, quits jobs to surf, or abuses drugs and alcohol — the core issue is an unwanted behavior that the parents do not want to support or encourage. If you have a child who is not mature or responsible enough to receive a complete inheritance today, a Will is not the appropriate estate tool for you.

You need the flexibility and control that only a Living Trust can provide, or as I like to call them when they are used in these situations, "motivational trusts." Control is the key advantage. You can add beneficiary requirements to your Living Trust. If you are concerned that a child will live off of their inheritance and lose all ambition to succeed on their own, you could structure the trust to pay out a percentage of your child's earned income. If Billy quits his job and decides not to work for a year, the trust wouldn't provide him with anything. If Billy gets his act together the following year and earns $40,000 at his job, the trust could pay out 50% of his income—another $20,000. This way, Billy has an incentive to develop a career rather than to live off of his trust fund. Or maybe you value higher education. Your motivational Living Trust could be written so that nothing is paid to your child until they graduate from college. Again, you can be as creative as you want to be with a Living Trust.

3. Spendthrift spouse. If you leave your assets to your spouse through a Will, your spouse will automatically receive your assets and be responsible for carefully managing them. If you are concerned that your spouse doesn't have the financial experience or skills to handle the family's finances if you pass away, a Will won't provide your family with the protection they need.

This is another example in which you need the control and flexibility of a Living Trust. In this situation, you can still leave all of your assets to your spouse, but with a Living Trust, you can require that an outside trustee manage the assets. This outside trustee would be hired at your passing to invest prudently and to supervise use of the assets. The outside trustee could be a friend or a bank with experience in these matters. This is an area fraught with emotional snares and should only be considered if you are comfortable discussing this option openly with your spouse and an experienced estate attorney.

4. Special-needs child. All loving parents want to protect and provide for their children. Parents of special-needs children often feel an even greater responsibility for their children because they know that even after their child becomes an adult, he or she may still require care, extra support, and supervision. As such, these parents have an increased need for advanced planning. Leaving your assets to your special-needs child through a Will has a couple of pitfalls. First, if you leave your assets to several of your children, they may all receive an equal share even though your special-needs child may have greater needs. Second, depending on the abilities of the special-needs child, he/she may have full access to his inheritance when he/she turns 18.

A Living Trust is a much better estate planning strategy when a special-needs child is involved. Instead of providing an inheritance of equal amount to each beneficiary, a trust can provide more support to the child with extra needs. For example, although one child may need funds to pay for summer camp, the special-needs child may require advanced treatment or the money to install an elevator. A Living Trust can adapt to changing needs whereas a Will cannot. As additional benefits, the assets in a Living Trust do not automatically pass to the child on their 18th birthday, and as a further precaution, a Living Trust can require an outside trustee to help manage the assets, regardless of the beneficiary's age.

5. Real estate owned out of state. If you own real estate in multiple states and use a simple Will, your loved ones will be forced to go through probate court in every state where you own property. As you've already read, probate court can be frustrating, time-consuming, complex, expensive, public, and your loved ones can experience significant delays in receiving their inheritance. These issues are magnified when your loved ones must probate assets in more than one state.

Real estate owned in a Living Trust avoids probate entirely, regardless of the state in which it is owned. If you have real estate in multiple states, a Living Trust is the only logical choice. You can save your loved ones an incredible amount of time and energy by avoiding multi-state probate proceedings.

When You <u>Don't</u> Want To See Your Advisor On TV

Large family offices and investors with significant assets often employ auditors who scour the deposits, withdrawals, fees, and transactions in their accounts to make sure they are being credited appropriately and to be sure there are no mistakes or maleficence. But employing a bookkeeper adept at detecting fraud does not come cheap, and for investors who cannot justify such a big expense, they have historically been on their own to comb through cash flow reports and monthly statements. Fortunately there are other options. See if your CPA is up to the task or hire an independent bookkeeper if they have experience in this area. Look for a Certified Fraud Examiner designation. Visit wealthdefend.com to learn about *WealthDefend* — a completely independent and out-sourced service that will audit your investment accounts to ensure you don't wake up one morning and see your advisor on CNBC being hauled off to jail for defrauding clients.

FAMILY LIMITED PARTNERSHIP

The use of a Family Limited Partnership (FLP) to protect your sudden wealth was discussed earlier, but FLPs can also minimize estate taxes. It's called a Family Limited Partnership because ownership of the partnership is typically limited to members of the same family. The

FLP is a partnership with two types of owners, at least one general partner and at least one limited partner. The general partner or partners have control of the partnership and are given voting and management responsibilities. Basically, the general partners call all of the shots — they have full and complete control of the assets in the FLP and the limited partners are along for the ride. They can't vote and have no control over how the assets are managed.

The primary objective of an FLP is to reduce the size of the family's estate in order to lessen the estate tax on the assets, while also allowing the parents to retain full control of the assets.

There are two ways an FLP can reduce or eliminate the estate tax:

1. **Discount for lack of marketability.** All things being equal, would you rather own an investment that you could quickly and easily sell through a large market of buyers or an investment that would be difficult or impossible to sell because there is no market of potential buyers? In other words, would you rather own $10,000 of Microsoft stock or $10,000 of a company that you've never heard of and that no one would ever buy from you? Of course, it would be better to own an investment you could actually sell. Owners of an FLP are at a disadvantage. Who in the world would ever buy your interest in Joe Smith's FLP? As a result of this limitation, the IRS lets you reduce the value of the FLP. For example, let's say assets valued at $2 million are transferred into an FLP. As soon as they are in the FLP, they are considered to be worth less than $2 million because the owners would have a hard time selling their partnership interest. The discount may be 15%, 20%, or even more.

2. **Discount for lack of control.** Control is valuable. The limited partners in an FLP have no control over the operations of the FLP, how the assets are invested, or when to distribute partnership income. The limited partners are essentially powerless. As a result of this lack of control, owning an interest in an FLP is not as valuable as owning an interest in an investment where you have complete control. The IRS allows a discount for lack of control, usually between 20% and 30%. To determine the "lack of marketability" or the "lack of control discount," work with an experienced estate attorney familiar with valuing FLPs.

Like all of the estate strategies discussed in this chapter, there are advantages and disadvantages to each. What may work well for one family and one situation may not work for another. That is why it is important for you to work with an experienced estate attorney to analyze the pros and cons of each strategy and to help create an estate plan that meets your needs and objectives.

IRREVOCABLE LIFE INSURANCE TRUST

An Irrevocable Life Insurance Trust (ILIT) sounds more complicated than it is. Life insurance proceeds are not subject to income tax. If you are the beneficiary of a $10 million life insurance policy, you don't have to pay a single dime of income tax. This is one of the tremendous advantages of life insurance.

Life insurance has a dark side that is rarely discussed. Although the beneficiary of a life insurance policy receives the sum without paying tax, the full value of the death benefit is included in the estate of the deceased. For example, Cathy is insured for $10 million and Beth is the beneficiary on the policy. When Cathy dies, the insurance company will issue a check payable to Beth for the full $10 million. Beth doesn't report the $10 million and isn't taxed on it. So far, so good. When it comes time to complete Cathy's estate tax return, the executor will list all of Cathy's assets—including the $10 million life insurance policy. Cathy's life insurance policy increased her estate by $10 million. Now, Cathy's loved ones may be subject to an estate tax approaching 50% on Cathy's estate.

This is where an ILIT is used. Instead of Cathy being the insured party and the owner of the policy, Cathy could create an ILIT and have it own the policy. At Cathy's death, Beth would still receive the $10 million tax-free, but it wouldn't be included in Cathy's estate because she didn't own it, the ILIT did.

If you already own a sizable life insurance policy and want to remove it from your estate, you can transfer it to an ILIT. Warning: Based on peculiar estate tax laws, if you die within three years following the policy's transfer to the ILIT, the value of the life insurance proceeds will still be included in your estate. If you haven't yet purchased the life insurance policy, have the ILIT purchase it, and then the three-year "look-back" rule won't apply. If you transfer a policy, you have to wait three years from when you owned it for the value to not be included in your estate, but if an ILIT purchases the policy, you never owned it so the three-year rule doesn't apply.

The theory behind an ILIT is pretty straightforward, but it can become much more complex. There are many rules and limitations that, if broken, can jeopardize the tax benefits of an ILIT. Be sure to consult with an experienced estate attorney if you think you might benefit from an ILIT.

This was a long chapter with new terminology and lots of details. It's natural to want to skip this principle, but I urge you to find good advisors to help you protect your assets. Your sudden wealth can abruptly vanish if you neglect this principle.

But for many sudden wealth recipients, it's not enough to just protect their new wealth. They want their money to appreciate over time to fund their lifestyle and to create a legacy for their family. The next chapter will help you grow your new wealth.

GROW WEALTH

Learn strategies to grow your wealth.

In this chapter, you will learn how to avoid many of the investing mistakes beginners and even experts alike make. After you pass through the anticipation of receiving the money (Stage 1), and the flurry of activity of getting accounts set up, taxes paid, and documents drafted (Stage 2), you enter Stage 3. Aside from occasional tweaks to your plan, investing and monitoring are what Stage 3 is all about. But for the uninitiated, investing can seem like gambling and too complicated to understand. I can assure you, investing is neither.

There are many excellent introductory books on investing, so I will leave the lesson on the basics of investing to others. But there are several topics related to investing that are unique to sudden wealth recipients that you should be aware of, including:

1. If you need to invest.
2. Which investments are okay and which are off limits.
3. How to create a monthly automatic paycheck.

DO YOU NEED TO INVEST?

The majority of sudden wealth recipients need their money to grow over time. There are those rare sudden wealth events when the windfall is so large that the client can pay for their lifestyle and do all the things they want without needing any growth. For everyone else, growth needs to come from investing. The question is, which camp are you in?

Clients have found it helpful and illuminating when we talk in terms of three possible scenarios: (1) they have more than enough money to meet their needs and fund their goals, (2) they have just enough money, or (3) they don't have enough money. The position you are in will dictate, at least in part, how you should invest your money.

HOW TO INVEST WHEN YOU HAVE MORE THAN ENOUGH MONEY

When you have more than enough money to meet your lifestyle needs and to fully cover all of your goals, you do not need to take as much risk with your investments. It's important that your financial advisor run and re-run several scenarios based on your living expenses and goals to ensure you have more than enough assets even with minimal growth in your portfolio. If you do indeed have more assets than you need, take a conservative approach with your money. There's no need to take too much risk because you don't need to rely on investment growth to cover the necessities.

Consider an asset allocation with a nominal percentage of stocks and growth assets and more individually held bonds and other sources of lower-risk fixed income. Your appetite for risk, the economic outlook, and current market fundamentals should dictate your allocation, but as a general rule of thumb, you can afford to take less risk with your portfolio. Ironically, you can also afford to take more risk. For example, some sudden wealth recipients with more money than they need will invest the majority of their portfolio conservatively, and then take a small percentage, an amount they could comfortably afford to lose, and invest it in higher risk ventures and investments such as private equity or limited partnerships. These kinds of investments take a greater degree of sophistication, not just on your part, but on the part of your advisors. Most financial advisors do not have the experience or expertise to determine whether they are good investments or how to value them.

HOW TO INVEST WHEN YOU HAVE JUST ENOUGH TO MEET YOUR GOALS

When you have just enough to meet your goals, you have to walk a fine line between taking too little and too much risk. If you are too conservative and don't make an investment return large enough to keep up with inflation or your living expenses, you may have to cut your expenses. On the other hand, if you take too much risk and lose part of your portfolio, you may also have to cut your expenses.

The key here is to create an asset allocation that provides the possibility for growth while providing enough cash to cover your living expenses in the short term. This strategy limits the possibility you will have to sell depreciated assets at a loss just to cover your expenses at the same time. The mechanics of this strategy will be discussed later in the chapter.

HOW TO INVEST WHEN YOU DON'T HAVE ENOUGH

If your sudden wealth is not enough to cover your living expenses and goals, you are in good company. This scenario is the most common and is what non-sudden wealth recipients face when they save for retirement. They know what they want their retirement life to look like, but they don't yet have enough saved. So they work, save, and invest to meet their target – often for several decades.

Some sudden wealth recipients who wish they could quit their jobs but can't afford it decide they want to become their own boss. They will start a business or invest in a franchise. In certain circumstances, this can work because it gives them more control while providing an income at the same time. There are numerous dangers in starting your own business and investing in a franchise (as you will read later), but it can work.

GREEN, YELLOW, AND RED INVESTMENTS

Investing doesn't have to be complicated and you don't need to take excessive amounts of risk to generate a decent return. The problem is that many sudden wealth recipients lose their money by making bad investments. If I had to guess, I'd say 95% or even more of bad investment decisions that end up losing all of their value could be avoided by sticking to a simple rule:

Invest in green investments, be cautious of yellow investments, and avoid red investments.

GREEN INVESTMENTS

Green investments, just like yellow, red, or any investment, can lose all of their value. In other words, a green investment can go to zero. What makes it a green investment is that it provides more liquidity, regulatory oversight, transparency, and accessible information than other investments.

The bulk of your investment portfolio should consist of green investments, such as:

1. **Mutual funds.** A mutual fund is a portfolio of other investments. For example, a single mutual fund may own 50, 100, or even 500 different stocks. Your one investment in the fund provides an investment into these holdings.

2. **Exchange traded funds.** Similar to a mutual fund, an exchange traded fund ("ETF") is a single security that contains other investments.

3. **Certificates of deposit.** Commonly referred to as CDs, these are loans mostly to banks that are typically FDIC insured.

4. **Fixed annuities.** A fixed annuity is an insurance contract that promises to pay you a certain amount of income, similar to a loan or bond. Fixed annuities are safe investments that can add stability and a fixed amount of income to a portfolio. Just be careful of high fees.

5. **Individual bonds.** If you have a large enough portfolio, owning individual bonds (as opposed to a mutual fund of bonds) has a couple of benefits. You can create a portfolio that is customized to your needs and if you hold until maturity, you get your principal back.

6. **REITs.** Real Estate Investment Trusts (REITs) are similar to mutual funds but this "basket" holds real estate.

7. **Money market accounts.** These are similar to cash accounts.

Invest Like Harvard

Most large pension funds and college endowments use an Investment Policy Statement to set certain restrictions on how their portfolio is to be invested. You should also consider setting parameters with your financial advisor on how your portfolio should be managed. For example, the following are good rules of thumb:

1. No more than 5% of your total investment assets should be invested in a single investment security. Exception: Fixed income investments explicitly guaranteed by the U.S. government.

2. No more than 20% of your total investment assets should be invested in a single mutual fund or ETF. Exception: Passively managed investment vehicles seeking to match the returns on a broadly diversified market index.

3. With respect to fixed income investments, for individual bonds, the minimum average credit quality of these investments shall be investment grade (Standard & Poor's BBB or Moody's Baa or higher).

YELLOW

Yellow investments can still make sense for *part* of your portfolio, but be careful not to have too much invested in these types of investments:

1. **Individual stocks.** Undoubtedly, you'll want ownership in stocks through mutual funds and/or ETFs, but be careful not to direct too large a percent of your portfolio in individual stocks unless you have a large enough portfolio where you can create a diversified allocation.

2. **Focused ETFs.** Be wary of double market exposure ETFs that provide two times the market returns, or those ETFs that are concentrated in a single sector.

3. **Precious metals.** Metals such as gold and silver can be good hedges against inflation, but you shouldn't have a large allocation of precious metals.

4. **Variable annuities.** Unlike fixed annuities (a green investment), variable annuities should be used less frequently and only in specific circumstances.

5. **Whole life insurance.** Based on the size of your estate and your estate tax projections, you may want a permanent whole life insurance policy. Often these are sold as "investments," and in some circumstances, they may be appropriate, but use only in moderation and if there is a need for the insurance.

6. **Hedge funds.** Hedge funds are like ice cream. There are hundreds of flavors. Some are conservative whereas others swing for the fences. The hedge fund as an investment vehicle is yellow because of the high fees, lack of transparency, and illiquidity. Be careful.

7. **Closed end mutual funds.** Like a regular open-ended mutual fund, closed funds invest in a basket of securities. However, closed-end funds have certain characteristics that make them less ideal for most investors. Use in moderation.

8. **Options (covered calls and long puts).** Options are a sophisticated investment that can be used to protect against losses and to increase your income.

RED

Investing and finance is fast-paced and exciting with high emotions and drama ... in the movies. In the real world, financial planning is slow and methodical. The glitz and glamour we think of on Wall Street doesn't translate into a good, long-term financial strategy. Red investments are sexy. They lure investors with their potential for huge returns and for their novelty. The following are Red because of the lack of liquidity, high volatility, and a track record for creating more bankruptcies than fortunes. Most sudden wealth recipients should avoid these unless you have a very large portfolio and can take a high amount of risk with 5% or so of your portfolio.

1. **Limited partnerships.** Limited partnerships ("LPs") are highly illiquid investments typically in private companies or real estate projects. Your money can be locked up for a decade or more and there will often be very little transparency.

2. **Private equity and venture capital.** The idea of getting into a hot tech company before it goes public is the dream of every investor, but the track record of private equity and venture capital is less than stellar. Your money can be locked up for years and you will have little idea what is going on behind the scenes.

3. **Individual private companies.** That company your brother-in-law wants to start or the iPhone app your personal trainer wants to create are both examples of private companies. If you haven't been already, you will be asked to invest in one (or probably many more) of these companies or ideas. Steer clear.

4. **Private loans.** Friends and family may also ask you to loan them money for business ventures or for personal reasons. Read and re-read Sudden Wealth Principle 6 and avoid personal loans.

5. **Options.** Covered calls and puts are yellow investments because they are good hedges for your portfolio, but selling puts and buying calls are considered red investments because they are an effective way to lose a lot of money. Avoid these kinds of options.

6. **Timeshares.** Now more euphemistically called "vacation ownership," these can barely be considered investments. Do not invest.

7. **Foreign currency.** Don't touch foreign currency investing or trading.

8. **Futures.** Avoid futures trading like the plague.

---

5 Ugly Investments To Avoid

Thinking about investing in one of these? Think again. Here are the top five private investments to avoid…

1. Restaurants. These take a lot of capital, time, and expertise and most do not make it more than a few years.

2. Mobile applications. Mark Cuban calls mobile apps the "most brutal business in the world."

3. Clothing. A few celebrities have done this successfully, but they usually have a big brand backing them. Fashion is fickle. Save your money.

4. Bars. If you want a place where everyone knows your name, invest in a bar. If you want to grow your money, don't.

5. Real estate development. Investing in real estate can be great way to build wealth, but investing in raw land with the hope of developing it is risky. It requires a substantial amount of capital and luck.

CREATING AN AUTOMATIC MONTHLY PAYCHECK

What happens when you've worked all your life and suddenly quit your job? When someone has a Level III Sudden Wealth event and decides to quit working, it can create a tremendous amount of anxiety because the paycheck they've come to expect disappears. "I know I have all of this money, but I'm worried that I don't have a check coming in," lamented one client. If you've relied on the certainty and predictability of a steady income your whole life, losing that can be difficult.

Many clients in this situation mistakenly think their income is tied to the stock market and how their investments do each month. If I had to rely on the week-to-week vagaries of the stock market to determine my monthly income, I'd be a nervous wreck, too! Fortunately, there is a solution that provides the same level of certainty and predictability of a paycheck without being tied to the stock market.

Your financial advisor can help you create a system that works best for you, but the general idea is as follows:

CASH BUCKET

Transfer cash equal to two years of living expenses into an account. Have your advisor schedule an automatic monthly transfer from this account into your checking account. This monthly transfer is your "paycheck." The monthly transfer is the same each month, so this provides certainty and also allows you to budget and not overspend. Another advantage is that you have two years' worth of cash so it doesn't matter how the market performs each month – you receive the same steady check.

LOW VOLATILITY BUCKET

Your next account should consist of CDs, low duration bonds, and other low volatility investments equal to three years' worth of living expenses. This is your feeder account, where you will shift funds from your Investment Bucket (described below) and your Cash Bucket. At the end of each year, convert one year's worth of living expenses to cash and transfer it to your Cash Bucket. This way, your Cash Bucket will always have sufficient cash to meet your monthly needs.

INVESTMENT BUCKET

This is your general investment account where you will have the rest and the bulk of your investments. Each year, you will convert one year's worth of living expenses to holdings that will be transferred into your Low Volatility Bucket.

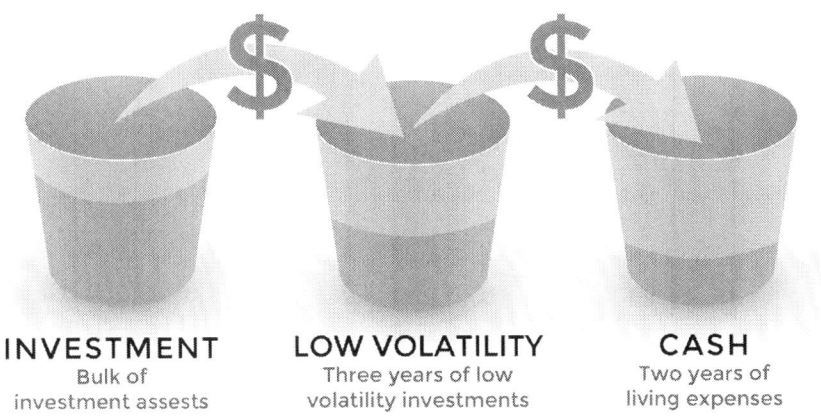

INVESTMENT   **LOW VOLATILITY**   **CASH**
Bulk of   Three years of low   Two years of
investment assests   volatility investments   living expenses

Each year, there is a shift of assets down the accounts to ensure you have plenty of cash and low risk investments to continue to fund your monthly paycheck.

Investment Cheat Sheet

With over 7,000 mutual funds, almost 5,000 ETFs, and over 10,000 individual stocks, it's hard to create hard and fast rules, but work with your advisor and do your best to keep these investment rules-of-thumb in mind…

1. Expense ratio of portfolio should be 1% or less. Use a combination of low-cost index funds and actively managed funds to get your investment expenses below 1% a year, and ideally, closer to 0.50%.

2. Management fee should be 1% or less. Fees advisors charge for financial planning and investment management vary widely based on the complexity of your situation and the amount of assets they will be investing. Stick to 1% or less.

3. Use no-load funds. Avoid mutual funds with front or back-end loads.

4. Seek daily liquidity. Unless you are investing in a CD, avoid investments that lock up your money for an extended period.

Once your financial and investment plan is in place, you should sit back and relax … but not for too long. Your plan needs constant attention, tweaking, and nurturing. It's one thing to start your journey in the right direction, but it's another to stay on track.

PRINCIPLE 12
STAY ON TRACK

Plug into an easy system to stay on track.

The goal of this Sudden Wealth Principle is to create an early warning detection system for your finances so if there is a problem, you become aware of it immediately and before it can cause too much damage. Sometimes, threats will come out of nowhere, and for these, you want to make sure your assets are protected, but many threats can be seen coming from a mile away. The problem is that many sudden wealth recipients (and their advisors) don't know what to look for and only see the problem after considerable, and sometimes irreparable, damage has been done.

Think of this last Sudden Wealth Principle as providing you with ongoing information about the state and health of your finances, like a dashboard provides you vital information about your car's oil pressure, temperature, and amount of gas you have left. Most people don't lose their sudden wealth overnight with one disastrous event – that is possible, but Sudden Wealth Principle 10 helped to minimize this risk. No, most sudden wealth is lost gradually over time as the bad decisions add up. But if you don't know how much you have, what you are spending, and how much you can afford, the red warning lights won't flash and you won't realize you have a problem until it's too late and you're on the side of the road with a dead car.

Sudden Wealth Principle 9 focused on making sure you know how much you have after taxes, expenses, and liabilities, as well as conservatively how much you could afford to spend each month without going broke. But you can't "set it and forget it." Things change and you need to adapt. It requires a continuous process, where you know how much you are spending each month and how much you can afford to spend.

Setting financial safeguards and staying on track is one of the most important principles of sudden wealth, but it is also one of the most neglected. The reason you read so many riches to rags stories is because either the sudden wealth recipients never created a financial plan or they created the financial plan but didn't stay on track. This chapter will help you (and your advisors) create the framework that provides the oversight, reports, and "early warning detection system" to ensure you make changes when necessary to stay on track.

Stop Before You HALT

If you've ever tried to break a bad habit or stop yourself from doing something you knew was harmful, you know how difficult it can be. If you find yourself driven to spend but cannot seem to control the urge, research by psychologist Dr. Roy Baumeister may provide important clues on how to create lasting willpower. Dr. Baumeister likens willpower to a gas tank. We wake up each morning with a fixed supply. Throughout the day, events and stress can "use up" our willpower, leaving us drained and less likely to stick to a plan. He has identified four states that suck the self-control from us with the aptly worded acronym HALT – Hunger, Anger, Loneliness, and Tiredness. If you are prone to over-spending and find that you go on spending binges, do whatever you can to prevent them. If you are hungry, angry, lonely, or tired, it can make sticking to a spending plan nearly impossible.

TRACK YOUR SPENDING AGAINST YOUR TARGET INCOME

In Sudden Wealth Principle 9, you determined how much you could comfortably withdraw from your portfolio each year to live on. If your goals and desired lifestyle exceeded your projected income, you needed to reduce your expenses to match the income you could withdraw. The danger I've witnessed time and time again is called expense creep. This is where a client will start off with expenses that match their income, but over time, their expenses increase and they start spending more than they can afford. This is why a "set it and forget it" approach is dangerous.

You must continuously track your spending against your withdrawal rate. Every month, you should see how much you've spent and how much you've withdrawn. A month or two does not make a trend, but if you see several months of increasing outflows, you can make adjustments before too much damage is done.

Again, the reason this Sudden Wealth Principle is so critical is because it can prevent large and unrecoverable financial losses. The statistics on sudden wealth are horrible – a large percentage of sudden wealth recipients go through all of their money quickly – but by tracking your spending against your income each month, you can avoid becoming another statistic.

One of the greatest joys sudden wealth recipients report is that they can stop clipping coupons and pinching pennies. It can be a burden to have to watch where every dollar goes each month, so it's natural for some to want to avoid all forms of budgeting after they receive their sudden wealth. Fortunately, most sudden wealth recipients don't need to budget or keep detailed notes of their spending in the same way, but you will want to keep abreast of where your money is going.

I prefer when a client, or their bookkeeper, keeps track of their expenses using a software program such as QuickBooks or Quicken because it provides the details. Clients may not care, but it allows me to spot trends and to make better projections. For example, it's a red flag when I see a client's basic living expenses increasing and/or when their fixed expenses are increasing. In either situation, the client loses his/her flexibility to reduce these expenses. If they remain high, especially if their basic living expenses are approaching the maximum portfolio withdrawal rate, we need to take immediate action.

At a minimum, review your monthly withdrawals with your advisor to make sure you are staying within the plan. This is especially important in the beginning, as you are becoming used to your new lifestyle and income level. With time and experience, you can review this every quarter.

MONTHLY REPORTS

Stay on track by reviewing a couple of key reports each month. The first is your net worth, which you calculated in chapter 9. You'll want to review your net worth at least once a month in the beginning, and then as you become more comfortable, at least once a quarter. Your net worth shows you your assets and your liabilities. If you are spending too much and having to withdraw funds from your investment accounts or if you increased your liabilities, this will be reflected in your net worth.

You shouldn't be concerned about fluctuations in your monthly net worth, but you are looking for trends and issues so you can make adjustments sooner rather than later. If you or your advisors don't track this closely, monthly declines could continue for months, or even years, and can erode your wealth.

In addition to a net worth report, you should also review your investment accounts. These accounts will experience volatility, going up and down each month, but you should still be aware of what is happening. I've found that the clients who are most nervous about investing become much more comfortable just by reviewing what is happening in their accounts.

Your advisor can create these reports for you or you can use an online system that will provide you with an updated net worth and investment snapshot at any time. My clients use a web-based system we call 360 WealthView to see real-time reports from their computer or phone. Regardless of the system you use, make sure you make a point to review it monthly.

FLASH ACCESS TO YOUR ADVISOR

Note: Not all financial advisors will agree to this, but I think it's invaluable for new sudden wealth recipients. Clients who experience a windfall are thrust into new and foreign situations. If they've never had to deal with complex tax, legal, or financial issues, it can all be overwhelming. The one thing that can alleviate their anxiety and uncertainty more than anything else is to be able to ask a question or voice a concern to someone who understands them and their situation.

As I've written about throughout this book, the worst thing you can do is make decisions when you are feeling stressed. If you are feeling unsure or stressed, contact your advisor to prevent bad decisions. I've talked many clients "off the ledge." Sometimes, they are considering a large purchase and want a second opinion, and other times, they just want reassurance.

Talk to your advisor and ask them if they will be available for after-hour emails, text messages, or phone calls. As long as it is not a daily occurrence, your advisor should agree to this. I want my clients to call me whenever they have an issue, even if it's Saturday at 9pm. I want them to know I'm always accessible, and often, it's enough just knowing that they can talk to someone if they get into a bind.

My firm created a mobile app that lets clients reach us immediately via email, text, or phone, but at a minimum, ask for your advisor's cell phone number and use it if you feel the need.

Spendbump?

I created a web-based mobile app called SpendBump that is designed to slow a client's spending. If they are going to make a big purchase or are concerned they are spending too much, they can reach an advisor immediately to discuss the details to make sure they stay on track financially.

REVIEW SYSTEM FOR LARGE EXPENSES

Another way to stay on track is to not get off track. Some sudden wealth recipients adapt quickly to their new situation and stick closely to their spending plan, but others struggle. If you find that you are making impulse purchases and/or are consistently spending too much, consider creating a spending review system with your advisor. For example, make a commitment that you will review all purchases over a certain amount with him before you buy, allow for a "cooling off" period between the impulse and the purchase, or both. If you find yourself trying on jewelry you know you can't afford, call your advisor or delay the purchase until you can talk to him.

When Shopping Hurts – How To Control Excessive Shopping

I've worked with people from vastly different backgrounds who have had excessive shopping issues, from sudden wealth recipients to the unemployed and destitute, who cannot control their shopping addiction. Dr. Drew and I recently worked with a young woman who was a self-diagnosed shopaholic. Her shopping addiction can provide valuable lessons for the rest of us.

First, it's important to understand what doesn't work. A shopping addiction is not a disease of intellect, it's a disease of emotion. Unfortunately, most family members, along with mental health and financial "experts," make things worse by focusing on the two areas that usually lead to even more shopping: shame and logic. What's wrong with you?! Don't you know better? How can you be so self-centered? Trying to use logic —if you spend too much, you won't have money to make the car payment—tends to be just as ineffective.

Such "cures" don't work. Shopaholics already feel badly about themselves, and they already know they can't afford it. Criticism often leads to people feeling even more socially isolated, which they "treat" by shopping. So what does work?

1. Identify the shopping trigger. What activates a person's urge to shop – boredom, guilt, shame, anger? Keep a written journal or electronic record and document what leads to the shopping.

2. Discover the need shopping fills. Excessive shopping doesn't serve a functional purpose as you probably don't need 15 purses. Instead, it serves a psychological purpose by meeting an unfilled or under-filled need. For the non-shopaholic, it may look like "crazy" or irrational behavior. It's not. The shopaholic is often entirely rational. They shop for a reason – it fulfills a need, so they keep doing it.

No matter what you do, if you don't find an alternative and healthier way to fill this need, the shopping urge won't fade. So the first step in halting compulsive shopping is to identify the psychological need driving it. Does the shopping provide pleasure, or does it help you avoid pain? In other words, do you shop to feel something you don't feel anywhere else throughout the day (a rush, excitement, variety, stimulation, being in control, feeling naughty), or do you shop to avoid feeling something negative, such as anxiety, loneliness, or fear? Determine what part of the shopping provides the reward. Is it going with friends (social)? Is it being around others (community)? Is it searching for things? Is it feeling significant? Does the shopping create relationship conflicts so you receive attention or feel a sense of connection, albeit negative? It takes an open mind and guts to analyze yourself like this, but it often provides the answer.

3. Replace shopping with something healthier. The shopaholic needs to find a healthier alternative to filling the need. Brainstorm how you could fill this need in other ways. Often, you'll find that someone with one addiction will trade it for another addiction. This is not a positive long-term solution. The goal is to trade in a negative and destructive addiction for one that is positive and healthy, or at least neutral. Sometimes, it's just not enough to replace shopping with a healthier habit. In this case, figure out what's more important than shopping. What do you value most in life? Your children, spouse, security, prestige? Whatever it is, you must link how continuing to shop will destroy what you value most. If you value the love from your family and friends, it's easy to see how that you will ruin these relationships if you keep borrowing and spending.

4. Change your environment. Our environment plays a huge role in our behavior. If you keep a bowl of jellybeans on your desk, it's clear what you will snack on throughout the day. Use the environment to your advantage. It makes no sense for the alcoholic to "test" their willpower by having a snack at their local bar, and it makes no sense for the shopaholic to be in shopping malls. Create "no-fly zones" – places you can't go, such as malls, stores, and other shopping areas. You want to remove any ambiguity in your rules. If you don't, then in the heat of the moment, the shopaholic will rationalize a way to shop. Make a list of the places you can and cannot go. Eliminate any TV watching (at least in the beginning), and stay away from magazines and newspapers. You basically want to remove any cues from the environment to shop.

5. Get support. Kicking an addiction is hard to do alone. Get some help from friends, family, or others. Debtors Anonymous is a great resource, and they have groups in cities across the country.

6 DEADLY SUDDEN WEALTH SINS

Sudden wealth can be a wonderful opportunity to create a better life for yourself and others. Many sudden wealth recipients manage this process deftly and with few issues. It's critically important to stay on track and to adjust your plan when necessary. It's also important to stay away from these six common sudden wealth sins, which have led to many bankruptcies...

1. **Spend too much.** It may be incomprehensible for someone who was making $50,000 a year to go broke after receiving a $10 million windfall, but it happens. It might not disappear in a year or two, but if the person is consistently making bad financial decisions, they can go through the money in less than a decade – and much quicker if they also engage in one of the other sudden wealth sins below.

The principles in this book will help you avoid this fate. Go slow, work with experts, figure out how much you can spend, and then stay on track. If you still have problems, work with a therapist or money psychologist. The few hundred you spend learning about your triggers and underlying issues will be one of the best investments you could make.

2.   **Give too much.** Sudden wealth recipients who spend too much on themselves will often give too much as well. When confronted with giving too much to family, one client confessed, "I feel guilty having this new house and stuff when the rest of my family is still struggling. I can't enjoy what I have unless I give them what I have." There are often familial pressures and hidden expectations to take care of the family that can weigh on the person. Helping those in need and others to create a better life for themselves can be one of the most rewarding uses of your windfall, but there is a limit to what you can do.

     Stick to your spending plan, help the right way, and stay on track with monthly reports. Work with your advisors to create a long-term and sustainable plan to assist your family. Have your advisors become involved in the discussions with your family, if necessary.

3.   **Divorce.** As was discussed in Sudden Wealth Principle 10, divorce can wipe out 50% or more of your wealth overnight. Divorce is also one of the most common reasons why sudden wealth recipients lose their money. Protect yourself with co-habitation, prenuptial, and postnuptial agreements. Work with a family law attorney to ensure you have some protection against separation or divorce.

4.   **Invest badly.** A common and large source of loss for sudden wealth recipients is making bad investment decisions. Many smart people have made bad decisions and have invested too much of their sudden wealth in red investments. Avoid these and stick to mostly green and occasionally some yellow investments. Work closely with your advisors to review each investment – especially those that are yellow or red.

5.   **Fraud.** The Bernie Madoff Ponzi scheme proved that you cannot trust anyone. Madoff was a highly respected investor and was once chairman of the NASDAQ stock market. The onus is on you to create a system of checks

and balances to protect your money. Follow the guide-lines in Sudden Wealth Principle 10 as a starting point. Also, never invest in a company or venture your advisor recommends in which he is also involved.

A few years ago, a wealthy client came to my firm for wealth management advice. Shortly in the relationship, the client presented us with an investment pitch he received from one of his advisors. We reviewed the pitch and spoke to the company, but we couldn't figure out how they were making money and they couldn't defend their lofty investment projections. We politely but firmly suggested to our new client that he not make the investment. Our relationship with the client was new, and he had a relationship with his other advisor for years. Therefore, he decided to make a substantial investment. Fast forward just a year later and the account was wiped out. The company squandered the money and our client was left with nothing but a costly civil lawsuit.

6.   **Lawsuit.** In an instant, all of your assets could be in jeop-ardy if they are not protected. Lawsuits are all too com-mon, especially for people who have wealth. Your sudden wealth makes you a larger and more visible target. Work with an asset protection attorney to shield your assets from creditors and lawsuits.

One of the most successful ways to stay lean is not diet. All it requires is weighing yourself each morning. If you are more than three pounds from your target weight, you simply eat less until you fall back into your ideal range. By weighing yourself each day, you can stay on track and make minor adjustments before too much time has passed and too much damage has been done.

Stay on track with your financial plan so you, too, can make minor adjustments and so you and your future generations can enjoy your sudden wealth.

THE SUDDEN
WEALTH EVENTS

THE SUDDEN WEALTH EVENTS

There are an unlimited number of ways to create gradual wealth, but only a handful of ways to create sudden wealth – each has its own characteristics, opportunities, and challenges. There are different ways to categorize these events, such as by most common, speed of the windfall, ability to anticipate the event, or emotional reaction, just to name a few. I've found, however, the best way to think of sudden wealth events is by splitting them into two categories: those where the money is a result of a loss and those where the money is the result of a gain.

For example, sudden wealth from a loss – the death of a spouse, an injury, or sale of a business – can create certain feelings and issues around the money that are often profoundly different from sudden wealth that arises from a gain, such as lottery proceeds, stock, or a performance contract.

LOSS

1. **Inheritance.** The advantage with an inheritance is that the process to receive the money is usually straightforward and there are few, if any, taxes due. Two potential issues with an inheritance are that the process can take a year or more, and depending on the source of the inheritance, there can be emotional baggage that comes with the money.

2. **Divorce.** It's important to note that only some divorces produce sudden wealth. If there are few assets or if both parties in the divorce have experience paying bills and managing the assets, this would not be considered sudden wealth. A divorce can be a type of sudden wealth when one spouse, often referred to as the "out spouse" – a term for the spouse that hasn't been involved in paying the bills, managing the investments, buying insurance, budgeting, or who doesn't have the relationship with the family attorney, CPA, or financial advisor – is now responsible for managing an amount of property and assets, which causes them anxiety and insecurity.

3. **Lawsuit.** Insurance settlements, lawsuit judgments, or lawsuit settlements are common sources of sudden

wealth. There are several challenges with lawsuits, however. The biggest complaint is that the legal process can be complicated, intrusive, and long – sometimes as long as several years or even a decade. Because of this, it keeps clients in limbo for an extended period, which is not healthy because they experience a roller-coaster ride of "they're going to settle" to "they decided to appeal." They never really know if they are going to get the money until it is wired into their accounts. Couple the long and often intrusive legal process with the fact that to receive an insurance settlement or judgment, you or a loved one had to have experienced some kind of loss, and you can see the challenges of lawsuit sudden wealth.

What About The Sale Of A Business?

When a business owner sells a business that they nurtured over years or even decades, and where the business represents a significant amount of their identity, it can feel like a profound loss when they sell it. Although all of the Sudden Wealth Principles apply to windfalls from a business sale, this type of sudden wealth will not be addressed specifically in Section II of this book for two reasons. First, the business owner has often spent years or even decades building their business and they possess the financial sophistication to handle the sudden wealth with much greater ease than others. Second, selling a business is highly technical, and I wouldn't be able to adequately address all of the tax, legal, and financial issues in a single chapter.

GAIN

1. **Lottery.** The lottery is typically what people think of when they think of sudden wealth, but comparatively speaking, the other types of sudden wealth are much more common. The lottery gets all of the attention, though, and this can create some unique challenges for the winner because most of the time, the lottery winner cannot remain anonymous. Winners are usually thrust into the spotlight, whether they want to or not. Additionally, much has been written about how most lottery winners lose it all, but this doesn't have to be the case. Yes, there are real challenges lottery winners face, but if they stick to

these 12 Sudden Wealth Principles, they can create a rich and sustainable life.

2. **Sports and entertainment contracts.** Athletes and entertainers have unique tax, legal, and financial challenges. This is a sudden wealth type that requires a great deal of management and coordination with the client's attorneys, accountants, agents, business managers, and financial advisors. One of the most important goals is to amass enough wealth in case their professional career is shortened.

3. **Stock options.** Stock options can turn an ordinary 9-5 employee into a multi-millionaire overnight. Tech IPOs are the most publicized, but there are many other industries that create sudden wealth. Stock option planning requires narrow but deep expertise in taxes and the law. As was mentioned earlier, many sudden wealth clients find they are in "Stage 1: Pre-Money" for a year or more. This provides the advantage of allowing them to prepare, but it also creates a great deal of uncertainty regarding how much money they will receive.

There are other types of sudden wealth events, such as windfalls from retirement packages, insurance settlements, and oil/gas rights. I'll include information on the specific tax, legal, and financial issues for these sudden wealth events at suddenwealthsolution.com. For now, the chapters that follow will use a question and answer format to dive deeper into some of the major issues unique to each of the six sudden wealth events discussed above.

SUDDEN WEALTH
INHERITANCE

Building a new financial plan.

The most common form of sudden wealth is from inheritance. According to the Boston College Center for Retirement Research, two-thirds of baby boomers will receive an inheritance and the figures are staggering – baby boomers alone will inherit $7.6 trillion over their lifetime! What's even more staggering is how quickly this wealth disappears. The *Wall Street Journal* reports that family money rarely survives the transfer for long, with 70% evaporated by the end of the second generation and 90% by the end of the third[13].

Why is so much family wealth spent down so quickly and how can you make the most of your inheritance? The goal of this book and this chapter is to help you make the best decisions you can with your sudden wealth. I've worked with many clients who have received their sudden wealth through an inheritance over the past two decades. Although each situation was different, what is common to nearly all of them is the weight of the inheritance the clients felt.

Unlike the other forms of sudden wealth, a death is necessary for an inheritance. There are stories of people receiving an unexpected phone call about a long-lost relative who passed away and left them a small fortune, but far more common is when the inheritor is close to the person who passed away. A death can be difficult for anyone to navigate, but add in a large inheritance and it can become even more complicated.

An inheritance can be a welcome surprise or it can be a sad reminder of who they lost. A large inheritance that pushes you out of your financial comfort zone can create anxiety about how to best manage the money. Clients have reported that they feel a sense of gravitas and responsibility – that they need to be extra careful with the inheritance. Some have said that even though they know it is their money and that they can do what they want with it, it feels borrowed.

Another critical factor with integrating the money into their life is the source of the inheritance. A death and subsequent inheritance can evoke a wide range of feelings that cause the recipient to treat the money differently, depending on their relationship with the deceased. If the relationship was troubled or if the death was premature, it is not uncommon to see the recipient consciously or unconsciously disown the money and divest it by spending lavishly or making risky investments.

HOW WE RESPOND TO AN INHERITANCE

However, not all sudden wealth recipients react the same to an inheritance. In my experience, beneficiaries respond to the money in one of three ways:

ACCEPTANCE

Good or neutral relationships with the deceased often generate a healthy response to new found wealth. They accept the money, and although they may still have a strong emotional connection to the deceased, they don't displace these feelings on the money. They view their grief separately and hold no grudge on the money. They hold a healthy view of what the inheritance means – it won't magically relieve their grief, but it isn't responsible for the loss either.

Accepting the money is the healthiest response. They are able to enjoy the benefits of the money without any negative emotions or guilt.

CONFLICTED

Others feel conflict over the money. They may appreciate the value it provides but it still creates feelings of anger, sadness, or guilt. They use the inheritance to better their lives, but the money feels like a bribe. It is hard for them to separate the money from the loss. The new house they were able to buy from the settlement is a constant reminder of the loss or injury. They have a hard time enjoying the money or what it has provided because it is a constant reminder of their pain.

Time and distance from the loss can help alleviate some of the conflict, as can speaking to a therapist or money psychologist, to separate the pain from the money.

REJECTION

A third response some inheritors take is to disassociate themselves from the inheritance. This can occur because of the grief surrounding the loss or if they inherited the money from an abusive parent, for example. Either consciously or unconsciously, instead of trying to separate the pain from the money, they simply try to separate themselves from the money. They are in so much pain that they think they will experience a reprieve by eliminating the money. This can take the form of giving the money away, spending recklessly, or taking excessive risk.

If their advisors aren't aware of what's happening, they will think the client is just being foolish with their money. They're not. What they're doing makes perfect sense, but if they continue, they will accomplish their "goal" and run out of money.

If you have strong negative feelings about your inheritance, start by putting a temporary freeze on your spending. Ask your financial advisor to help you create systems that will support your desire to spend less. Then work with a therapist or money psychologist. You won't get emotional clarity around the money overnight – it will take time and work – but the sooner you get started, the sooner you will have a healthier reaction to the money and can start to use it to improve your life and the lives of those around you. If you are going to spend part of your inheritance, you should at least be able to enjoy it.

Q—*I inherited an investment account. What should I do with it?*

A—One of the pitfalls you want to avoid when inheriting investments is hanging on to assets that aren't appropriate for your asset allocation or risk profile. A few years ago, a client inherited a $65 million position in a large and well known technology company. After several months of meetings and deliberation, we were finally able to convince her that having most of her net worth tied to one company's stock was too risky. We entered into a variable prepaid forward contract hedging strategy to lock in the value of the stock and to protect against losses. Today, it's no longer a publicly traded stock. By looking at the inherited investment objectively in light of her other assets, the client was able to make a rational decision, which ended up saving her over $40 million in investment losses. Although you probably didn't inherit $65 million of stock from a single company, whatever you did inherit needs to be analyzed for appropriateness. Have your financial advisor run a risk analysis of each holding and the inherited portfolio as a whole. Look for investments that are too risky or just not appropriate. For example, if you live in California and inherited a portfolio of New York municipal bonds, they may not be right for you. Likewise, if you inherited municipal bonds but pay little income tax, you may be better off with taxable bonds.

> *If you inherited an investment you wouldn't have purchased yourself, sell it.*

In addition, often, an inheritance of investment assets will shift your asset allocation. For example, if your allocation is 60% to stocks and 40% to bonds and you inherit an all stock portfolio, this could bump your stock allocation to 80% and drag down your bond allocation to just 20%. Work with your financial advisor to make sure the influx of new assets doesn't shift your allocation beyond your target percentages in each asset class.

Also, make sure that each investment you inherited doesn't violate your investment parameters. For example, if you have a rule that you will not invest more than 20% of your total portfolio in any single mutual fund and you inherited a fund that represents 30% of your portfolio, you will need to sell part of the fund to bring its percentage down to, at most, 20%.

Lastly, review each investment to make sure it fits within your investment beliefs. For example, a client recently inherited a large portfolio of stocks, including a position in McDonalds. The problem with owning McDonald's stock? It didn't violate her risk tolerance or investment parameters, but it did violate her ethics . . . she is a vegan and doesn't support the eating of meat. If you feel strongly about tobacco, energy, defense, or other companies, carefully review what you inherited to be sure your investments reflect your investment morals.

Q—*I inherited a stock from my dad and my advisor thinks I should sell it, but I don't want to. What should I do?*

A—It's easy to see how someone could have an emotional attachment to the chair Dad always sat in, his fishing pool, or even the house in which you grew up in, but a stock? Yes, it is quite common to have an emotional attachment to a stock.

I'm never surprised when a client says, "I can't sell that stock. It was Dad's favorite." So, now I ask if there are any holdings that have an emotional connection, and more often than not, there are. If the stock holds sentimental value, and if it fits within your asset allocation and risk profile, then, by all means, keep it. However, if it doesn't fit or if it is too concentrated, sell it. If you can't bring yourself to sell all of it, sell some of it. Keep a handful of shares. Does it really matter if you have 100 shares or 10,000? Would the deceased want you to own it if he knew it wasn't right for you? Are there other ways to keep his legacy without jeopardizing your finances?

Q—*I received a large inheritance some time ago but haven't done anything with it. Is this okay?*

A—Absolutely. Don't feel pressured to do anything with your inheritance until you are ready. It's perfectly fine to take your time and, as Sudden Wealth Principle 2 encourages, to slow down. However, I've also seen people leave their inheritance in cash for decades or more. If you are pushing a year or two and haven't done anything with the inheritance, this may be fine, but it also may be because you are scared to do anything or are trying to pretend it isn't there. In either case, there is too much emotion wrapped around the money. It's normal to feel a sense of responsibility to do the right thing, but if you are feeling so much that it is paralyzing you from enjoying the inheritance or investing it, work with your advisor or therapist to get free of the weight it has over you. Consider starting small and gradually investing. Take a small part of your inheritance and invest it so you can see how the stock market works and so you can get a level of comfort. Buy CDs and have the interest deposited into your checking account so you can witness first-hand the power of investing. Use some of the inheritance on a trip or a toy. The idea is to break the emotional grip the inheritance has on you and for you to enjoy it.

Career Planning For The Multimillionaire

Receiving an inheritance at a young age can pose certain challenges. If you are young and have just inherited a large amount of money or have reached adulthood and now have access to a trust fund for your benefit, your friends may be planning their careers, but you may be conflicted. Do you get an entry level job and start your career even though you have millions in the bank and can afford to not work? Work with a therapist or career coach and brainstorm your passions and possibilities. You have the financial ability to focus on a life path that focuses on meaning and purpose and less on finances.

Q—*My spouse is pressuring me to use the inheritance to pay off credit card debt. What should I do?*

A—Financially speaking, if you are paying 16% credit card interest but have a bank account with several hundred thousand dollars in cash, it's best to pay off the credit card debt. If you are feeling pressure because it's not what you want to do, explore why you don't. Often, in these situations, it's because paying off credit card debt seems like a "waste" of the inheritance and that there is guilt around using the money in this way. It's best to share these feelings with your spouse and to talk to your financial advisor. If I've learned anything over the years, it's that humans are not always rational, but we always have a reason for what we do . . . even if it's only logical to us.

Q—*I'm married and I'm expecting to get an inheritance shortly. What should I do?*

A—If it's a small inheritance (Level I), you are probably fine having the money deposited in a joint account with your spouse. If it's a larger inheritance, or you think you'll be getting a divorce, seriously consider keeping the money in a separate account in your name only. Even if you are married, inheritances are special in that if you keep the money separate, your spouse will not have any ownership over it or claim to it. If you mix the inherited money with jointly owned money (e.g., depositing it in a joint bank account), it's difficult to later make the case that it is your separate property. It's best to keep the account clean by not commingling the inheritance with other assets. This is easily accomplished by opening a new, separate (i.e., non-joint) bank and investment account and depositing the assets into it. Have a conversation with your financial advisor and estate attorney to make sure everything is indeed kept separate. Also, consider creating a post-nuptial agreement to further protect your assets.

Q—*I'm only 22 years old and I'm inheriting several million dollars. Is there anything special I should know?*

A—You have a wonderful opportunity to use the money to create the best life you can imagine. Read and re-read this book and work with a good group of advisors you feel comfortable with. One of the challenges with inheriting so much wealth at such a young age is that your identity hasn't fully formed yet. The money can be a tool to help you experience new things and help you grow into the person you want to become. The money can also be a hindrance by acting like a crutch. I've seen young sudden wealth recipients lose their motivation to finish school and contribute to the world, but this doesn't have to be your fate if you see money as a means to an end and use it to better yourself.

One of the best things you can do is to find others going through the same thing you are, somewhere you can share your fears and struggles and also learn how others are successfully navigating their new wealth. There are many programs available. We are developing groups across the country, so go to so we can help connect you with a group.

Q—*I inherited some art and jewelry. Is there anything special I should do?*

A—Yes, contact your property and casualty insurance agent. You'll want to take photos of each item as well as video. Get copies of the purchase receipts or appraisals that were done for the estate. Schedule each of the items so they are protected. If you don't have one already, consider getting a safe deposit box at your bank to store the jewelry.

Q—*What other things should I do after receiving an inheritance?*

A—Call your property and casualty insurance agent and boost your umbrella liability policy limits. At a minimum, have $5 million worth of coverage, but most sudden wealth recipients should have $10 million or more of protection.

Also, check your own beneficiary designations on IRAs, 401(k)s, and life insurance policies. If the deceased is one of your beneficiaries, make sure you replace them with someone else.

Similarly, review your Will and estate plan documents. If the deceased was named as guardian for your children, executor of your estate, or trust beneficiary, have these documents updated.

Inherit Wise

The quickest and easist way to gain money confidence is to participate in our online wealth prep course. Through videos, drawings, and real world examples, you'll gain the money confidence and skills you need to make the right financial decisions so that your inheritance becomes lasting wealth. Go to suddenwealthsolution.com to get wealth ready!

Q—*I'm the executor of my parent's estate. How can I avoid disputes with my siblings over my parent's things?*

A—The death of a parent can either bring siblings closer together or pull them apart. I've seen many situations where siblings have become enemies, disputing an inheritance or fighting over seemingly insignificant items. Even the strongest and tightest bonds can be tested in the highly emotional aftermath of a loss. And if the relationship is already tenuous, a parent dying can break a relationship. Obviously, you'll want to minimize any disputes with family members and retain your relationships.

There is no single solution, but here are a few ideas I've found to be effective in keeping everyone civil and committed to a positive resolution. First, the executor/trustee should keep everyone apprised of what is happening. If that's your role, you can never provide too much information. Create an email list and send regular updates on the progress of the estate. Aim for a weekly summary so your siblings and relatives know what to expect. Even if there has been nothing that has changed since your last communication, send a notice letting everyone know nothing has changed. Again, err on the side of providing too many updates/information. The heirs to the estate often have no idea what is going on. This lack of knowledge can create tension and uncertainty. It's better to let them know precisely what's happening at each step in the process.

A Little Known But Important Type Of Insurance

If you are the executor of a large estate and/or think one or more beneficiaries will dispute your decisions and handling of the estate, consider purchasing trustee errors and omissions liability insurance to protect yourself from claims against you.

Second, a common cause of sibling disputes occurs when someone takes sentimental items from the parent's house. For example, I've seen situations where heirs have taken fine china, sterling silver flatware, paintings, and other items. Sometimes, these items have significant financial value, but they almost always have significant emotional value. You want to prevent anyone from taking anything at this early stage. As the executor/trustee, send out a message to the family members, asking if there are specific items they would like. Often, there will be items that hold sentimental value for one person but not another. If multiple people want the same item, have them work out an acceptable resolution – maybe they can trade one item for another. The goal is to create a process for requesting items and resolving disputes instead of a free for all.

Another area of contention is when one person feels they are not getting their fair value of assets. For example, if one sister has an emotional connection to the fine china and sterling silver flatware, both valued at $25,000, but the brother only wants a .22 caliber rifle, valued at $250, this is not equitable. In this situation, there would need to be additional assets or cash to compensate the brother.

Ideally, the parents would have had a conversation with the family and earmarked certain items in the Will or trust, but if this wasn't done, then do your best to create a fair and equitable system that everyone understands rather than one where it appears you are playing favorites.

Q—*What is the best way to divide illiquid assets between heirs?*

A—The easiest estates to divide are those consisting of cash, stocks, bonds, and mutual funds because you can simply divide the holdings into equal shares. However, most estates are not this straightforward. Often, there will be multiple heirs and illiquid assets such as a house, raw land, apartment building, or even a business that needs to be divided. It's easy to divide a $2 million investment account three ways, but how do you divide a commercial rental property?

If you have a unanimous agreement, it may make the most sense to sell the asset and divide the proceeds. This is especially true if there are several heirs and if the asset, such as real estate, is out of state. If everyone agrees, it becomes an easy solution.

However, often, not everyone agrees on what should be done. For example, what do you do if the family has a vacation property with high emotional value that one of the heirs doesn't want to sell? Or, what if two siblings want to sell a property but the third doesn't? If there are significant assets, it may be possible to trade assets, where some heirs receive cash and others receive illiquid assets. For example, the heir who wants to keep the vacation property may be able to "buy out" the other two heirs by taking less cash as an inheritance.

Again, it's best to get everyone on the same page. Explore various options with the heirs and see if you have a consensus. Even if you don't, you can see how close you are to a resolution rather than unilaterally making decisions that may not be desired by anyone.

Overseeing an estate and dividing assets can be challenging. Work closely with your advisors and get their ideas and input on how to best present the options. Also, consider holding a family retreat to update the heirs on the estate and to go through the various options. These day long or multi-day retreats with everyone in attendance can resolve issues that otherwise could have taken months to do via emails and conference calls. For larger and more complicated estates, these are incredibly valuable.

Q—*If I don't need the inheritance, what are my options?*

A—If you already have a large estate and/or want to pass the estate on to other beneficiaries, you can consider disclaiming the asset(s). When you disclaim a gift or inheritance, you do not get to decide who gets it. Instead, it passes to the next beneficiary. Why not just accept the inheritance and then gift it to the next beneficiary in line? It's much easier and tax efficient to disclaim it and have it pass directly to the beneficiary.

There are specific IRS rules you must follow to disclaim an inheritance, including putting the disclaimer in writing, completing the disclaimer within nine months of the death of the person leaving the property, and making sure you have not received any benefit from the property you are disclaiming.

Instead of blindly accepting the inheritance, work with your advisors to see if it makes more sense to disclaim the assets.

Q—*Won't I pay a lot of tax if I receive an inheritance?*

A—Generally speaking, the beneficiaries will pay very little, if any, income tax on an inheritance. However, the estate may pay estate tax, which would decrease the amount of inheritance that is ultimately transferred to the heirs. Also, there may be a small amount of tax on income for which the decedent never paid income tax.

Watch Out For The 50% Tax!

If you inherit an IRA and don't take the required minimum distribution set by the IRS, you will be subject to a penalty equal to 50% of the amount you should have withdrawn. Don't let this technicality cost you thousands of dollars in unnecessary fees. Work with your financial advisor and CPA to make sure you are withdrawing at least the minimum amount each year.

Another tax advantage of receiving an inheritance is the step-up basis rule, which minimizes and often eliminates capital gains tax. Capital gains tax is a tax assessed on an asset that you sell for more than you originally purchased it for. For example, if your mom sold the house she bought for $100,000 30 years ago for $3 million today, she would have a gain of $2.9 million ($3 million sales price - $100,000 basis). However, if you inherited the house, the IRS lets you "step-up" the basis amount to the value of the asset on the day she died. In this case, if she died when it was worth $3 million, your basis is stepped-up to the $3 million instead of the $100,000 amount. If you were to then immediately sell it for $3 million, you'd have no taxable gain. The step-up basis rule can save millions of dollars of capital gains tax. Work with your advisors to make sure you are taking full advantage of this benefit.

Need Help Or More Information?

Are you anticipating an inheritance in an amount that is making you uneasy or are you feeling pressure because of the responsibility and are not sure what to do? We can help. We are known nationally for our expertise in working with inheritors and have developed a national network of experts from different law, accounting, and financial firms. We can point you in the right direction to help you get back in control and feeling confident and secure. Go to suddenwealthsolution.com for more information and up-to-date strategies on managing your inheritance and to learn about our online wealth prep course.

SUDDEN WEALTH
DIVORCE

Ensuring financial security.

Divorce hits close to home for me. When I was six years old, my father left my mother to raise me and my four siblings. Our lives and our finances were turned upside down overnight. I witnessed firsthand what can happen without proper guidance and planning. As a result of my personal experience, I am passionate about working with women who are going through, or have gone through, a divorce.

Divorce can create fear and uncertainty. Regardless of how affluent the couple is, there is often a great deal of worry about the financial future. If you are preparing for, are in the middle of, or have finalized your divorce, you need immediate clarity as to what you have and how your new life will look financially.

People are often surprised when I talk about divorce as a form of sudden wealth. Divorce can often create financial hardship through the splitting of assets and attorney's fees. Families are often divided and finances are pushed to the limits – one of the most common predictors of bankruptcy is divorce. In my own experience as a child who was affected by my parents' divorce, we had very little to begin with, and so there was no windfall for us. However, for those with significant assets, a divorce can elicit many of the same characteristics of other sudden wealth events.

For the spouse with financial experience and relationships with advisors, this can be an easy transition. But for the spouse who either hasn't had a job or been in charge of managing the finances, this influx of money and responsibility can feel like a windfall. Even though they were in a marriage where they had substantial assets, they didn't control the wealth. It is common to feel overwhelmed, confused, and unsure of who to turn to, which are all classic characteristics of a sudden wealth experience. The 12 Sudden Wealth Principles apply to the divorcee just the same as if the money came from a lawsuit, lottery win, or inheritance.

Q—*What does the term "out spouse" mean?*

A—The term "out spouse" is commonly used by family law and divorce lawyers. When a couple is getting a divorce, sometimes both spouses have been involved equally in the financial decisions throughout the marriage. Maybe one paid the bills and worked with the CPA on the taxes while the other was in charge of investing the assets and getting insurance. They may have also met with their attorney, investment advisor, and CPA together. In this situation, both have shared many of the legal, tax, and financial responsibilities. If this couple separates, they can both confidently pick up the financial duties their ex-spouse was doing and take over with little worry or uncertainty.

But what happens if one spouse has all of the relationships with the professionals and is responsible for paying the bills, investing the money, and all things financial, legal, and tax related, and the other spouse doesn't? In this situation, the spouse with the relationships and the experience is called the "in spouse" because they have an "in" with the CPA, the attorney, and the investment advisor and because they feel confident in their ability to seamlessly take over their own finances.

The "out spouse," then, is the other spouse — the spouse who doesn't have the relationships or the day-to-day experience managing the legal, tax, and financial matters. Maybe before marriage they did these things, but because it's been so many years where they didn't have to think about it, they feel "out of it." Even though the out spouse certainly can re-learn the practical skills and develop the relationships, there can be a period of time during and after the divorce that some feel paralyzed. Often, this is the result of not knowing who to trust. Which attorney is right for them? Which financial advisor has their best interests at heart? During and after a divorce, you want to surround yourself with people you know and can trust. The in spouse has this, but the out spouse has to create this from scratch. This can take time and cause some anxiety.

Is Collaborative Divorce An Oxymoron?

Hundreds of thousands, if not millions, of dollars can be lost in legal fees in a prolonged and heavily disputed divorce. The old joke is that the only people who win in a divorce are the attorneys. There are many forms of divorce that can be less expensive and can lead to a more amicable and faster settlement. Consider collaborative divorce or mediated divorce, as they can be effective and relatively inexpensive solutions to the traditional response of "lawyering up."

Q—*I'm terrified about what my financial life will look like after my divorce. How can I get clarity?*

A—Divorce can feel like a full time job. Between the (sometimes) contentious texts with your ex-partner, phone calls to your attorney, and figuring out child custody, where you are going to live, and how your new life will look, there is almost always a sense of uncertainty or fear just below the surface. And regardless of how affluent the couple is, there is often a great deal of worry about the financial future.

As a divorce financial advisor who has specialized in working with the out spouse, three fears have emerged as the most common. Although some degree of worry and apprehension is to be expected, with a little work and planning, these three common divorce fears can be eliminated and can help the out spouse feel more confident and secure:

1. **Fear of not getting a fair share.** If your finances are simple, it can be easy to evenly divide the assets, but if your finances are more complex (e.g., multiple homes, employer stock options, closely-held business, illiquid investments, separate property), this can become much more difficult. The solution is to answer these two questions: What do we own and what is it worth? If you are concerned that assets are not being disclosed, discuss this with your attorney and consider hiring a forensic accountant, basically a financial detective, to help uncover any undisclosed assets. The next issue is to arrive at a fair value for each asset. This is an area that is ripe for abuse. The valuation of family-owned or other privately-held companies is inherently prone to subjectivity and, particularly in the divorce context, manipulation.

2. **Fear of not knowing what you'll have.** This is a pervasive fear...and it's completely justified! In a divorce, it is easy to become lost in the details and lose sight of the bigger picture. It's critical to stay focused on what your finances will look like post-divorce. This starts by knowing not only how much you have, but also what you have and where you will have it. For example, $600,000 equity in your house is very different from $600,000 of cash in the bank or $600,000 worth of stock in your ex-spouse's business. Get rid of the fear by getting clear on your assets. Work with a financial advisor before the divorce is finalized so you can make sure you are not only receiving

your fair share, but that you also don't get stuck with illiquid assets while your ex gets the cash.

3. **Fear of not knowing how your lifestyle will change.**
    This fear comes down to cash flow. After alimony, child support, employment income, investment income, and basic living expenses, how much will I have left? What value of house can I afford? These are real concerns that keep many soon-to-be divorcees up at night. To squash this fear, have a financial advisor create a post-divorce income and expense report for you so you can quickly see how your new finances will affect your lifestyle. Just make sure the advisor factors in all of the new post-divorce expenses such as health insurance, rent, car loans, etc.

It's common and natural to experience a wide range of emotions when going through a divorce, from worry to excitement, to anger to contentment. For the out spouse who isn't as financially savvy or who wasn't involved in the couple's finances, fear and uncertainty regarding money are all too common. But with some planning and a few good people to help guide you, you can feel more confident and secure about your future and your finances.

Q—*What should I do immediately following a divorce?*

A—If you are going through or have recently gone through a divorce, make sure you update the following right away…

1. **Will/Estate plan.** Your old Will and estate plan most likely lists your ex-spouse throughout. You'll want to update this to reflect your new intentions.

2. **Power of attorney/directives.** Along with your Will, you'll want to update your living will, power of attorney documents, and other such forms.

3. **Deeds/Titles.** It's likely you have already transferred the title on your property, but verify that what you should own is listed in your name only.

4. **Beneficiary designations.** Change these on IRAs, 401(k)s, life insurance policies, annuities, and other accounts.

5. **Various accounts.** Don't forget to update your credit cards, brokerage accounts, bank accounts, auto/home policies, driver's license, and other documents.

Protect Yourself

Divorce is stressful, emotional, and can bring out the worst in us. During and after a divorce, it's natural and common for both men and women to seek out comfort and reassurance from family, friends, or new partners. Take things slowly. We are highly susceptible to being taken advantage of. Do not loan money to a new partner, invest in their company or projects, or open joint accounts. Run your financial decisions by your financial advisor.

Q—*My husband has his own business. What are some issues I should be aware of during the divorce?*

A—Closely held businesses represent a real challenge during a divorce. They can be difficult to value because they are ripe for manipulation by your spouse. It's common to see businesses that had been providing a good deal of income for years suddenly and inexplicably face hardship once a divorce is initiated. There is always a valid sounding explanation for the unexpected downturn, but in my experience, the reasons are usually fictional so one spouse can undermine the value of the couple's largest asset and so the spouse won't have to pay as much financial support.

If your spouse operates a business and the business produces the majority of your income, it behooves you to get an expert to dig deeper into the business. Forensic accountants can analyze the books to see how much money is coming in and where it is going as well as be able to spot fraud and other conspicuous wrongdoings. Often, however, a forensic accountant is not enough. There are countless ways for the owner/operator to hide or postpone income as well as inflate expenses. For example, a company that was making $1 million in net profit one year can easily be shown to lose money the next year with a little manipulation.

Privately-held companies can take considerable liberties with respect to salary levels, employee perks, and expenses. In addition, the owner/operator may have knowledge of potential new clients, pending product developments, or other business opportunities that could significantly increase the valuation of the business, which would not be known by the out spouse or detected by a valuation expert or forensic accountant.

Q—*What are my options for not being taken advantage of and receiving the most value from our business?*

A—There are a couple of options available if you have a privately-held business. First, you could suggest co-ownership. In situations where the business represents the majority of the marital assets and it is not feasible for one spouse to buy out the other spouse, both can continue to co-own and operate the business. This works best when both spouses are amicable and both have a role in the company.

Additionally, you can sell to the highest bidder. In this scenario, the interests of both the in-spouse and out-spouse are aligned – they both want to receive the most for their business. The spouse who may be inclined to undervalue the business now has the incentive to maximize its value.

Q—*What major decisions do I need to make after a divorce?*

A—Once you find good advisors and you map out your income and expenses, you should do very little else. As you've read in Sudden Wealth Principle 2, it is difficult for humans to make good long-term decisions when they are under stress or in an emotionally charged situation. In a divorce, stress and emotions are the rule, not the exception. This makes it even more important to slow down and to not make any decisions you do not have to make. There will be plenty of time to decide where you want to live and what you can afford. Do not make the mistake of rushing into a big decision like buying a home. Rent for a period. Although a divorce can create feelings of uncertainty, and many jump at wanting the stability of their own home, it's often best to rent for several months, if not longer. Adjust to your new situation so you can make a clear and rational decision, not one based on emotions. For example, it's not uncommon to see a newly divorced person rush to buy a new sports car or an oceanfront condo. It can sound good in the moment, but once the thrill fades, they usually find their choices were not very practical.

Q—*Should I assume my expenses will be about what they were before the divorce?*

A—They may stay the same, but in my experience, I often see expenses go up dramatically in areas such as entertainment, dining out, and travel, as well as areas that enhance how the person looks and feels, such as personal trainers, facials, haircuts, new clothes, and even cosmetic surgeries. When you work with your financial advisor, think realistically about these potential expenses to see how much you can afford.

Q—*I've noticed I'm spending more money on myself than I did pre-divorce. Is this normal?*

A—It is common, and if you can afford it, then it's probably fine. If you can't afford it, then you are jeopardizing your finances. I've seen several divorcees use shopping as a form of therapy because it provides them with a distraction and a neurotransmitter-induced euphoria. Emotional spending rarely helps in the long-term, especially when you can't afford it. You may also be locked into a pre-divorce lifestyle you cannot afford. After years of enjoying a particular level of lifestyle, it can be difficult to quickly adjust to a budgeted one. If you find that you are spending too much and can't control yourself, re-read Sudden Wealth Principles 4, 9, and 12.

Q—*I've noticed I'm spending more on my children after the divorce. Is this common?*

A—Yes. Many newly divorced individuals who feel guilt about their divorce, or badly for their children, will shower their kids with gifts. It's natural to want to take the pain away and to help your children, but seldom does "stuff" make things better. If you feel badly and/or if your children are having a difficult time, instead of buying things for them, consider using that money for personal experiences or family therapy.

Q—*I'm getting spousal support and child support. Are there any issues I should be concerned with?*

A—The biggest and most under-addressed issue with spousal and child support is not preparing for when the support stops. When you get comfortable with receiving a check every month, it can be a shock when that time comes to an end. Make sure you are saving some of the support money, so you can continue to afford your lifestyle even after the support payments stop. As always, make a plan with your financial advisor so you are prepared and not surprised.

Don't Get Stuck With Ferns

Ferns require lots of water whereas cacti do not. Some assets require a substantial amount of upkeep and expense while others do not. For example, the Maserati is going to have high insurance and maintenance expenses. The timeshare might be worth $25,000, but it's better to let your spouse have it while you get a different asset that doesn't have monthly and annual fees associated with it. Don't just look at the value of the assets, but also consider the ongoing costs for each to make sure you aren't being stuck with the ferns.

Q—*I'm going to be getting a divorce, what should I know?*

A—At a minimum, consider the following:

1. **Make a copy of your records.** If at all possible, before your divorce, make a copy of any and all records including such things as tax returns, bank statements, brokerage statements, 401(k) statements, mortgage documents, credit card statements, and insurance policies. When in doubt, make a copy. This is especially true if you will be moving out, as you may not have easy access during the divorce.

2. **Cancel joint credit accounts.** If you have joint credit cards or lines of credit, cancel these. If there are existing balances, freeze the accounts and tell the institution they are not allowed to re-open or increase the credit line.

3. **Run a credit report.** This serves two purposes. First, you want to know if you have any credit issues that will prevent you from renting an apartment or buying a house. Second, it may list accounts you didn't know existed, which will need to be closed or frozen.

4. **Get recent credit/loan applications.** Credit and loan applications such as for a mortgage or refinance will often have a full list of accounts as well as their values. This can be valuable information, especially if your spouse tries to hide assets.

5. **Open new bank and credit card accounts.** It may be important to start building credit in your name and to have an emergency financial back-up until the divorce is finalized.

Q—*My spouse is suggesting a 50/50 split. Should I accept it?*

A—Not all assets are created equally. If you get $5 million and your spouse gets $5 million, is this fair? Maybe, but maybe not. For example, receiving a $5 million 401(k) while your spouse receives a $5 million taxable investment account is not an equal distribution. Why? You have to pay income tax on the withdrawals from the 401(k). So when your ex-spouse receives $5 million after tax, your $5 million 401(k) is really only worth about $3 million. This is an obvious example, but there are others just as inequitable that are not so obvious. Work closely with your financial advisor and family law attorney. Hire valuation experts when needed. Lastly, don't just look at the value of the assets upon divorce, run scenarios based on the expected growth rates for each asset to obtain a clearer picture of what each asset is truly worth.

Need Help Or More Information?

Are you preparing for, in the middle of, or have finalized your divorce and are looking for immediate clarity into what you have and how your new life will look? We can help. We are known nationally for our expertise in supporting divorcees and have developed a national network of experts from different law, accounting, and financial firms. We can point you in the right direction to help you get back in control and feeling confident and secure. Go to suddenwealthsolution.com for more information and up-to-date strategies on managing your finances and lives after a divorce and to learn about our online wealth prep course.

SUDDEN WEALTH LOTTERY

WIN

Making the right decisions.

Winning the lottery is an amazing thing. Congratulations, if you have won. And as you've probably realized, nothing could have prepared you for the rush of emotions and adrenaline. Winning a large lottery has to be one of the most exciting events that can happen to a person. Their day starts like any other, but by the time they go to bed, their life has forever changed. If you've just won, you may feel a little anxiety mixed in with the excitement because of the many legal, tax, and financial decisions you have to make right away.

The 12 Sudden Wealth Principles give you a solid foundation and this chapter will highlight some of the main issues you should explore and challenges you may face as a lottery winner.

BEFORE YOU'VE CLAIMED THE PRIZE

If you haven't claimed your win, there are several things you should do to protect yourself:

Q—*I have the winning ticket, but I haven't claimed the prize yet. What should I do first?*

A—Call the Lottery Commission in the state where you bought the ticket (do not give them your name) and ask if you are allowed to sign the back of the ticket. If you are, immediately sign the ticket in ink. Lottery tickets are "bearer" instruments. This means that whoever holds the ticket is the winner. I would also suggest you take a photo and video of yourself with the ticket. If something unforeseen happens, these steps can go a long way to prove you are the winner.

When You Shouldn't Sign The Ticket

If you have creditor issues or are going through a lawsuit or divorce, photograph and store the ticket in a bank safe deposit box, but do not sign the back of it. There may be strategies to legally shield your win. Work with an asset protection attorney to see which options you have available to you.

Q—*What should I do with the ticket?*

A—Keep it safe . . . in a safe! Once you've signed the back of the ticket, go to your local bank and open a safe deposit box. Tell a family member where the ticket is but do not give anyone else authorization to the safe deposit box.

Q—*Who can help me?*

A—The clock is ticking. Depending on the lottery and the state in which you purchased the ticket, you have a limited amount of time to claim the prize and often even less time to decide if you want the lump sum payment option or the annuity – as little as 180 days from the drawing to claim the prize and as few as 60 days if you want a lump-sum check. Go through the guidelines in Sudden Wealth Principle 3. You'll want an attorney - actually, you'll undoubtedly use many attorneys (e.g., business, tax, trusts and estate), but don't worry about finding everyone on day one. Find a good attorney to guide you through the initial steps and introduce you to others as needed. And, at minimum, you will also want a CPA and a Certified Financial Planner™ practitioner who have experience guiding clients who have received sudden wealth.

Q—*Should I choose the cash lump sum option or the annuity?*

A—Most lotteries allow the winner to take a lump sum or an annuity. The lump sum is a single cash transfer whereas the annuity is a series of annual payments. Most lottery winners, if given the choice, take the lump sum payment. They want all of the money immediately, and that is the main advantage. You have full and complete access to the money. The lump sum payment can have disadvantages, however.

First, if your lottery win is less than $10 million, you may be in a better income tax position if you receive the proceeds over several years via an annuity rather than up front. Why? Lottery wins are subject to income tax in the year you receive the money. If you take the lump sum option, the entire $10 million is subject to income tax in that year. However, if you choose the annuity option, the payments could come to you over several decades. For example, instead of $10 million of income in one year, your annuity payment might be $300,000 a year. Although the $300,000 would be subject to income tax, it would keep you out of the highest state/federal income tax brackets.

Second, I strongly believe that for certain people who are more prone to spending, won't get help from advisors, and/or have certain familial pressures (take the quiz at), the lump sum option can create more problems. There are lots of lottery winners who you never hear about who do just fine, but there are others who ruin their finances, relationships, and lives after they win. For them, having less access to the full amount of the win is better. Instead of having to manage $15 million, they may be much better at managing $800,000 a year.

The annual annuity option is often scoffed at by winners, but the big advantage for taking the money over time is that it provides you with a "do over" card. We've all heard the stories of lottery winners who have lost it all in a few short years. By receiving a check every year, even if things go badly the first year, you will have many more chances to get it right. This is a significant advantage of the annuity, but it's often difficult to convince the winner of the merits of an annuity. Couple the winner's reluctance to spread their win over time with the financial advisor's desire to manage a bigger pool of assets and you can see why so many choose the lump sum option.

What option is best for you? Take the quiz at suddenwealthsolutions. If the results strongly favor the annuity, share the quiz with your advisors and ask them what they recommend. The annuity is not as sexy as a big check, but I've never heard anyone complain about receiving a check in the mail every year.

There is a third option, however. If you like the idea of having access to all the money but also like the comfort, predictability, and security of a check, you can use some of the lump sum win to buy a private fixed annuity. This lump sum private annuity option doesn't have the advantage of spreading your income out over time to minimize income taxes, but for the winner who is concerned that they will face pressure or make questionable financial decisions, the annuity can alleviate much of their concern. One strategy that works well for some clients is to get a private annuity that pays an amount each year to cover their basic living expenses (e.g., property taxes, insurance, food, clothing, medical, etc.). This strategy provides anxious winners the comfort of knowing they will never go broke and will always have a certain standard of living covered.

Lump Sum vs. Annuity

From a strictly financial perspective, is it better to take the annuity or the lump sum? This is a complex tax question that depends on the size of the lottery win, current income tax rates, projected income tax rates, your state of residency when you win, in which state you will live after the win, how much you will withdraw from your portfolio each year, and the rate of return you will receive on your investments. You will want to work with your financial advisors, tax attorney, and CPA to determine which option is best for you, but as a rule of thumb, if you can earn an annual return of more than 3% to 4%, the lump sum option may make more sense over the annuity at the end of 30 years.

Q—*I'm worried about the media attention. What should I do?*

A—Make a publicity plan. In many states, you don't have the option of remaining anonymous if you win the lottery. As soon as you claim the prize, the whole world will know your name. Journalists and TV reporters will come from far and wide and will all want to talk to you. The best approach is to develop a public relations strategy before you claim the prize. Decide what you want to share, when you want to share it, and if you will be your own spokesperson or if you want to have someone else speak on your behalf.

For sudden wealth lottery winners who are bombarded with TV cameras and questions, it can be overwhelming and intimidating. "I felt like I was under attack even in my own home," complained one lottery winner. "I felt holed up like I was barricaded in my house and afraid to leave."

You can use one of your advisors, such as your attorney or financial advisor, to act as your spokesperson. In some situations – especially large and heavily covered lottery wins by the national media – consider hiring a temporary public relations firm to advise you and to help control the message.

How Not To Run Out Of Money

It's common for lottery winners to quickly adapt to their new lifestyle, but when their lifestyle is tied to an annual annuity check, it's critical to plan for when those annual annuity payments stop. For example, if you are used to spending down your annual annuity payment of $800,000, you need to have a plan when the $800,000 annuity payments end. Work with your financial advisor to set aside and invest some of your annuity payments each year so that when your lottery annuity terminates, you have enough in savings to generate a sufficient amount of income to continue to live on.

Q—*How can I remain anonymous?*

A—If you thought winning the Powerball lottery was difficult, try remaining anonymous! Although it may be difficult to remain anonymous, it's not impossible. But first, why would you want to remain anonymous? Why not raise the big cardboard check high in the air for millions of people on TV to see? If you've always wanted to be in the spotlight, this could certainly be your opportunity. Reporters will come far and wide to snap your photo and interview you, especially if you won a large lottery. They will shower you with praise and congratulations and will want to learn all about you and how you'll use the money. For some, this part of winning the Powerball lottery can be as much fun and as exciting as winning itself. But for most, this part of winning the lottery can be scary and cause anxiety.

Should You Change Your Name?

Is it possible to remain anonymous by changing your name, claiming the lottery prize, and then changing your name back? Probably not. As you can imagine, when you claim your win, the lottery commission requires you to complete various documents, which includes an affidavit that you have been known by no other names. And because the lottery association is run by the state, all of these documents are subject to Freedom of Information Act requests and are, therefore, available to the public. Although it may be possible, this strategy, like all of the others, requires a good team of advisors.

When you have a lot of assets, you can become a target for lawsuits, harassment, and requests for money — from family, friends, and often complete strangers. The Multi-State Lottery Association, which runs the Powerball Lottery, explicitly states that if you purchase the winning ticket in following five states, you have the legal right to remain anonymous:

1. Delaware (DE)
2. Kansas (KS)
3. Maryland (MD)
4. North Dakota (ND)
5. Ohio (OH)

Q—*What are my options to protect my privacy if I buy the winning ticket in a state where I can remain anonymous?*

A—If you want to remain anonymous but didn't purchase the winning ticket in one of those states, it makes the job harder, but there are strategies and legal entities you can create that will help:

BLIND TRUST

There are a lot of misconceptions and potential problems with blind trusts. Federal officeholders, such as senators or governors, are required to either fully disclose all their financial holdings and any possible conflicts of interest, or place their holdings in a blind trust with a financial institution as the trustee. To prevent the perception that they are voting on legislation from which they could personally benefit, their assets are managed independently and by a third party, without their knowledge or control (i.e., the politician is blind to their investments). But you're not a politician and you don't want to give up control of your assets to someone else.

Recently, the term blind trust has grown to include a trust or entity that attempts to hide the true ownership from the public and asset searches. In this case, "blind" refers not to the owner of the trust but to everyone else.

Here you create an entity, a trust, or LLC, and name it something other than your name. For example, one of my actor clients titled his trust using an obscure quote from a former president of the United States. Unlike a politician's blind trust, he has 100% control of the trust, assets, and decisions. This doesn't completely cloak the account, but it can make tying the trust to my client more difficult in an asset search.

Louise White, the winner of a $210 million lottery, named her trust the "Rainbow Sherbert Trust" after the ice cream flavor that led her to the grocery store where she purchased the winning ticket.

TRUST WITHIN A TRUST

For high profile lottery winners who want even greater anonymity, a trust within a trust structure is recommended. This is an advanced strategy that should only be taken with competent and experienced legal counsel.

The trust within a trust requires two trusts:

1. CLAIMING TRUST

It's called the Claiming Trust because this is the entity that claims the prize. As the winner, you assign the ticket to the trust. The trust, which now holds the winning ticket, can claim the prize. The Claiming Trust is a short-term trust that simply claims the prize and then distributes the win to the Bridge Trust. To keep your win as private as possible, the Claiming Trust should have a unique title not at all related or traceable to you. For example, you wouldn't want the trust to have your name, address, or other identifiable information as the title.

Handing over ownership of a million dollar winning ticket to a trust that is not in your name can seem reckless and scary. Why is this strategy recommended? Rest assured, even though the name of the Claiming Trust won't have your name, the trust will be directly tied to you. The Claiming Trust, like most trusts, include three types of people: (1) grantor – this is you, the creator of the trust and the individual whose assets are put into the trust, (2) trustee – this is also you, the person who manages the trust and makes decisions regarding investments and distributions and (3) beneficiary – again, also you, the person for whom the trust was created and who receives the benefits of the trust.

The astute reader may be wondering how anonymous the Claiming Trust is when your name is listed as grantor, trustee, and beneficiary

Need Help Or More Information?

Not sure where to start? We can help. We are known nationally for our expertise in working with lottery winners and have developed a national network of experts from different law, account, and financial firms to help clients build their team, determine whether it makes sense to take the lump-sum or the annuity, protect their winnings, minimize taxes, handle the media, grow their assets, and work through the emotions to help lottery winners make the best decisions they can so that winning the lottery doesn't just change their lives, but improves them. For more information and up-to-date strategies on managing your lottery win and to learn about our online wealth prep course, go to suddenwealthsolution.com.

throughout the trust document. It's possible to create an irrevocable trust and name a trusted family member, attorney, or financial advisor as trustee who's only function is to immediately transfer the trust assets into the Bridge Trust for which you will have control. For the winner who wants to remain as private as possible, this is a potential strategy, but for most, I don't recommend giving up control.

Bulletproof Privacy

If you wanted to remain completely anonymous, you can create an irrevocable Claiming Trust with your attorney to act as sole grantor, trustee, and beneficiary. The Claiming Trust would explicitly limit the trustee's power to only being able to distribute the income and principal of the Claiming Trust to the Bridge Trust. You would be the grantor, trustee, and beneficiary of the revocable Bridge Trust and as such, have full and complete control over the assets and be able to do anything with the lottery win that you wanted. The "winner" of the lottery would be the Claiming Trust, and if someone did some snooping, they would see that the owner of the trust was your attorney and not you. What you gain in privacy, you give up in control, which is why I caution against this strategy.

Although most revocable trusts use the Social Security Number of the grantor (i.e., you – the person setting up the trust), you want to avoid this. Why? State lottery commissions are state agencies, and as such, all of their records are subject to the Freedom of Information Act, which makes it easy for a reporter (or anyone else!) to request these documents and trace the Social Security Number back to you. For greater anonymity, depending on the state lottery commission's rules, you may be able to have a limited liability company (LLC) act as the grantor. Using this strategy, the winning lottery ticket would be owned by the LLC and the LLC would be the grantor of the Claiming Trust. If a nosy reporter gets a hold of the Claiming Trust, they wouldn't see your name but would see the name of the LLC instead. However, some states have reporting requirements when forming an LLC that would identify the name of the person who owns the LLC. For example, in California, a Statement of Information for domestic and foreign corporations must be filed within 90 days of forming the LLC, which requires the complete name and addresses of its managers and officers. This is where it is important to work with an attorney well versed in the laws of your state.

2. BRIDGE TRUST

The lottery proceeds are paid into the Claiming Trust and then almost immediately transferred into the Bridge Trust. The reason the lottery proceeds aren't simply paid to the Bridge Trust is because the Claiming Trust shields the true identity of the winner – it is cloaked to avoid determining the true owner. The Bridge Trust, however, is not designed to protect the identity of the winner. The details of this trust are not subject to Freedom of Information Act requests, so your name can be listed as grantor and trustee, but because the trust name will be listed as beneficiary of the Claiming Trust, which is subject to Freedom of Information Act requests, it's best not to name the Bridge Trust with personally identifiable information. It's called a "bridge" trust because this is the vehicle that holds and manages the assets for you while you determine if there needs to be more complex estate, charitable, and asset protection trusts/entities. But if you do not need more complex planning, the Bridge Trust is perfectly sufficient as your "living trust" and to serve as your main estate planning document, because unlike the Claiming Trust, it will have all of the necessary estate planning provisions.

Don't Give Up Control!

Do not sacrifice control for privacy! If an advisor is requesting you give them control of the trust or entity and manage it for you, be very careful. Can they claim the prize on your behalf? Absolutely, but don't give them irrevocable control of your lottery win. If it were me, I'd want full control at all times and wouldn't give up control just to remain anonymous.

Q—*How can I protect my assets?*

A—Boost your umbrella liability coverage. You'll want to create a comprehensive asset protection plan as discussed in Sudden Wealth Principle 10, but this can take time. As soon as you know you've won, call the insurance company that handles your homeowner's and auto policies and get an umbrella liability insurance policy. The amount of the coverage will depend on several factors, but I suggest at least $5 million and $10 million may be more adequate. Again, you'll want to create a more comprehensive asset protection plan, but this is a quick phone call and will provide some immediate protection.

AFTER YOU'VE CLAIMED THE PRIZE

Once you've claimed your lottery win, you and your advisors still have work to do. Go through each of the 12 Sudden Wealth Principles in detail. Also, consider these additional notes:

Q—*Do I have to pay taxes on my lottery win?*

A—Lottery winnings are taxable income and subject to federal income tax. They may also be subject to state income tax, although there are several states that do not tax lottery prizes (e.g., California, Florida, Texas, Washington). For winnings over $600 and up to $5,000, you will be issued a W-2G form to report your winnings on your federal income tax form. For lottery winnings of more than $5,000, your state's Department of Revenue deducts the 25% federal withholding before you receive your lump sum check or annuity checks.

For example, if your lump sum payout is $100 million, the automatic withholding would be $25 million and you would receive a deposit into your account of $75 million. At this point, many lottery winners think they are worth $75 million, but they are not! Why? They owe more tax. The top federal income tax bracket is 39.6%, but the withholding was only 25%. When it's time to pay taxes, they will owe another $15 million in federal tax and may owe state income tax as well.

Free Money?

Would you like to earn another $500,000 risk-free? The U.S. tax system is a "pay as you go" system, where you are required to pay taxes on your income as you earn it. For people who receive their income from employment, they have tax withheld from their paychecks. But if you have rental income, interest, or other sources of income where tax is not automatically withheld, you may need to make estimated tax payments each quarter. When you win the lottery, 25% is automatically withheld to cover your taxes, but you may still owe a significant amount of tax. Fortunately, there is an exception to having to pay estimated taxes. If the current year's withholding is at least 100% of last year's tax, then you don't have to pay estimates. In other words, if you had $25 million withheld this year because of a lottery win, you won't have to pay any estimated taxes unless you somehow owed more than $25 million in tax last year. Instead of paying the tax early, set the $15 million aside and earn 2% or 3% until it's time to pay the tax, which could be over 16 months later.

Q—*I'm worried about my family's safety. What can I do?*

A—If your lottery win was highly publicized, you have now become a target; not just for lawsuits but worse. At a minimum, install a home security system. If you've won a large jackpot, you can also consider hiring a 24/7 security detail for your home at least for the first week or two after you've claimed your prize and are the center of attention. Costs can range from $250 to $1,500 a day. This is certainly not a requirement for every lottery winner, but if you are receiving threats, it is well worth the cost for the extra peace of mind.

Q—*Anything else I should consider to protect myself and loved ones?*

A—Consider kidnap and ransom protection. The odds of being a kidnapping and ransom victim are remote, but your lottery win is a testament to how even the longest odds can hit. If you travel internationally, it may be wise to consider a kidnap and ransom insurance policy. These are not for everyone, but if you are going to be traveling to high risk countries, I strongly suggest these policies. Read the eBook, *Kidnap & Ransom: How to Protect Yourself* at .

Additionally, your estate plan should include a pour-over will, which is a document that calls for any asset not placed in your living trust (or Bridge Trust) to automatically "pour over" into the trust at your death. This is an important document because if the assets you purchase throughout your life (e.g., houses, cars, art, investment property) are not owned by the trust, they will be subject to probate and to the direction of your will.

The media loves a good rags-to-riches story, but what really gets ratings is a riches-to-rags story. There are plenty of stories of lottery winners who lose it all, but there are many more who have successfully navigated this exciting but stressful time. Stick to the 12 Sudden Wealth Principles and you will also be a success story.

When someone hears I specialize in working with people who receive windfalls, they usually get excited and tell me how much fun it must be to help lottery winners, professional athletes, and actors plan their lives, buy houses, give to friends, and all the things we dream of when we think about striking it rich, and they're right. It can be exciting and quite rewarding to help shape someone's life for the better. But there is another side to sudden wealth that is less celebratory.

My work over the years with clients who have received a lawsuit judgment or settlement has humbled me. These clients have been wronged—usually twice. First by the defendant, and then again by a slow and sometimes unjust legal system. And their "windfall" is not because they won a prize or starred in a film, it is compensation for an injury, for pain, or from a loss they endured. And sometimes, the wrong can never be made right even if they "win" or regardless of the amount of money they receive.

RESPONDING TO A LAWSUIT/SETTLEMENT

However, not all sudden wealth recipients react the same in the aftermath of a judgment/settlement. In my experience, beneficiaries of litigation – similar to inheritors – respond to the money in one of three ways:

ACCEPTANCE

Some view the money as just compensation for damaged incurred – a legitimate payoff. They accept the money, and although they may still hold strong feelings about the wrong they suffered, they don't displace these feelings on the money, they view the hurt separately and hold no grudge on the money. The settlement doesn't undermine their recovery or lessen their pain, but more importantly, the money doesn't cause additional pain or guilt.

Accepting the money is often the healthiest response to a financial settlement. They are able to enjoy the benefits of the money without the negative emotions and guilt that plagues the others.

CONFLICTED

Others feel conflict over the money. They may appreciate the value it provides, but it still creates feelings of anger, sadness, or guilt. They use the settlement to better their lives, but the money feels like a bribe. It is hard for them to separate the money from the injury. The new house they were able to buy from the settlement is a constant reminder of the loss or injury. They have a hard time enjoying the money or what it has provided because it is a constant reminder of their pain.

Time and distance from the injury can help alleviate some of the conflict, as can therapy. Some do well by doing good deeds, such as using some of the money to support a cause they feel strongly about, which is connected to the injury or loss they experienced. Others may benefit from speaking to a therapist or money psychologist to try to separate the pain from the money.

REJECTION

A third response some sudden wealth recipients take is to disassociate from the settlement proceeds. Either consciously or unconsciously, instead of trying to separate the pain from the money, they simply try to separate themselves from the money. They are in so much pain that they think they will experience a reprieve by eliminating the money. This can take the form of giving the money away, spending recklessly, or taking excessive risk.

If their advisors aren't aware of what's happening, they will think the client is just being foolish with their money. They're not. What they're doing makes perfect sense, but if they continue, they will accomplish their "goal" and run out of money.

If you have strong negative feelings about the lawsuit judgment/settlement and find that you are spending or giving away too much money, start by putting a temporary freeze on your spending. Ask your financial advisor to help you create systems that will support your desire to spend less. Then work with a therapist or money psychologist. You won't get emotional clarity about the money overnight – it will take time and work – but the sooner you get started, the sooner you will have a healthier reaction to the money and can start to use it to improve your life and the lives of those around you.

It is a great honor and responsibility to guide sudden wealth lawsuit judgment/settlement clients, to help them navigate the countless legal, tax, and financial decisions they and their attorneys have to make before and after they are awarded a settlement. If you're in the process of receiving a legal settlement or have already received one, follow the 12 Sudden Wealth Principles and consider the following…

Q—*I'm involved in a lawsuit and I will be receiving a substantial amount of money. What should I do?*

A—Prepare yourself for not winning a judgment or settling the case. I'd love to tell you that everyone who deserves to win does, but they don't. Even the most promising cases end up defeated. Even if your attorney tells you it is a slam dunk case, do not assume you will prevail. Chances are exceptionally high that you will not win, or if you do, you will receive much less than the big windfall you expected.

The risk you face if you put too much weight on a win is that you may begin to shift your life and finances in anticipation. For example, I've seen situations where those who are waiting on a big win will quit or put in only half effort at their job. I've seen people buy cars, take trips, upgrade their homes, and give money they couldn't afford.

Hope for the best and do all within your power to claim victory, but do not change your lifestyle or expenses. Work just as hard at your job and continue in school. Keep your expenses in check and save for retirement. Live your life with the expectation you will not win the judgment/settlement.

Q—*My attorney thinks the case will settle in the next couple of months. What should I do?*

A—Nothing. Expect your case, if you win, to take five times as long as you (or your attorney) expect. I've had clients who have waited years for a successful resolution. I'm not sure I've ever heard a client or attorney say they were surprised at how quickly the case closed. Each lawsuit is different, but with a trial and appeals, it would not be out of the ordinary if your case took several years before you receive the money. Think marathon, not a sprint.

Q—I just filed the lawsuit. What should I expect?

A—Prepare yourself for a slow and seemingly unjust legal system. Lawsuits are plagued by fits and starts, flurries of activity followed by months of waiting. High hopes (and high fives) one day and despair the next. This process is an emotional roller coaster. You and your attorney will be certain you are days, or even hours, away from a settlement, only to lose hope. Unlike many of the other forms of sudden wealth, there is a great deal of uncertainty with a lawsuit judgment/settlement, and you may not receive any money.

The legal process is not just slow, it can also be invasive. You may be required to sit through difficult depositions. Your friends and family may be interviewed. Your personal life may be exposed. Even though you are the victim, it may feel like you are the one on trial.

This process can break even the strongest person. It's important to know what you are getting yourself into so you can "prepare for war" as one client recounted his experience.

Free Money?

Would you like to earn another $500,000 risk-free? The U.S. tax system is a "pay as you go" system, where you are required to pay taxes on your income as you earn it. For people who receive their income from employment, they have tax withheld from their paychecks. But if you have rental income, interest, or other sources of income where tax is not automatically withheld, you may need to make estimated tax payments each quarter. When you are awarded a settlement, you may owe a significant amount of tax. Fortunately, there is an exception to having to pay estimated taxes. If the current year's withholding is at least 100% of last year's tax, then you don't have to pay estimates. So instead of paying the tax early, set the tax money aside and invest it in CDs or other interest bearing investments to earn 2% or 3% until it's time to pay the tax, which could be over 16 months later. One client used this strategy and earned another $2.2 million.

Q—How can I avoid the emotional ups and downs?

A—They will be impossible to avoid, but you can minimize the emotional highs and lows. It is natural to sigh with relief when your attorney tells you the settlement is eminent, but resist. Until the money is wired into your bank account, assume the case will take another three years and that you are going to lose. It sounds dreadfully pessimistic, but it's the best way to keep you focused on your life and not becoming caught up in the details of the case.

You will receive many mini victories throughout the process, which your attorney will be all too happy to share with you. There will be depositions, court proceedings, and maybe even a summary judgment that goes your way. You will win battles, and it's natural to want to celebrate these wins. My advice is to acknowledge them but not to become excited or to daydream about a win. Winning a few battles does not win the war.

Q—*Are settlements taxed differently from judgments?*

A—No, they are taxed the same.

Q—*Does it make any difference whether I settle the case or if it goes to a judgment?*

A—Even though they are both taxed the same, it can make a big difference. Why? Settlements and judgments are taxed based on the "origin of claim." This means they are taxed based on what you are suing for. For example, if you are suing your employer because you were fired and it was discriminatory, the origin of the claim is lost wages, and because wages are fully taxable, the proceeds from a lawsuit win would also likely be taxable as wages and subject to income tax and payroll taxes.

With a judgment, you have very little flexibility in how the money is apportioned for tax purposes, but you may have much more flexibility in a settlement because you may be able to assign part of the settlement to areas with more favorable tax treatment. For example, in the employment discrimination suit discussed above, part of the settlement might be in wages, but some could be classified as emotional distress damages (taxable as income but not subject to employment taxes) and some to pension benefits (nontaxable). So instead of the full damages being taxed and subjected to payroll taxes, in a settlement, you may have the flexibility to appropriate some damages to non-wage categories and reduce your taxes.

Q—*How are damages for physical injury and sickness taxed?*

A—There is a specific section in the IRS tax code, Section 104, that excludes damages paid on the account of physical injury, sickness, or wrongful death from taxation. It's important to note, however, that your injuries must be visible. Emotional distress and the like are not considered physical and are, therefore, taxable.

Again, it may be advantageous to settle because in a settlement, you have more control and flexibility in how the damages are allocated. Your attorney can work to get an agreement with the defendant that will substantiate the tax position you will take on your return. Although, in an audit, the IRS may disagree with your classification of damages, it can benefit you to have the settlement agreement corroborate your position.

Q—*Are punitive damages taxed the same as compensatory damages?*

A—No. Compensatory damages are tax-free and punitive damages are fully taxable. This is another reason it may behoove you to settle. If you're in a car crash and about to receive $100,000 in compensatory (tax-free) damages and $6 million in punitive damages, can you settle at $3 million that is all tax-free? A settlement can be a win for you and for the defendant.

Q—*I have an attorney working on my case. Won't she know what's best for me when it comes to taxes?*

A—Maybe, but probably not. The practice of law is as highly specialized as the practice of medicine. There are narrow areas of expertise. The attorney representing you in the lawsuit may not have expertise in tax law. I highly suggest you at least get a review of your case by a tax attorney. The larger the possible judgment/settlement, the more important this analysis becomes.

My clients have saved literally tens of millions of dollars because of pre- and post-judgment/settlement tax planning. When the combined federal, state, and payroll tax rate can exceed 50%, expert tax planning should be your top priority. And because there is much more tax planning and maneuvering you can do before a judgment/settlement, it's never too early to get good tax advice. Ask for a complimentary review of your case early on, and as things get closer to a possible resolution, have your litigation attorney work more closely with your tax attorney.

Q—*What is a structured settlement?*

A—Instead of receiving your injury settlement in a single lump-sum, a structured settlement is an annuity that provides your settlement over time. Why would anyone choose (structured settlements are voluntary agreements, unless required by a court order) to have their settlement money come in over time instead of all at once? Structured settlements have several unique advantages:

STRUCTURED SETTLEMENT ADVANTAGES

1. **Tax-free payments.** The biggest advantage with a qualified structured settlement is that the payments are free from federal and state income tax as well as the Alternative Minimum Tax (AMT) on injury claims. Tax-free structured settlements are typically available only if the settlement is made on account of physical injury, physical sickness, or wrongful death, but you may be able to avoid taxes using a non-qualified structured settlement on **non-injury** damages (see the Pro Tip below on non-qualified structured annuities). But certain damages such as personal injury damages are already tax-free, so what's the benefit of a structured settlement? Let's say you are involved in a car accident and you receive a lump sum $1 million settlement. This comes to you tax-free. If you invest the $1 million, then the dividends, interest, and gains are taxable. With a structured settlement annuity, part of each payment is your original principal (the $1 million award) and part is interest paid on the annuity. Normally, interest is taxable, but in a structured settlement, the entire payment is tax-free to you.

2. **Flexibility.** Another big advantage of structured settlements is their flexibility. If you are awarded a $1 million settlement, you can choose to have all, none, or just part of the award structured. Additionally, you can have the payments customized for your needs. For example, you may choose to receive a monthly payment now or wait until retirement. You can choose to begin with a small monthly payment that increases each year, or you can schedule one or more larger payments to cover projected expenses. For example, you may want a $100,000 payment in nine years to coincide with your child starting college. The variations on the payments are limitless and can (should) be customized for your specific needs.

3. **Safety.** Structured settlements are annuities issued by insurance companies that guarantee payments. Unlike investing in the stock market, structured annuities pay out regardless of what happens in the economy or if interest rates go up or down. This can provide a great deal of comfort knowing that no matter what happens, you will always receive your check every month.

4. **Foolproof.** Similar to lottery winners who have the choice of lump sum payment or an annuity, I strongly believe that for certain people who are more prone to spending, won't get help from advisors, and/or have certain familial pressures (take the quiz at suddenwealthsolution.com), the lump sum option can create more problems. You may benefit from having less access to the money. Instead of having to manage $1 million, you may be much better at managing $50,000 a year.

    The big advantage for structuring all or part of your settlement is that taking the money over time provides you with a "do over" card. It's not uncommon for settlements to be lost in a few short years because of bad financial decisions. By getting a check every year, even if things go badly the first year, you will have many more chances to get it right. This is a significant advantage of the structured annuity.

5. **Facilitate settlement.** If a plaintiff and defendant are far apart in their settlement negotiations, a structured settlement may provide a win-win for each party and lead to a faster and better resolution.

6. **Continuation of payments at death.** If the recipient dies prematurely, the annuity's beneficiaries may be able to continue to receive guaranteed payments.

Pro Tip

A non-qualified assignment with respect to non-injury or sickness damages allows a plaintiff to receive periodic payments from a third-party assignee. Provided that a plaintiff's settlement is structured properly, these periodic payments only need to be included in the taxpayer's income in the years they are actually received.

In a non-qualified assignment, the third-party assignees are usually off-shore corporations that receive the funds from the defendant. The third party assignee buys an annuity from a U.S. life insurance company that is a parent or affiliate of the off-shore entity. The third-party assignee makes the periodic payments to the plaintiff, in accordance with the requirements of the settlement agreement.

In 2008, the IRS issued a Private Letter Ruling (PLR 200836019) that confirmed that in the case of a non-qualified assignment, the plaintiff/taxpayer did not recognize gross income in the year the settlement agreement was signed, but only in the years they actually received the payments. So long as the plaintiff/taxpayer abides by the terms of the structured settlement, the non-qualified assignment can provide valuable tax deferral advantages.

~ Bruce Givner, tax attorney with Givner & Kaye

STRUCTURED SETTLEMENT DISADVANTAGES

1. **Highly technical.** To retain the tax-free nature of the annuity payments, it is critical that you structure the award *before* signing the settlement agreement. It's important to work closely with the attorney representing your case, a tax attorney, and a qualified structured settlement broker.

2. **Limits financial resources.** The amount of the award you structure becomes locked away in an annuity. Unlike the lump-sum payout, where you have full and unfettered access to the money, the money in the annuity cannot be accessed. It can be difficult to pay for large one-time expenses (e.g., new car, house, medical bills) if your entire award is tied up in an annuity.

3. **Difficult to modify.** Once you lock in a structured settlement annuity, it can be very difficult, if not impossible, to make any changes to the amount or timing of the payments. Section 130 of the tax code specifically states that the payment schedule cannot be "accelerated, deferred, increased, or decreased."

4. **Lower investment returns.** You may be able to invest the lump-sum award in investments that produce a higher long-term return.

5. **Costly to cash out.** You've undoubtedly heard late-night commercials offering to buy structured settlements. They offer "cash now," but cashing out your annuity comes at a high cost. Most states have required court hearings before you are allowed to sell.

Do You Need A Special Needs Trust?

If you've been injured and have a disability, you may qualify for Medicaid, Social Security Income, and other means-tested or asset-tested programs. In other words, to qualify you have to either have limited assets and/or income, sometimes as low as $2,000 in assets. But if you receive a settlement, this could prevent you from receiving these benefits. A possible solution is to set up a special needs trust and to have it funded with a structured settlement. Structured properly, this keeps the settlement award out of your hands and allows you to continue to receive benefits.

Q—*Based on the advantages and disadvantages of structured settlements, should I do one?*

A—The first step is to see if your settlement is able to be structured. Aside from injury awards, there are few exceptions. Second, generally speaking, I wouldn't structure the entire award. Work with a financial advisor to determine your immediate cash needs and your ongoing expenses. One option that can work well is to structure just enough to cover your basic living expenses. This ensures you will always be able to cover your standard expenses. You can take the rest of the award as a lump-sum and invest it in potentially higher returning investments. Consider increasing your annuity payment each year to keep up with inflation and the rising cost of your living expenses. Also, in addition to working with a financial advisor, you will want to work with a structuring specialist. I suggest working with a Certified Structure Settlement Consultants (CSSC) awarded by the National Structure Settlements Trade Association.

Pro Tip

Personal injury victims are faced with a once-in-a-lifetime decision. Should they receive their settlement as a single lump sum or in the form of a tax-free, structured settlement annuity guaranteed by an insurance company? Personal injury victims are "unique investors" who must focus on leveraging their capital into long-term income and safeguarding it from a complex and volatile maketplace. Such unique investors have an opportunity to ensure both their future needs and their peace-of-mind with a safe and secure structured settlement plan.

~ Bill Wakelee, Chief Strategy Officer, Chronovo

Q—*I have a structured settlement annuity, but I need cash. What should I do?*

A—Do not use the structured settlement as collateral for a loan unless you've received advice from a tax attorney, CSSC, or both. Generally, you are not allowed to assign or encumber a structured annuity without losing its valuable tax-free status. When in doubt, get help.

You may be tempted to sell part or all of your annuity. If you do, be prepared for it to take time. It's not as fast and easy as the commercials suggest. Most states require a judicial review to make sure you, the annuity holder, are not being taken advantage of. Also, expect to lose quite a bit of the value when you sell it. Ideally, look for alternatives. Do you have other sources of funds you can tap first? Selling your tax-free, guaranteed annuity should be a last resort after you've exhausted all of your other options.

Q—*My attorney says I will have to pay income tax on the fees he receives. Is this true?*

A—Sadly, it may be true. Let's say you hire an attorney on contingency and agree to pay her/him 40% of any damages she/he wins for you. If your $2 million award is non-taxable, the entire $2 million comes to you tax free and then you pay your attorney $800,000 in contingency fees. But if your award is taxable, you may have a problem. Here's why. Even though $800,000 of your award goes to your attorney, the full $2 million is considered income to you. The IRS may let you deduct the $800,000, but it is subject to several limitations, including the dreaded Alternative Minimum Tax (AMT), which could render the deduction worthless. So you will be taxed on the full $2 million but still have to cut a check to your attorney for $800,000 (your attorney will also have to pay income tax on this!).

There may be strategies to limit or even eliminate this double taxation, but the rules are quite complex. One of my clients saved close to $3 million in taxes by capitalizing on several advanced strategies. If you have a large settlement subject to double-taxation, consult with an expert in this area.

Pro Tip

Pursuing a claim is often a long process. One cannot underestimate the need for early settlement planning. For instance, answering questions like:

- What is a reasonable expectation for recovery? What is the range of money I am likely to net (be available after liens, expenses, fees)?

- What will support a reasonable lifestyle? What are my basic needs? What would I like to have/do?

- How will I pay my mortgage, taxes, monthly bills, etc.?

- What ongoing medical expenses will I have?

- What health/other insurance/government benefits are available? At what cost?

- How will I save/budget for my future?

- What is obtainable to make my life easier?

- Does a trust make sense?

- Does taking some of the money over time (structured settlement) help fulfill some of my needs?

- What experts are needed to help me/us?

Beginning to answer these and other questions early in the process will put you ahead of the game at settlement. Waiting until the last minute guarantees confusion and less desirable results.

~ Karen Meyers, founding partner at Little, Meyers & Associates, Ltd.

Q—*I'm worried about the media attention. What should I do?*

A—Most lawsuit judgments/settlements go unnoticed, but there are others that capture the media's attention. If your lawsuit win was highly publicized, you may be contacted by the press and you may have TV cameras on your front lawn. If you think your case will make news, consider creating a publicity plan. Decide what, if anything, you want to share, when you want to share it, and if you will be your own spokesperson or if you want to have someone else speak on your behalf.

You can use one of your advisors, such as your attorney or financial advisor, to act as your spokesperson. In some situations, especially large and heavily covered lawsuits by the national media, consider hiring a temporary public relations firm to advise you and to help control the message.

Q—*I'm worried about my family's safety. What can I do?*

A—If your lawsuit win was highly publicized, you have now become a target. At a minimum, install a home security system. If you've won a large judgment/settlement, you can also consider hiring a 24/7 security detail for your home, at least for the first week or two after you've made the news and are the center of attention. Costs can range from $250 to $1,500 a day. Obviously, this is not a requirement in most lawsuits, but if you are receiving threats, it is well worth the cost for the extra peace of mind.

Q—*How can I protect my assets?*

A—Boost your umbrella liability coverage. You'll want to create a comprehensive asset protection plan as discussed in Sudden Wealth Principle 10, but this can take time. As soon as the judgment/settlement award has reached your account, call the insurance company that handles your homeowner's and auto policies and get an umbrella liability insurance policy. The amount of the coverage will depend on several factors, but I suggest at least $5 million, but $10 million may be more adequate. Again, you'll want to create a more comprehensive asset protection plan, but this is a quick phone call and will provide some immediate protection.

Need Help Or More Information?

Are you in the process of receiving a legal settlement or have already received one and are unsure who to turn to? We can help. We are known nationally for our sudden wealth expertise regarding lawsuits and settlement and have developed a national network of experts from different law, accounting, and financial firms. We can point you in the right direction to help you find the right team for your needs. For more information and up-to-date strategies on managing your lawsuit or settlement, go to suddenwealthsolution.com.

STOCK OPTIONS

Creating maximum value.

If there is one area that requires impeccable attention to details, a proper strategy, and knowledge of taxes, it is stock option planning. Stock options can create sudden wealth overnight. A client's stock options can represent 80% to 90% of their net worth, but if they are unvested or un-exercised, extracting this value takes a great deal of planning. A simple oversight, such as not exercising the options in the proper amount of time after you leave your employer, can cost hundreds of thousands of dollars or more. Failing to account for your income tax bracket or AMT can have you paying more than you need to in taxes. If you have substantial wealth in stock options, it is critical that you have a team of advisors who understand the tax, legal, and financial implications.

Stock options create many sudden wealth recipients each year. Although big technology companies such as Facebook and Twitter often get the media's attention, there are countless other companies both public and private that create windfalls for their employees each year. The research shows that approximately 19 million employees of stock-based companies owned company stock in 2010 and that 9.3 million held stock options[14]. Additionally, according to the National Center for Employee Ownership, of the publicly traded companies, some 36% of employees own stock in their employers through one kind of plan or another[15]

The Dangers Of Company Stock

Enron employees lost over $1 billion in retirement assets as a result of investing in company stock. If you have too much wealth concentrated in your employer, consider divesting or hedging a portion to reduce your risk.

COMMON STOCK OPTION MISTAKES

Stock option planning can be complex and is often fraught with mistakes. The most common and most egregious mistakes I see are the following:

1. **Too heavily concentrated.** Whether you are a founder, an executive, or a rank and file employee, your stock options could be worth a considerable deal of money, sometimes as much as 100% of an employee's net worth. Any time you have so much of your wealth tied up in a single asset, in particular a single company, you are rolling the dice. Great fortunes have been made and lost betting everything on the performance of a company. Most recently, this occurred during the 2008-2009 financial crisis and before that with Enron, Worldcom, Tyco, and the dot com Internet bubble. It's okay to take some money off the table, but as you'll read later in the chapter, many founders/employees do not. They ride the stock up and down without exercising any of their stock.

2. **Miss key expiration dates.** Your stock options are like a gallon of milk: they have an expiration date. If you miss the date, your milk goes bad and your options are worthless. Mark your calendar with your option schedule and revisit it often – at least twice a year with your advisors.

3. **Exercising too early.** Many employees exercise their options too early. The research shows it is often best to sell employee stock options near expiration, when the value of the time premium is lowest.

4. **Lose your job and your options.** What happens if you quit your job or are fired? What happens if you get a job with the competitor? Become an expert (or have your advisors become experts) on your stock option plan document so you know what happens when you terminate your employment. Many employers will allow employees to exercise their options 90 days after termination, but you need to read your plan documents to be sure. If you think you will be quitting or that you may be fired, some planning and strategic exercising may be warranted. Also, don't confuse the length of your severance package with the amount of time you have to exercise your options after you leave your employer. Check the dates for each as they may be two different lengths of time.

5. **Change in control of company effects option plan.** What happens to your un-exercised options if your company is acquired by a competitor or if you merge with another company? What happens if a private equity company takes over or if your public company goes private? Each stock option plan is different, so it's important to know what happens to your plan. In the event your company announces a forthcoming change in control, work quickly with your advisors to capitalize on any opportunities you may have.

6. **Divorce ownership issues.** Generally, in community property states, stock options that were granted and vested during marriage are considered community property. But what if stock options were granted but not yet vested after date of separation? Or, what if the options were granted before the marriage but vest during the marriage? Or, if the options were granted after separation but were awarded for service by the employee during the marriage? As you can see, there are no hard and fast rules for determining ownership or value in a divorce. It's critical that you work with competent legal counsel well versed in stock option planning to avoid making mistakes and to reach an equitable compromise.

7. **Trying to be a market timer.** If there is one guarantee in investing, it is this: it's impossible to successfully time the market consistently. Much wealth has been lost by not sticking to a pre-planned option exercise schedule. Besides, if you are successful at timing the exercising and selling of company stock, you may attract the attention of the SEC and be questioned on insider trading issues.

Q—*What is the best employee stock option strategy?*

A—Unfortunately, there isn't a single "best" strategy, but there is a process you and your advisors can follow to help you determine the best strategy for you.

First, learn about your stock option plan. You'd be surprised how few people have read their employer's stock option plan. You and your advisors will want to know how your options vest and expire, what type(s) of options you have or will be receiving, if you are subject to special corporate rules, as well as what happens if you retire, quit, become disabled, are terminated, die, etc.

Next, you'll want to integrate the stock option planning in with your financial goals (e.g., retirement, college funding, career changes). Although taxes are usually a big driver with stock option planning, your financial and life goals should be paramount when deciding when to exercise and sell stock.

How Not To Be Gordon Gekko

Be careful when exercising and selling company stock. If you trade on non-public information that the general public does not have, this can be considered insider trading by the Securities and Exchange Commission and can lead to fines and jail time.

You will also want to analyze your company and its stock. Have your financial advisor do a comprehensive analysis of the company as well as its competitors and industry. Is it a solid company with a strong balance sheet or is it struggling? Is it a leader in its space or is it on the wane? The goal is to determine the expected performance of the stock relative to its current value. For example, if the company is in growth mode, you'd want a different strategy than if it were in decline.

Lastly, you'll want to determine the optimum exercise and selling schedule based on the above research and analysis. If you are a high-level executive, you may be able to sell at predetermined amounts at regular intervals per SEC rule 10b5-1.

Q—How do I know if I am too heavily concentrated in company stock?

A—Having too much company stock is fine . . . until it isn't. Unfortunately, it's impossible to accurately predict when to get out. It's better to limit your exposure to a reasonable level. First, determine how much exposure you currently have. Add the value of all restricted stock, publicly traded stock, stock converted from options, company stock in your 401(k), in-the-money options, and stock owned in an ESOP. Next, compare this to your overall investment net worth (do not include the equity in your home or personal belongings). If the total of your company stock exceeds 10% to 15%, work with your financial advisor to reduce your exposure. Start by selling the stock in your 401(k) and any shares you own in your own brokerage account. If you still have too much exposure, consider one of the hedging strategies discussed later in the chapter.

Pay Now To Receive More Later

Pay tax now to minimize taxes later with an 83(b) election. If you work for a start-up company whose stock is relatively inexpensive now but that has a good chance of going public or being acquired in the future, you can opt to pay tax on the exercise so that all future appreciation is taxed as capital gains rather than waiting until the options vest and presumably the value of the stock is much higher. As with most stock option planning, the rules are complex. Work with your advisors to determine if an 83(b) election makes sense for you.

Q—*Other than selling company stock, how else can I limit my exposure?*

A—There are several hedging strategies you and your advisors may want to explore, but be careful. These strategies can be expensive and you want to avoid "constructive sales rules" that can trigger taxes as if you sold the stock outright.

1. **Reduce exposure to industry.** If you have a substantial portion of your investments in your company, you can reduce/eliminate ownership in other companies in your industry. For example, if you work for an Internet company and have a large allocation of its stock, you could direct your financial advisor to reduce your exposure to other Internet companies. The idea is that companies within an industry often perform similarly. If your employer's stock tumbles, there is a good chance others in the same space will also suffer.

2. **Short your competitors.** In addition to eliminating exposure with other investments in the same industry as your employer's, you can select the top two or three direct competitors and sell their shares short. Your financial advisor should select competitors whose stocks move as closely in unison to your company's stock (i.e., high correlation). This way, if your company stock goes down (e.g., you lose money), there is a good chance your competitor's stock will also decrease (e.g., you'll make money).

3. **Short an index.** If you work for a booming technology company, instead of trying to select an individual competitor's stock to short, you can select a technology index to short or buy an inverse technology ETF. The strategy

is the same – if your company stock goes down, you are also hoping the companies in your industry also go down. As you lose money on your company stock, you are making money on the short position.

4. **Use options.** In addition to private stock options offered by companies, there is also a large public stock option market where you can buy/sell call and put contracts. You could buy put options on your company stock to protect against losses, but using options is an expensive long-term hedge. You can reduce your cost with a collar option strategy, where you buy a put option and sell a call option. By selling the call option, you generate income, which can be used to at least partially offset the cost of the put purchase. Additionally, you can sell exchange traded long-dated calls and use the un-exercised options as collateral (you will need your employer's approval and participation to do this effectively).

5. **Use a variable prepaid forward.** As discussed earlier, this hedging strategy saved my client approximately $40 million in losses. The strategy is complex and requires all your advisors work together to ensure it makes sense for you. Basically, you agree to give a pre-determined number of shares of stock to a brokerage firm at a future date. The brokerage firm gives you cash in the amount of 75% to 90% of the value of the stock right now, even though you won't be providing the stock to the brokerage firm for months or even years. If the stock declines, the brokerage firm takes the losses. If the stock goes up, you can participate in some of the gain. You have a great deal of flexibility when structuring these deals.

Get Wealth Ready

The quickest and easist way to gain money confidence is to participate in our online wealth prep course. Through videos, drawings, and real world examples, you'll gain the money confidence and skills you need to make the right financial decisions so that your sudden wealth becomes lasting wealth. Go to suddenwealthsolution.com to get wealth ready!

Q—*When should you exercise and sell your stock early?*

A—There are many reasons why you may want or need to exercise your stock options early and sell the underlying stock. The following are the most common:

1. **Too concentrated.** Again, if you have more than 10% to 15% of your investable net worth in company stock, you should consider selling early to reduce your exposure.

2. **Challenges at the company.** If you are not optimistic about your company and its stock, you may want to sell early. Do not try to time the market and do not trade on insider information, but if you no longer have faith in your company, then it may be a good time to reduce your ownership. I always ask clients if they didn't work for the company, would they still want to own it?

3. **Minimizing taxes.** Exercising options can be a taxable event. You may want to spread when you exercise your options over time to minimize being pushed into a higher tax bracket. Work closely with your CPA to exercise just enough, but not too many so you don't jump to a new tax bracket.

4. **Personal reasons.** There are countless personal reasons you may want to exercise and sell your stock early. You may need to fund a college expense or a big one-time purchase.

Q—*What is the problem with owning a large percentage of my company's stock?*

A—Even after the collapse of Enron, Worldcom, Global Crossing, and countless other less high-profile bankruptcies, 40% of employees in defined-contribution retirement plans are still allowed to invest in employer stock[16]. Millions of employees, knowingly or unknowingly, have a high concentration of their employer's stock in their retirement accounts. In fact, over 10.6 million employees' retirement accounts are composed of more than 20% of employer stock[17].

Ignorance is one explanation. Many people just don't know any better or know that they can change their allocation, but it is not your employer's responsibility to ensure that your asset allocation is appropriate for your needs. In fact, your employer may have an incentive to keep you ignorant because the more their employees buy public company stock, the greater the potential return of the stock price.

How To Avoid The Social Security Tax

If you are over or near the yearly maximum contribution for Social Security, consider exercising non-qualified stock options or stock appreciation rights by the end of the year to avoid the additional 6.3% Social Security tax. If you wait until January to exercise the options, your yearly wage base starts at $0 and the Social Security tax will again apply on the exercise spread and the vesting value of restricted stock up to the new maximum for that year.

No matter how much you like your job or your employer, do not expect your employer to act in your best interest. Laurence J. Kotlikoff and Scott Burns write in *The Coming Generational Storm*, "The largest and, presumably, the most responsible U.S. companies are systematically inducing, enabling, or encouraging their workers to hold huge fractions of their defined-contribution portfolios in company stock." Smart investing is solely your responsibility.

The other explanation I often hear is that investing is scary and that it is the same as gambling. "Why invest in companies I don't know anything about when I can invest in a company with whom I am familiar and with whom I can help improve?" This line of thinking seems logical, but it is a mistake and can be a costly one. Intelligent investing doesn't have to be scary and it most certainly doesn't have to be a gamble. The dangers of having too much exposure to your employer's stock are fourfold:

1. **Lack of diversification.** Investing in individual stocks is generally a bad idea. By doing so, you are subjecting yourself to avoidable risk and greater chances of incurring losses for a large part of your portfolio.

2. **When it rains, it pours.** If your employer's industry falters, as it did for technology in the early 2000s and real estate in 2008-2009, you could be hit with a double whammy. First, your chance of experiencing a lay-off dramatically increases, and second, the performance of your company's stock will most likely also suffer. When you are out of a job, you may need to tap into your investment accounts, and because they contained an abundance of company stock, you could find they hold a fraction of their former value. When you invest in your company's stock, too much of your livelihood is tied to the success of the company, both your income and your investments. I

recommend investing not only outside of your company, but outside of your company's industry.

3. **Lack of rational perspective.** When you are too close to a subject, you lose the ability to think rationally. Do any of your friends believe their children are gifted when you know that they are average kids? The same thing can happen when you work for and invest in the same company – you lose perspective. You may think the company is strong and innovative when it is actually average or an under-performer.

Groupthink is also another major problem. The dictionary defines *groupthink* as, "The act or practice of reasoning or decision-making by a group, especially when characterized by uncritical acceptance or conformity to prevailing points of view." In other words, if your boss and all of your co-workers are investors, you may feel real or perceived pressure to continue to invest or not sell when you should. An excellent example of groupthink occurred at Enron. At an all-employee meeting on December 1, 1999, Cindy Olson, an Enron vice president and fiduciary of the Savings Plan and ESOP encouraged employees to invest in Enron stock when she told the crowd:

OLSON: "Should we invest all of our 401(k) in Enron stock? Absolutely. Don't you guys agree? … We're having a great year … We expect to finish it up in very fine fashion here over the next few weeks and, of course, enter the new millennium, the year 2000, in very strong shape. … But if we do the right things, there's no reason to think that we couldn't see a $15, $20, $25 increase in stock price over the next 12 months or so."

4. **Cognitive dissonance.** Cognitive dissonance is what happens when you are committed to something and you discover something wrong with it. It is the feeling of psychological discomfort created by having two competing thoughts. When this state of dissonance exists, our natural tendency is to disregard the negative news and reinforce our existing position. By dismissing the competing thought, we create a sense of cognitive harmony again.

If you get up every morning, drive to the office, and put in a full work day, you justify this behavior by thinking the company is good, that you are making a difference, and that the service/products the company produces benefit society. If you invest in the company and you see, hear, or read negative, albeit true, reports about your employer, cognitive dissonance theory tells us it will be difficult for you to sell your company stock. If you do sell, you admit that the company for whom you work so hard is not worth an investment. Instead of selling on the negative news, you might be inclined to dismiss the report as untrue, biased, or even fabricated to maintain cognitive harmony.

Q—*How should I keep track of my option schedule?*

A—Your financial advisor should create a spreadsheet or document with the following information:

1. Date of each option granted

2. Number of options granted at each date

3. Type of options granted (i.e., ISO or NSO)[4]. Exercise price for each option[5]. Expiration date of each set of options[6]. Date of vesting for each set of options[7]. Date, number of shares, and price of each exercise

This matrix will provide you with a quick snapshot of the most important dates and information. There are also many Excel templates and software programs available online that can help you keep track of your options schedule.

Need Help Or More Information?

If you have stock options from your employer and want to create the most after-tax value, we can help. We are known nationally for our expertise in working with stock options and have developed a national network of experts from different law, accounting, and financial firms. We can point you in the right direction to help you take maximum advantage of your opportunity. For more information and up-to-date strategies on managing your stock options, go to suddenwealthsolution.com.

SPORTS & ENTERTAINMENT

Creating certainty in an uncertain world.

Do professional athletes or entertainers really have legal, tax, and financial needs that are different from others? Absolutely! Unlike the other forms of sudden wealth, where there is just one windfall event (e.g., inheritance, lawsuit, lottery), the athlete/entertainer may receive several windfalls over the course of their career from signing bonuses, contract payments, or sponsorship royalties. As a result, this requires unique planning.

I've worked with enough athletes, writers, musicians, directors, producers, and actors over the years to know that they have distinct needs from the salaried employee, from the business owner, and even from other sudden wealth recipients.

How much money did you make last year? For most people, this is highly private and known only by their spouse, CPA, and financial advisor. If you're an athlete or celebrity, I can look on Wikipedia and find out how much you made in less than 20 seconds. People with money are targets for lawsuits, and celebrities with money are even bigger targets. It's important to have privacy agreements with household staff and nannies.

It's also important to have proper insurance coverage, such as employment practices liability insurance, and for some clients who are higher profile, even kidnap and ransom insurance. In addition to tight legal agreements and insurance, LLCs for homes and other assets can protect the client's privacy and assets.

Cash flow for athletes and entertainers can be volatile, so income and expense planning for living expenses, taxes, and savings is critical. If you're an athlete or entertainer, you need a team to protect your assets and plan for an uncertain future. This chapter will dig deeper into the unique opportunities and challenges of the professional athlete and entertainer.

Q—*What is one of the biggest financial challenges facing athletes and entertainers?*

A—Myopia. The dream for many is to get the big contract and to perform on the big stage, but this should be just a milestone on their financial path to the ultimate goal – financial independence. The mistake most athletes and entertainers make is confusing their career success with financial success. Although they have achieved what few have done and made it where few go, the ultimate victory is not playing for the NFL or getting the lead in a feature film. A lucrative contract gets you on the right track, but it does not get you to the destination.

Your ultimate financial goal should be to save and invest enough so that you are financially secure, so if you are injured or don't get another contract, you can continue to live your life without financial worries.

Don't confuse where you are now with where you want to go. Keep your eye on the prize and achieve financial independence by saving and investing.

Q—*How should I view my sudden wealth?*

A—To become a professional athlete or entertainer takes a tremendous amount of hard work, determination, and sacrifice. Your "sudden" wealth is often anything but sudden. Although you may look like an overnight success, you know it can take years of blood, sweat, and tears before you sign the big contract. The quickest way to upset an athlete or entertainer is to call them an overnight success or attribute their success to luck. So why do I encourage you, the athlete/entertainer, to view your windfall like hitting the lottery, which requires no skill, talent, or hard work? It shifts your mindset so you can take maximum advantage of your opportunity. When you are one of the very best in the world at your craft, it can become difficult to objectively see any potential threats that could jeopardize your career. View your success as a result of hard work and skill, but view the money as a lottery to focus on the ephemeral nature of your career.

Q—*How much should I be saving?*

A—Many professional athletes and entertainers have short careers. Either from injury, bad luck, or the public's obsession with the next big thing, it is not uncommon to make a large amount of money in a short period of time and then to make nothing. It's all too common for athletes/entertainers to ramp up their lifestyle expenses to meet, or even exceed, their newly inflated incomes. As long as they can continue to perform and the checks keep coming, they can pay for their new lifestyle, but if the checks stop, they find themselves with few savings and no ability to meet their monthly nut – the basic living expenses they must pay every month.

Here's how to avoid that scenario and create financial independence instead:

First, you want to determine your baseline spending before the big contract. How much were your lifestyle costs? Once you get the signing bonus or contract payment, you will likely want to upgrade your car and living situation, but do not increase your baseline costs by greater than $100,000 or 25%.

Next, determine a lifestyle you would be content with if you had to retire. Work with your financial advisor to figure out how much this lifestyle would cost and how much you would need saved in order for your investments to produce enough income to pay for this desired lifestyle. This represents your savings target.

Finally, save all excess money and do not spend more than your baseline plus 25% until you reach this targeted savings level. Once you reach the savings target, but no sooner, you can increase your current living expenses.

Here's how this looks in the real world. Let's say you are an athlete/entertainer getting by on $40,000 a year, when you sign a contract that pays you $2 million over three years. Your baseline is $40,000. You are allowed to increase your baseline expenses by 25% or $100,000. In this case, the greater is between $50,000 (25% more than the baseline) or $100,000. Therefore, you would be allowed to increase your living expenses to $100,000 a year. Next, you would determine how much your desired lifestyle would cost. In this example, we'll assume it is $400,000 a year. To generate $400,000 a year conservatively, you would need to have saved approximately $10 million. You would keep your current lifestyle expenses at no more than $100,000 a year until you saved $10 million. Once you saved that amount, which represents your financial independence, you could then increase your lifestyle expenses and save less. Although the numbers are not set in stone, the strategy is. Figure out what you need to be financially independent and instead of consuming your income on toys early in your career, do your best to save until you hit your targeted savings goal. Once you hit that goal, regardless of what happens to your career, you will have enough assets and income to support you for the rest of your life.

SUDDEN WEALTH EXPERIENCE

First, understand one thing: Pro football players as a whole are terrible money managers. Oh, they earn plenty. They just don't keep it. NFL players have the lowest salaries in team sports, the shortest careers, and the worst injury and disability rates in team sports.

I almost became one of those negative statistics. I have had to re-invent myself, beginning an entirely new career. It wasn't always easy. First, I had to recognize that there was life beyond sports. That's hard for any athlete to deal with. Most of us are young and unschooled in the real challenges we have to face off the playing field.

In my book, New Money: Staying Rich, I dispense some valuable advice so young athletes and other suddenly wealthy people don't make the same mistakes I did. Here are a few of the points I make:

• New Money is like a newborn baby, it doesn't come with an instruction manual. You have to write your own. You'd better learn how to deal with it – fast – because no financial advisor, no genius with money, is going to care about your money more than you do.

• Your "fun friends" and your family will look at you as an ATM. Trust me, they will hit you up for money whenever they see you. They will plead poverty, wearing the newest sneakers, while sneaking off to the dog track with money from your bankroll. You had better learn the difference between "I truly need it" and "I'd really like it" when dealing with those closest to you.

• While the Self-Made Millionaires were calculating how to grow their money, I was calculating how to spend my money. The sooner you learn this is a bad plan, the better. Yes, I had fun. But then, maybe, just maybe, I should not have blown so much cash on VIP rooms, parties, and weekend jaunts to the Caribbean. Enjoy yourself, but be sane about your spending.

If you disrespect your money, the money is going to disrespect you.

~ Former NFL Cornerback, Phillip Buchanon

Q—*What else should I be doing to secure my financial future?*

A—One of the most damaging and common financial challenges is failing to plan for act two. Because many athletes/entertainers reach their prime at an early age and because their careers are typically short, when they retire, they are often quite young, usually in their 20s or 30s. While others their age are just getting started with their careers, theirs are ending. It doesn't have to be that way, though. As you read in Sudden Wealth Principle 8, work can not only provide an income but also provides purpose. The end of one career can be the start of a new career. Many professional athletes and entertainers have gone on to have successful second careers. It's never too early to start thinking of your act two.

There are many options you can consider, everything from starting your own company to buying and operating a business to using your fame to obtain sponsorships or spokesperson roles. Work with your agent, manager, and other advisors to lay out the possibilities and the game plan.

Q—*How can I resist buying toys and stay on track financially?*

A—Find a mentor. Is there someone who has beaten the odds in your field and zigged when others have zagged? Is there someone who has avoided conspicuous consumption for financial security? One of the most important factors for financial success is surrounding yourself with others who share your money values. All it takes is one positive role model to make the difference. You can have a half dozen "suits" giving you suggestions, but it might sink in deeper if a friend you look up to gives you the same advice. If a good role model is hard to find, contact your players association or guild, or ask your agent/manager for a connection. You are looking for someone to provide you with a counter example to the consumption messages you are undoubtedly facing. Fortunately, more and more players and entertainers are making the news, not for their over-the-top MTV *Cribs* appearance, but for their positive financial choices. For example, NBA point guard, Michael Carter-Williams, recently announced he will keep all of the earnings from his rookie contract in a trust that he can't access for three years until he is 25 years old.

Pro Tip

To ensure long-term success, it's essential that professional athletes view themselves as high net worth business executives. How many executives of Fortune 500 companies are represented by one, singular individual? Typically, the legal and business issues facing high net worth individuals are complex and multifaceted, requiring top-notch expertise in each particular area of concern. Consequently, high net worth individuals are usually represented by a team of very skilled legal and business minds. The "Jack of all trades" model simply does not work. It is most often a recipe for disaster. Think of it this way, when the athlete is injured, he or she doesn't seek medical counsel from a "do-it-all," general practitioner. Rather, the athlete usually seeks the opinion of an expert whose practice centers on the body part that's injured. So, it's not enough to simply have a sports agent, even if the agent is an attorney. To be adequately protected, the professional athlete needs a team of competent legal advisors to oversee matters involving tax law, intellectual property protection, trusts and estates, real estate matters, corporate and general business law matters, charitable trust planning, and litigation. Moreover, the professional athlete requires competent financial and investment advisors. Assuming the athlete allows the aforementioned experts to do their respective jobs, the athlete can reasonably expect to attain both short and long-term financial success. Play like an athlete, but think like an executive!

~ Adisa P. Bakari, sports agent and Chair of The Sports Entertainment Group at Kelley Drye & Warren, LLP

Q—*Shouldn't professional sports player's associations be doing more?*

A—The stats regarding athlete bankruptcies are both shocking and sickening. There are countless stories of well-known athletes who have earned $20 million, $40 million, and even more than a $100 million over their careers and have filed for bankruptcy. It's not right when someone works so hard the way athletes do each week and then end up penniless. The player's associations have taken notice. For example, the National Basketball Association holds a three-day Rookie Transition Program with some emphasis on financial literacy and has recently instituted a forced retirement annuity as well as an optional savings program to help its players save for retirement. The National Football League has a Financial Education Program for its players to help answer their questions and educate them on financial best practices.

These are well-needed programs and a great start, but if you want true financial independence, they are not enough.

The best advice for an athlete is to take what they do best on the field – "Sudden Wealth Principle 1: Take Control" – and put it to work off the field to get control and to improve their finances. Professional athletes don't sit passively hoping for and daydreaming about success. They get out there and make it happen. When it comes to their finances, they should take that same zeal and energy to become financially successful. Don't hope your player's association, agent, manager, or financial advisor will take care of you. It's your life. It's your money. Take control.

WHY DO SO MANY ATHLETES GO BROKE?

Over the years, I've read countless articles about a world-class athlete going bankrupt and the authors' inevitable big conclusion is that they go broke because they are young and dumb. Although they may be young, in my experience working with athletes, they are most definitely not dumb. I wanted to defend athletes and get to the real reasons athletes go broke. The following appeared in my CBS column and was one of my most popular articles:

Did you hear about the professional athlete who just declared bankruptcy? Of course you have. Because when it comes to professional athletes and money, we tend to only hear about how large their new contract is worth or how much they just lost – and unfortunately, there is no shortage of examples of the latter. A *Sports Illustrated* article reports the grim statistics that 78 percent of NFL players face bankruptcy or serious financial stress within just two years of leaving the game, and 60 percent of NBA players face the same dire results in five years[18]. Although the statistics are not in dispute, the reasons why so many athletes face financial problems are. It often boils down to the "dumb jock" stereotype - these guys are superstars on the field but completely clueless off. Sure, that may explain some of the athletes who have gone broke, but this is not a valid or useful explanation of why so many professional athletes end up without money. In fact, NFL players score above average on intelligence measures[19]. Many professional athletes suffer financial problems – not because they aren't smart, but for a number of more nuanced reasons.

In my work managing the finances of sudden wealth recipients and advising professional athletes, the best way to help is to overcome the common barriers that prevent windfall recipients from doing the right thing. Here are a few issues that are common to the professional athlete, any one of which can wreak havoc on one's finances:

TRUST ISSUES

Think Goldilocks. Too much or too little can be a problem. For the athlete who doesn't trust anyone, he won't be open to good tax, legal, and financial advice that could protect his wealth and ensure a lifetime of financial stability. On the other hand, more than a few professional athletes have been duped, taken advantage of, or downright defrauded because they blindly trusted a smooth talking "suit."

WIRED DIFFERENTLY

It's pretty easy to spot a professional athlete in a lineup. Physically, they are quite different from you and me. But psychologically, they may be different as well. Research found significant differences between athletes and non-athletes across personality characteristics such as inhibition, emotionality, and aggressiveness. Good characteristics on the field, but not necessarily optimum for making financial decisions.

FOCUSED ON TODAY

Research published in the *Journal of Judgment and Decision Making* shows professional athletes are more present focused rather than future focused as compared to non-athletes[20]. In other words, there is much greater emphasis placed on today than there is on tomorrow. This may help support the athletes' winner-take-all mindset needed to excel, but can impede any attempt at saving and investing for their future.

FAMILIAL PRESSURE

"If you haven't experienced it yourself, there is no way to describe it" is how one client expressed the rush of a windfall and the ensuing pressure from friends and family to "spread the love." The star we see on the field is often the proverbial tip of the iceberg. What we don't see are the family or friends who may have encouraged and even supported the athlete. For some athletes, they feel a sense of duty to buy houses and cars or invest in the business ideas of those who helped them get to where they are. They may do this to the extreme to assuage the idea that money has changed them. "Look at me," they'll say. "Money hasn't changed me and I'll prove it."

EGO BLEED

For professional athletes, it's the Lake Wobegon Effect – the tendency for everyone to think they are above average, but on steroids! Because in this case, these athletes are truly the very best in the world at what they do. The problem is when this over confidence bleeds into their finances, thinking they don't need advice and that they have some special insight or talent in areas beyond their athletic expertise.

NEED EXCITEMENT

Investing and finance is fast-paced and exciting with high emotions and drama... in the movies. In the real world, financial planning is slow and methodical. The glitz and glamour we think of on Wall Street doesn't translate into a good, long-term financial strategy. But some athletes want and expect the drama. A steady return in the stock market just isn't exciting enough, so some seek high-risk, winner-takes-all (sound familiar?) investments, which often leave them high on adrenaline but low on funds.

TWO WORLDS

As foreign as it would feel for you to enter their world, it is often just as alien for the athlete to discuss asset allocations, family limited partnerships, and the alternative minimum tax. According to former professional baseball player, Bobby Grich, "Players are not trained in wealth management and that world can be totally intimidating, as I know from firsthand experience."

Athletes suffer financially for many reasons, but the dumb jock explanation is not one of them. Professional athletes are intelligent and talented in ways the rest of us cannot fathom. Sometimes, all it takes is recognizing and overcoming some of these barriers, entering their world, and providing a little guidance.

Q—*What cash flow issues should I be aware of?*

A—Unlike a traditional 9-5 job with a steady paycheck, athletes/entertainers have erratic cash flows. It's common to have large signing bonuses followed by little to no income for months. It's natural to want to spend the large check, especially if it's been many months since you've had income. However, to minimize the cash flow ups and downs, you'll want to work with your financial advisor and CPA to help you budget for the flush times and the dry times. The solution that works best is to have a plan for the money before you receive it, to know exactly what you are going to do with it.

Before you spend a dime, you should set aside the amount of tax you will owe on the income in a separate account. I've seen people get into trouble thinking their windfall was all theirs and not having enough money to cover taxes. This is easily solved by pulling out the amount you will owe in taxes and keeping it safe in a separate account.

Next, consider paying off debts, particularly credit card debts. It's common for athletes/entertainers to charge their lifestyle expenses on their credit cards when they are short on cash. Use your windfall to pay these high interest cards off.

Set aside money to cover your basic living expenses and don't forget to budget for the one-time or occasional expenses, such as property taxes and auto insurance. This money is for living expenses during the off season or between projects and designed to get you through erratic paydays.

With a proper budget and a little foresight, you can avoid big tax surprises and the stomach-churning roller coaster of having lots of excess cash and running out of money.

Q—*How can I focus on saving and avoid spending my money?*

A—For non-athletes/non-entertainers, it's hard to understand the special dynamics at play that make saving difficult and spending the norm. First, it's important to understand how powerful our environment shapes and influences our thoughts, beliefs, and behaviors. Who we are is often less important than where we are and who we are with.

As was discussed in Sudden Wealth Principle 4, we adopt the characteristics of the group we belong to. We often sound like them, dress like them, and even vote like them. Amazingly, Nicholas Christakis' research shows we may even weigh the same as them. If your friend is obese, you have a 57% greater chance of being obese, and if your close friend is obese, you have a 171% greater chance of being obese. As personal development godfather, Jim Rohn, once remarked, "You are the average of the five people you spend the most time with."

So what is the environment of a typical athlete/entertainer? They spend an inordinate amount of time with other athletes/entertainers. They live in what one client referred to as a "bubble." Athletes spend hours practicing, traveling, and surrounded by other athletes. Actors, directors, and others often live together for months at a time on set. It is common for negative money beliefs to be formed or reinforced in such tight circles through a process called groupthink.

Groupthink is when individual creativity, uniqueness, differences, and independent thinking is secondary to the group's cohesiveness and mission. The stronger and tighter the group, the easier it is for groupthink to rear its ugly head. In other words, groupthink is what happens when its members check their individuality and ideas at the door and succumb to the will of the group. At the extreme, groupthink is what is required for cults to form and function. Dr. Clark McCauley, a psychologist and one of the main contributors to groupthink research, says groupthink is the "isolation of the group from outside sources of information and analysis."

In other words, if you are surrounded by others with poor money habits, you may easily adopt the same habits yourself. This bubble atmosphere helps to explain how so many athletes/entertainers can become sucked into bad investments or conned by bad advisors. When all of your peers are doing one thing, it's hard to resist. Even if you would never dream of spending lavishly on a vacation, if all of your friends are taking a $100,000 trip to the Caribbean to celebrate the end of a season or the end of a shoot, it's easy to lose perspective and to rationalize why the excursion makes sense.

This is why it is critical to find friends/mentors who are making smart choices with their money and to get a plan and stick to it. No matter how good something sounds, run it by your advisors and listen to their feedback.

Q—*Why does it seem like so many athletes/entertainers are duped out of their money by crooked advisors?*

A—This is a real issue and valid concern. For the reasons discussed above, once an advisor breaks into the group and convinces one or two people, many others often follow their lead – something called herd behavior. If you walk down the street and you see a man staring up at the sky, you might think he's a little off, but if you walk down the street and see three or four people staring up at the sky, you'll suddenly stop and find yourself staring, too. Psychologists call this tendency to look to others to determine appropriate behavior as "social proof," and it happens not just on street corners but also on film sets and in locker rooms.

We especially look to see what others are doing if we are in a new situation, where we don't know what to do or are unsure. If your peer praises his investment advisor and you don't know anything about investing or how to evaluate an advisor, it's easier to follow his lead.

This is where you need to do your own research, though. Remember, trust but verify everything. Go through Sudden Wealth Principle 3 to evaluate any advisor you are considering. Be especially careful of financial advisors and business managers as they often have the most access to your funds.

Q—*I feel pressure to take care of my family and friends, but I don't think I can afford it. What should I do?*

A—There is a simple solution, but it's not easy. If you can't afford it, you shouldn't do it. Helping when it hurts doesn't do anyone any good in the long-term. It can alleviate guilt and pressure momentarily, but it will only cause problems for you and your family/friends down the road. Work closely with your advisors and figure out how you can help. Focus on Sudden Wealth Principle 7.

Q—*How else can I protect myself?*

A—Athletes/Entertainers have a double target on their backs – not only are they wealthy, but they are also in the spotlight. Because of this, some people may want to take advantage of you. Make sure that all of your household help sign non-disclosure agreements and other privacy documents prepared by your attorney and that you have ample amounts of employment practices liability insurance coverage. Also, if you travel to exotic destinations around the world, consider kidnap and ransom insurance. If you broadcast your whereabouts on social networking sites, it can be easy to be a victim.

Also, because of your fame and affluence, you may be asked to join non-profit organizations. If you decide to participate, make sure they provide directors and officers insurance with sufficient liability limits.

Need Help Or More Information?

If you're an athlete or entertainer who wants a team to protect your assets and plan for an uncertain future, we can help. We are known nationally for our expertise in working with athletes/entertainers and have developed a national network of experts from different law, accounting, and financial firms. We can point you in the right direction. For more information and up-to-date strategies for athletes/entertainers, go to suddenwealthsolution.com.

FINAL THOUGHTS

I have been honored to work with sudden wealth recipients for nearly two decades, and although each client and situation is different, the 12 Sudden Wealth Principles provide the foundation for my work. They have worked for me and my clients over the years, and I am confident they will help you create more peace, comfort, happiness, and a lifetime of financial security.

Although these principles are the basis of my work with clients, they are simply the starting point; there is much more that is required. This is why it is so important to work with the best advisors you can find. These 12 Sudden Wealth Principles are the beginning, not the end.

Sudden wealth planning is a constantly evolving field. Although the 12 Sudden Wealth Principles are what exist today, they are not carved in stone. They will, and should, adapt as we learn more about human psychology, behavioral finance, and decision making. Every new sudden wealth recipient is an opportunity to test these principles and to refine the strategies.

I've found that it is one thing to read a book and something quite different to implement the strategies recommended. If, after reading this book, you have a good handle on what you need to do, my mission will be accomplished. If you have additional questions or need help making the ideas in this book work for you, please do not hesitate to contact me. People are often surprised when I personally respond to an email or phone call. I do what I do because I love it. I love helping clients who are going through one of the most exciting and nerve-wracking events in their lives. I'm happy to answer a question or point you in the right direction. Contact me at robert@pacificawealth.com or 949-305-0500 and share your sudden wealth questions, successes, and challenges – what's worked and what needs to be improved. Together, we can continue to refine this field and ensure that anyone who comes into a windfall has the best tools and strategies to make the most of their opportunity.

ACKNOWLEDGEMENTS

Sometimes when I am writing on of my financial columns, the words s-l-o-w-l-y trickle out. Each word and sentence is labored. That was definitely *not* the case for me with *The Sudden Wealth Solution.* Writing this book was a thrill! Having worked with sudden wealth recipients for so many years, the book seemed to write itself, and for that, I have to thank my clients. All of the men, women, and young adults across the globe who have opened their hearts and their souls to me, who, at a time of high emotion and stress, have trusted me to walk beside them and to guide them. It has been an honor to wake up every morning and to be able to serve such good people. Each of you have allowed me to do what I love. Thank you for that.

I want to extend my gratitude to all who provided such glowing endorsements for the book. Honestly, asking someone to review your book is never easy. All of the people who were kind enough to review this book are successful and busy professionals. I'm deeply indebted to them for taking the time to read such a long and sometimes technical book. They didn't have to, but they believed in the message and the work.

I also want to thank the professionals who shared their Pro Tips throughout the book. They have a depth of knowledge that is unsurpassed. We are fortunate they shared their wisdom.

A special thank you to those who wrote the Sudden Wealth Stories and for sharing your personal experience with the world. Allowing me to include your triumphs and struggles have helped make this book even more special for me.

And, of course, I also want to thank my wonderful family for giving me support and encouragement. I tend to go "all in" when working with clients and on big projects like writing a book. They give me the freedom to create, take risks, and pursue my passions. I couldn't ask for a more supportive and inspiring two gals.

READ THIS FIRST

Do you want access to exclusive content, videos, worksheets, tax, legal & financial tips, and breaking news?

ARE YOU AN ADVISOR?

We want you! We are looking for financial advisors, attorneys, CPAs, therapists and other service professionals who are currently serving or want to serve sudden wealth recipients to join our growing nationwide community of experts dedicated to working with sudden wealth recipients.

▸ Receive referrals to sudden wealth recipients in your area looking for advice

▸ Network with other professionals

▸ Learn the latest tax, legal, and financial strategies

▸ Get access to exclusive content

▸ Watch educational videos and listen to podcasts

▸ Download forms and worksheets to help you work with clients

ABOUT THE AUTHOR

Hello. My name is Robert Pagliarini. I have the great honor of helping people during one of the most exciting and nerve-wracking times in their lives. I have specialized in managing, growing, and protecting clients' sudden wealth for nearly two decades. My investment and wealth management firm, Pacifica Wealth Advisors, serves clients across the country and around the globe. We have developed a reputation for our specialized work with sudden wealth from inheritance, divorce, legal judgment/settlement, stock options, business sale, sport/entertainment contract, and the lottery.

ALWAYS LEARNING

Sudden wealth is an area with always-changing tax, legal, and financial issues. I've made it my mission to become a life-long learner and student, sometimes to the dismay of my family. I have several photos of me on my honeymoon lounging poolside reading a thick book on wealth management. When on a non-profit trip to Myanmar, I studied on the plane for the IRS Enrolled Agent exam. When on vacation in Europe with my wife, I was caught highlighting a journal column on the taxation of lawsuit damages. I have a large purple folder marked "To Read," filled with columns and papers on investing, taxes, asset protection, and estate planning that I bring with me nearly everywhere. I love to learn, and I think it is a necessity if you want to provide the best advice and current strategies to clients. This probably explains all of the letters after my name. I am a Certified Financial Planner™ practitioner, a Certified Divorce Financial Analyst, a Certified Structured Settlement Consultant, an Enrolled Agent with the IRS, and have a Master's Degree in Financial Services. I have also earned a Ph.D. in financial and retirement planning.

PSYCHOLOGY OF MONEY

Although I've spent a great deal of time learning the financial, tax, and legal aspects of sudden wealth, I would be doing my clients a huge disservice if I stopped there. I tell my clients that successfully managing sudden wealth is often less, at least initially, about managing the money and more about managing emotions and relationships. The sad riches-to-rags tales you hear are rarely from a single bad investment or from paying too much tax. The real cause is how money changes us and how it changes those around us. Although I'm a financial advisor, I learned quickly that if I was going to really help my clients, I needed to understand the psychology of money, motivation, emotions, and relationships. To that end, I went back to school and earned a Master's Degree in Psychology with an emphasis in marriage and family therapy. This program required I conduct hundreds of hours of face-to-face counseling. To better connect with clients, I've graduated from business and personal coaching programs as well as workshops in Solution Focused Therapy and others. My goal is *not* to be a therapist for my clients. My goal is to better understand what drives them and to help them make the best financial decisions they can.

LOVE OF TEACHING

This is the third book I've written (fourth, if you count a free eBook I wrote during the 2008-2009 financial crisis). My first was the #1 bestselling *The Six-Day Financial Makeover: Transform Your Financial Life in Less Than a Week* (St. Martin's Press, 2006). I wrote this as a general guide for anyone who wasn't quite sure what they should be doing with their finances. Although the book is almost a decade old, the advice is

still as relevant today as it was when I wrote it. My second book was *The Other 8 Hours: Maximize Your Free Time to Create New Wealth & Purpose* (St. Martin's Press, 2010). This book was a departure from traditional personal financial advice and was more focused on investing your human capital rather than investment capital.

In 2018 I published my fourth book. It is titled *Get Money Smart: Simple Lessons to Kickstart Your Financial Confidence & Grow Your Wealth*. This book was born from my work with a young sudden wealth recipient. We had weekly money coaching calls and I turned those lessons into the Get Money Smart book.

DADDY ON TV

Over the years, I've had the privilege of appearing on Dr. Phil, 20/20, Good Morning America, Fox Business, Katie Couric, and many others. I always have a good time on these shows, and my daughter gets a kick out of seeing Daddy on TV.

HELPING THE LESS FORTUNATE

I'm not sure if it was because of my own experience as a child seeing my family struggle financially, but I've always been interested in helping those with less. I got in the habit of writing checks and sup-porting causes, but there was something missing – I wanted to do more. A few years ago, a couple of friends and I started a non-profit organization called The Band of Brothers Foundation. Our charity supports poor and often parent-less children around the world. We currently have active school, orphanage, and other projects in Thai-land, Vietnam, Myanmar, Cambodia, Indonesia, and the Philippines. Visiting these countries and helping these kids has been one of the best things I've ever done.

MANY ADVENTURES

Traveling around South East Asia over the past several years ignited the adventurer in me. A couple of times a year, I travel to exotic places around the world. I've climbed Mt. Kilimanjaro, hiked the Inca Trail to Machu Picchu, hang-glided in Brazil, ice-climbed in Colorado, camped at the bottom of the Grand Canyon, mountain biked in Burma, trekked to the Great Wall of China, and explored the jungles of Thailand and Malaysia with friends and clients. Not all clients are interested in these trips, but they are always welcome.

MY WEALTH MANAGEMENT FIRM

We are experienced independent investment managers who get up each morning with the unwavering mission to help our clients make more money through low-cost investing, reduce the taxes they pay, and implement comprehensive and creative financial strategies tailored to meet their needs.

We are honored that our clients put their trust in us to help them create a better future. We are passionate about always doing what is right, honest, and ethical for our clients—putting their needs above all others. And we never forget that we are here for our clients and because of our clients.

I WANT TO HEAR FROM YOU

I've found that it is one thing to read a book and something quite different to implement the strategies recommended. If, after reading this book, you have a good handle on what you need to do, my mission will be accomplished. If you have additional questions or need help making the ideas in this book work for you, please do not hesitate to contact me. People are often surprised when I personally respond to an email or phone call. I do what I do because I love it. I'm happy to answer a question or point you in the right direction. At the very least, go to http://suddenwealthsolution.com and signup to receive our free newsletter, read new articles, watch videos, and listen to Sudden Wealth Radio.

With warm regards,

Robert Pagliarini
Business Website: www.pacificawealth.com
Book Website: www.suddenwealthsolution.com
Email: robert@pacificawealth.com

ENDNOTES

1 Ripley, Amanda. "A Survival Guide to Catastrophe," Time. Time Inc., 29 May 2008. Web: 4 December 2013.."

2 Strauss, Eric M., Denise Martinez-Ramundo, and Lauren Effron, "20 From 20/20: Former Navy SEAL's Guide to Surviving Almost Anything," *ABC News*. ABC 20/20, 23 Aug. 2013. Web: 4 December 2013.

3 Fisher, Anne. "Being a Mentor Could Boost Your Own Career." CNN. CNN Money, 13 Mar. 2007. Web: 6 November 2013.

4 Driskell, James E., Carolyn Copper, and Aidan Moran, "Does Mental Practice Enhance Performance?" *APA PyschNet*. American Psychological Association, Aug. 1994. Web: 8 November 2013. <http%3A%2F%2Fpsycnet.apa.org%2Findex.cfm%3Ffa%3Dbuy.op tionToBuy%26id%3D1995-00363-001>.

5 Baumeister, Roy F. "Yielding to Temptation: Self-Control Failure, Impulsive Purchasing, and Consumer Behavior." The Journal of Consumer, 28.4 (2002): 1}Print.

6 Yi, Youjae, and Grace Yuna Lee, "The Effect of Shopping Emotions and Perceived Risk on Impulsive Buying: The Moderating Role of Buying Impulsiveness Trait." *Seoul Journal of Business* 14.2 (2008): Print.

7 Arkes, Hal R., Cynthia A. Joyner, Mark V. Pezzo, Jane Gradwohl Nash, Karen Siegel-Jacobs, and Eric Stone. "The Psychology of Windfall Gains, *"Organizational Behavior and Human Decision Processes* 59.3 (1994): 331-47.

8 Arkes, Hal R., Cynthia A. Joyner, Mark V. Pezzo, Jane Gradwohl Nash, Karen Siegel-Jacobs, and Eric Stone. "The Psychology of Windfall Gains, *"Organizational Behavior and Human Decision Processes* 59.3 (1994): 331-47. Web: 12 November 2013. < http://www.science-direct.com/science/article/pii/S0749597884710636>

9 "Suicide in Youth," *NAMI: National Alliance on Mental Health*. Ed. David Brent. NAMI, June 2003. Web: 22 November 2013. <https://www.nami.org/Content/ContentGroups/Illnesses/Suicide_Teens.htm>.

10 Csikszentmihalyi, M., and J. LeFevre. "Optimal Experience in Work and Leisure," *J Pers Soc Psychol* 56.5 (1989): 815-22. *NCBI*, Web: 16 December 2013.

11 Jordan, B. "Science-Based Assessment of Animal Welfare: Wild and Captive Animals." 24.2 (2005): 515-28, Foundation for Wildlife, 2005. Web: 6 December 2013. <http://www.oie.int/doc/ged/D2048.PDF>.

12 Maglich, Jordan D. "2013 Ponzi Schemes In Review: Nearly $3 Billion of Ponzi Schemes, Over 1,000 Years Of Prison Time." *Ponzitracker*: The Ponzi scheme Authority, 23 Dec. 2013. Web: 18 November 2013. <http%3A%2F%2Fwww.ponzitracker.com%2Fmain%2F2013%2F1 2%2F23%2F2013-ponzi-schemes-in-review-nearly-3-billion-of-ponzi-schem.html>.

13 Sullivan, Missy. "Lost Inheritance:" *The Wall Street Journal*. Dow Jones & Company, 8 Mar. 2013. Web: 5 January 2014.

14 Levisohn, Ben. "Playing Your Options:" *The Wall Street Journal*. Dow Jones & Company, 6 July 2012. Web: 18 February 2014.

15 "A Brief Overview of Employee Ownership in the U.S." *NCEO*, the National Center for Employee Ownership, n.d. Web: 6 February 2014..

16 Kotlikoff, Laurence J., and Scott Burns, *The Coming Generational Storm: What You Need to Know about America's Economic Future*. Cambridge, MA: MIT, 2004. Print.

17 Kotlikoff, Laurence J., and Scott Burns, *The Coming Generational Storm: What You Need to Know about America's Economic Future*. Cambridge, MA: MIT, 2004. Print.

18 Torre, Pablo. "How (and Why) Athletes Go Broke," Sports Illustrated, 23 March 2009. Web: 27 July 2014. <http://www.si.com/vault/2009/03/23/105789480/how-and-why-athletes-go-broke>

19 Merron, Jeff. "Taking Your Wonderlics." *ESPN*, ESPN Internet Ventures, n.d. Web: 19 November 2013.

20 Krumer, Alex, Tal Shavit, and Mosi Rosenboim. "Why Do Professional Athletes Have Different Time Preferences than Non-athletes?" *Journal of Behavioral Decision Making* 6.6 (2011): 542-51. SJDM. Aug. 2011. Web: 9 December 2013. <http://journal.sjdm.org/11/11315 /jdm11315.html>.

INDEX

Printed in Great Britain
by Amazon